YouTube™ Marketing

by Will Eagle
YouTube Brand & Marketing Strategist

[Business]
658.872
Eag

for
dummies®
A Wiley Brand

TWINSBURG LIBRARY
TWINSBURG OHIO 44087

YouTube™ Marketing For Dummies®

Published by: **John Wiley & Sons, Inc.,** 111 River Street, Hoboken, NJ 07030-5774, www.wiley.com

Copyright © 2019 by John Wiley & Sons, Inc., Hoboken, New Jersey

Published simultaneously in Canada

No part of this publication may be reproduced, stored in a retrieval system or transmitted in any form or by any means, electronic, mechanical, photocopying, recording, scanning or otherwise, except as permitted under Sections 107 or 108 of the 1976 United States Copyright Act, without the prior written permission of the Publisher. Requests to the Publisher for permission should be addressed to the Permissions Department, John Wiley & Sons, Inc., 111 River Street, Hoboken, NJ 07030, (201) 748-6011, fax (201) 748-6008, or online at http://www.wiley.com/go/permissions.

Trademarks: Wiley, For Dummies, the Dummies Man logo, Dummies.com, Making Everything Easier, and related trade dress are trademarks or registered trademarks of John Wiley & Sons, Inc. and may not be used without written permission. YouTube is a trademark of Google, LLC. All other trademarks are the property of their respective owners. John Wiley & Sons, Inc. is not associated with any product or vendor mentioned in this book.

LIMIT OF LIABILITY/DISCLAIMER OF WARRANTY: THE PUBLISHER AND THE AUTHOR MAKE NO REPRESENTATIONS OR WARRANTIES WITH RESPECT TO THE ACCURACY OR COMPLETENESS OF THE CONTENTS OF THIS WORK AND SPECIFICALLY DISCLAIM ALL WARRANTIES, INCLUDING WITHOUT LIMITATION WARRANTIES OF FITNESS FOR A PARTICULAR PURPOSE. NO WARRANTY MAY BE CREATED OR EXTENDED BY SALES OR PROMOTIONAL MATERIALS. THE ADVICE AND STRATEGIES CONTAINED HEREIN MAY NOT BE SUITABLE FOR EVERY SITUATION. THIS WORK IS SOLD WITH THE UNDERSTANDING THAT THE PUBLISHER IS NOT ENGAGED IN RENDERING LEGAL, ACCOUNTING, OR OTHER PROFESSIONAL SERVICES. IF PROFESSIONAL ASSISTANCE IS REQUIRED, THE SERVICES OF A COMPETENT PROFESSIONAL PERSON SHOULD BE SOUGHT. NEITHER THE PUBLISHER NOR THE AUTHOR SHALL BE LIABLE FOR DAMAGES ARISING HEREFROM. THE FACT THAT AN ORGANIZATION OR WEBSITE IS REFERRED TO IN THIS WORK AS A CITATION AND/OR A POTENTIAL SOURCE OF FURTHER INFORMATION DOES NOT MEAN THAT THE AUTHOR OR THE PUBLISHER ENDORSES THE INFORMATION THE ORGANIZATION OR WEBSITE MAY PROVIDE OR RECOMMENDATIONS IT MAY MAKE. FURTHER, READERS SHOULD BE AWARE THAT INTERNET WEBSITES LISTED IN THIS WORK MAY HAVE CHANGED OR DISAPPEARED BETWEEN WHEN THIS WORK WAS WRITTEN AND WHEN IT IS READ.

For general information on our other products and services, please contact our Customer Care Department within the U.S. at 877-762-2974, outside the U.S. at 317-572-3993, or fax 317-572-4002. For technical support, please visit https://hub.wiley.com/community/support/dummies.

Wiley publishes in a variety of print and electronic formats and by print-on-demand. Some material included with standard print versions of this book may not be included in e-books or in print-on-demand. If this book refers to media such as a CD or DVD that is not included in the version you purchased, you may download this material at http://booksupport.wiley.com. For more information about Wiley products, visit www.wiley.com.

Library of Congress Control Number: 2018968030

ISBN 978-1-119-54134-9 (pbk); ISBN 978-1-119-54135-6 (ePDF); ISBN 978-1-119-54136-3 (epub)

Manufactured in the United States of America

C10007553_011419

Contents at a Glance

Table of Contents

To help you navigate this book and absorb the key concepts, I did follow a few conventions:

>> If I provide an example of how to say something, I use *italics* to indicate a placeholder, as in *your company name*, which means that you need to replace the italics with your own information.

>> I also use *italics* for terms that are being defined.

>> I also use *italics* for phrases you need to search for on Google.

>> Web addresses appear in <u>monofont</u>. If you're reading a digital version of this book on a device connected to the Internet, you can click the live link to visit a website, like this: `www.youtube.com`

YouTube is improving the platform every day, and so things may change, but don't worry: The principles stay the same, even if a button has moved. This book is as much about the theory and practical principles behind how to use YouTube successfully as it is about providing a step-by-step guide to navigate YouTube's tools and features.

Foolish Assumptions

I've made a few assumptions about you as I've written this book:

>> **You're a marketer who has specific goals you need to achieve.** Perhaps you need to sell more of your products, encourage more signups to a service you offer, to get more people to visit your bricks and mortar store, or want to let more people know about your brand.

>> **You've tried other marketing techniques.** Some of these techniques have worked well, while others haven't performed how you'd hoped. You're now considering YouTube to see what it can do for your marketing needs.

>> **You like a plain speaker.** While the industry excels at creating overly complicated terms for simple concepts, you're interested in delivering results. You know that plainly spoken, practical advice with guiding steps is the easiest way to get from A to B. I call out jargon when it's useful to know but keep things as straightforward as possible.

>> **You're willing to give YouTube a go.** This last one is the most important assumption I've made. Even though I firmly believe YouTube is a crucial part of the marketing mix and that it offers simple solutions to get started, you can easily feel overwhelmed by all the options YouTube offers. My advice is to start somewhere simple. You don't have to do everything all at once.

Icons Used in This Book

Icons in this book are used to mark important things along the way:

TIP

The Tip icon calls out my top tips and shortcuts for success,.

REMEMBER

The Remember icon identifies key concepts and foundational principles that you'll want to keep in mind.

WARNING

The Warning icon appears to warn you about common mistakes — and the threat of certain doom.

TECHNICAL
STUFF

The Technical Stuff icon marks high-level information that you don't have to know to understand the concept at hand (but you may be interested in it!). Feel free to skip any text marked with this icon.

Beyond the Book

In addition to what you're reading right now, this product also comes with a free access-anywhere Cheat Sheet that gives you pointers on responding to comments on your videos, optimizing your SEO, using thumbnails and titles to get more clicks, using YouTube as a marketing channel, and creating viral videos. To get this Cheat Sheet, simply go to www.dummies.com and search for "YouTube Marketing For Dummies Cheat Sheet" in the Search box.

Where to Go from Here

You don't need to read this book from start to finish, although you can. Instead, you can scan the table of contents and pick where it makes sense to start. Here are a few more suggestions:

» If you're completely new to the idea that YouTube is a marketing tool, check out Part 1.

» To find out more about YouTube's advertising platform, see Part 2.

» For help developing a content strategy, go to Part 3 .

» Check out Part 4 when you're ready to make a video.

» Make sure you measure the success of your marketing efforts by going to Part 5.

1

Getting Started with YouTube Marketing

IN THIS PART . . .

Discover why YouTube is an important marketing channel.

Choose how you'll use YouTube for your business and marketing needs.

Distinguish between advertising and content strategies.

Make campaign choices and determine your budget.

Create your marketing brief to guide all your efforts.

Develop actionable insights about your target audience.

Chapter **1**

YouTube in the Marketing Mix

I n this chapter, I demystify some misconceptions about YouTube as a marketing tool and explain why YouTube (along with Google search) is probably the most important and sophisticated marketing channel available to marketers today. Few other platforms offer the depth of potential offered by YouTube.

I also ask you to pick your lane to decide how you'd like to use YouTube in a way that's manageable for you, walk through the differences between advertising and content as marketing approaches, and show how YouTube will fit into your marketing calendar.

YouTube Is Important for Marketers

The first thing to know about YouTube as a marketing channel is that the people you'd like to talk visit YouTube anywhere from several times a month to several times a day.

The second thing to know is that they spend a lot of time on YouTube. People watching videos on YouTube are engaged, sometimes watching one video, sometimes staying for an hour or more watching many videos.

Third, they are receptive to messages. YouTube works hard to provide a great viewing experience while finding ways to provide advertising options to marketers that aren't overly intrusive. People vote with their eyeballs and attention, and poorly targeted ads or disruptive ad formats turn people off. YouTube knows that the ads must be a complementary experience to watching videos, or they risk losing audience.

YouTube is often the last channel marketers tackle because video requires a bit more effort than just an image, some text, and a link, but the potential to reach your audience with compelling video ads and content is well worth the effort.

YouTube is big and growing fast

YouTube is massive. With more than 1 billion users visiting the site every month and 400 hours of video content uploaded every minute, YouTube is more massive than you may at first think, especially when you consider that both those numbers are increasing. YouTube is also the second largest search engine in the world, after, of course, its big brother Google.

People watch videos on YouTube on their computers at home, their tablets during dinner, on their mobile phones, with friends on a TV screen in the living room, and even on gaming consoles. YouTube is everywhere, and it's set to be (if it isn't already) the most watched format in the United States, beating out TV for time spent viewing.

The benefits of YouTube's big data

You may have read a lot of articles about the benefits of big data for marketers, but sometimes the term *big data* is used without it being really clear what it means. Big data can mean a few different things:

>> **Volume of data:** A massive volume of data reveals things like audience content consumption habits and confirms them with the sheer volume. Think of YouTube as a giant survey where people are voting for the content they like every day. That's a powerful tool to have access to!

>> **Velocity of data:** Velocity in big data means that enough data over a set period, often a short period, of time reveals when something is trending or emerging. For example, the Center for Disease Control (CDC) uses data from

Google's search engine to help track flu outbreaks in the United States. The YouTube equivalent would be the trending videos pages, which uses data to float to the top the videos with the most velocity of views.

» **Variety of data:** Big data can simply mean variety. If YouTube is a survey tool, it's asking millions of questions every day about everything; what people want to watch, how and where they watch it, what makes it shareable, which devices they use, and more.

YouTube is so big, it has some of the biggest big data around. It has volume, velocity, and variety of data and uses learnings from its data to deliver advantages to marketers.

YouTube's big data helps deliver cost savings to marketers; you have the choice to reach specific audiences who will convert into a click or purchase best, ultimately benefitting from cost savings as you'll only be buying the media that works best for you. It is no longer the case that any part of your marketing campaign's performance is unknown.

You'll find efficiencies in the time it takes to create and execute marketing campaigns, tools, and features that do the thinking for you, such as where media should run, how much money should be spent to give the best return, and analyses of which creative works best and why. These features and options are born from deep research based on YouTube's big data repository. YouTube develops things like advanced audience targeting methods that are so sophisticated and yet easy to action, making your marketing budget work harder and more efficiently.

You also get access to constantly evolving tools that help you uncover insights about your audience, giving you a deeper understanding than in the past. YouTube comes with incredibly sophisticated analytics tools, developed from millions of experiments and tons of feedback, to learn what you can do to deliver more results. YouTube has used its big data to create the simplest solutions for marketers to get the maximum results.

YouTube's place in your marketing mix

Whether you're an established marketer or just starting out, it's important to regularly review all the channels available to you, decide whether they can help deliver to your goals, and choose how you'll spend your time, efforts, and budget.

Many marketers, especially small businesses and independents, may start with digital channels like Facebook and Instagram. These channels provide easy, self-serve solutions to get started and typically require only simple creative, such as an image, text, and link. This simplicity is great, but sometimes YouTube is left until last to be explored and exploited by marketers, primarily because creating video takes a bit more work. As evidenced by the fact that Facebook, Instagram, and other social media channels are increasingly turning to video as part of their offering, it's rapidly becoming clear that video is a required component of any marketer's plan. Given that video is becoming an essential in all marketing plans and YouTube is the most powerful video platform available, YouTube needs to be a part of your mix.

Sure, you have to make a lot of choices. You need to make decisions about your media spending and production budget, work through your resources, and decide what video you can make. Fortunately, throughout this book, I break out everything you need to consider into easy-to-manage steps so that you can easily make YouTube a part of your marketing mix.

Using YouTube in Marketing

As a marketer, YouTube gives you choices. You can use YouTube to create more leads, let people know about your brand, solve your customer service inquires, and more. The opportunities are endless.

Advertising versus content marketing

YouTube offers both an *advertising platform,* a place to run ads in paid media, and a *content platform,* a place to post your video content for people to discover and watch.

Think of *advertising* as a classic ad served up when you're watching another video; it may be a short ad, running in paid media, that tells you about a product or service and encourages you to buy or act. You may like the ad; you may not. Part 2 details everything you'll need to know about advertising on YouTube.

Think of *content* as something you may choose to watch, such as a recipe video or a comedy skit. You're probably watching the video because you want to, not because a marketer paid to make you watch it. Part 3 covers content strategy development.

The best way to maximize YouTube as a marketing channel is to tackle both advertising and content. You can simply run ads, or you can make great content, or you can do both. If you do both, they can work in tandem and deliver a marketing channel essentially unlike any other.

With the proliferation of digital channels and the increasing demands from consumers for smart, compelling, targeted ads, the best marketing messages manifest increasingly as formats and creative that feel more like content than ads. Essentially, great ads are more like content. The best advertisers make ads that are so good they don't feel like an ad,; they feel like content, and people choose to watch them

To keep things simple, I break down how to run advertising on YouTube in Part 2 and how to make content for YouTube in Part 3. I treat these topics as two separate things altogether. Just know that the best marketers make ads that are as good as content.

Picking a lane

You may think the first step in getting started on YouTube is setting up a YouTube channel, but planning how you want to use YouTube can save you time, money, and effort, and should be your first task.

Before you get started, you need to pick a lane. Are you

TIP

>> **An advertiser:** The simplest lane a marketer can choose is to be an advertiser on YouTube, meaning that you make ads that run in paid media on YouTube. Advertising is a great place to start, especially if you're a marketer with existing video ad creative who wants to test how YouTube can work for you.

Choose this approach if you have some video ads you'd like to run on YouTube or, want to create some video ads to test. (Refer to Chapter 7 to get your campaign started.)

>> **A sponsor:** If you're an advanced marketer who wants to run your ads against specific content, then choose this lane. Some marketers want their ads to be appear in specific placements — for example, only against sports video content or premium content from the top YouTubers. You're still running ads, but you're more selective with your placements because association is important to you. (See Chapter 7 to find out about the extensive placement options available to you.)

>> **A content creator:** An even more advanced lane to choose is to be a content creator. As a content creator, you make and run your ads, but you also create content for your YouTube channel. Creating video content takes more time and budget and is often used by marketers to deliver a fuller YouTube strategy. Using YouTube to run ads and deliver content is a sophisticated strategy. (Chapter 8 covers different video content formats. Chapter 9 breaks out how to develop a content strategy.)

>> **A publisher:** The most advanced lane to choose is to be a publisher. Think of Red Bull, GoPro, and any brand that has turned content creation into the core strategy of their marketing initiatives. Content has become the focus of almost everything they do in marketing. These marketers have mastered the art of great content, leveraging many of the content fundamentals described in Chapter 10.

The Secret Formula for YouTube Success

When using YouTube as a marketing channel, you can do certain things that will help increase your video's chances of success. A handful of key components to the secret formula include

>> Creating a brief to reach the right people

>> Harnessing the power of video ads

>> Developing your content strategy

>> Making great videos

>> Mastering YouTube management

>> Measuring success

Creating a brief to reach the right people

Don't even think about making an ad or a video until you've written a brief. A *brief* is a guiding document that marketers use to collect all the necessary information to create a successful ad or piece of content.

In the brief, you answer questions about what you want to achieve, how you'd like to go about executing your marketing program, and who you want to target — which is perhaps the most important part of a brief,. As you create your brief, you'll uncover deep insights about your target audience to inform your marketing. (Chapters 2 and 3 cover everything you need to know about creating a brief.)

When you know who you want to reach and what you want to communicate to them, you'll be able to use the targeting options YouTube makes available to speak to exactly the people you want to reach. You won't have to waste your media spend reaching people you don't want to talk to.

After your campaign or first video is live, something magical happens: Every day you'll be able to learn something new about your audience by looking at the rich analytics available and you'll be able to talk to the people watching your ads and videos, hearing directly from them. (For more on how to use analytics, see Part 6) This information helps you make choices that make your work on YouTube and all your marketing efforts better every day. You can use the gems you uncover in your reports to develop new briefs for your marketing campaigns and content strategies.

Harnessing the power of video ads

It's a competitive time for marketers. With the proliferation of digital channels, the bar has been raised for the quality of ads and content, and because there's so much noise, you need to work harder than ever to stand out. Marketers have many opportunities throughout the course of an average day to reach their audience, but it takes quality work to truly stand out in a sea of messages bombarding people every day.

Decent ads aren't good enough anymore; they have to be great ads. Marketers must work hard to deliver a compelling ad that catches your attention, stands out, has a clear message, and makes some kind of connection with the viewer so that they'll think or feel or do something afterwards. The good news is that video is the best medium to make truly great ads with. Sure, video takes a bit more work than a static image and some text, but if a picture is worth a thousand words, then video must be virtually priceless.

The Google Ads solution, described in Chapter 7, is possibly the most powerful advertising platform on the planet and is your gateway to uncovering what works best in your video ads.

Developing your content strategy

Just like ads, there's a lot of competition for content viewership. Think of all the moments during the day where you reach for your phone to read the news, watch a video, check a social channel, post a photo, comment on something, or message a friend. Hundreds of content moments occur throughout the course of a day, and people have become experts at sifting the wheat from the chaff. Their thumbs and eyes work in perfect partnership to merciless scroll past hundreds of pieces of content, slowing to dwell on only the best. The writing of headlines has become an expert skill close to a form of art, designed to catch your eye and maximize the chances of a click and more time spent.

Time spent is the currency of attention, the very thing marketers are trading in. Chapter 9 can help you develop a content strategy that makes sense for your organization.

Making great videos

It's no surprise that making video is crucially important to success with YouTube! Chapter 11 details how you can get started making videos, avoid pitfalls, and produce something that delivers. Making videos has never been easier as most people have the necessary equipment right in their pockets. Today's smartphones have such capable cameras that you can make movies with them.

If you're not familiar with creating video, head to Chapter 12, which gives you options for how you can get help from others to create content for your channel.

Mastering YouTube management

Marketers are handling more channels than ever, with the added challenge that digital channels are giving daily feedback, while constantly changing and evolving. Magazines are, for the most part, the same as they've always been, with the basic rules of how print marketing works remaining the same for decades. The only way to succeed with digital channels, especially the most powerful and advanced digital channels like YouTube, is to actively manage them. That process requires understanding them, experimenting with them, and regularly reevaluating and maximizing your usage of all the tools they offer.

I've seen clients, time and again, who think that a small burst of effort to kickstart their YouTube channel will be sufficient. They then move on to other projects, revisiting YouTube a year later. Succeeding on YouTube just doesn't work like that. (What does?)

An even worse crime is a common misconception by even the biggest clients that a good strategy for YouTube is to use it as a repository for their TV ads. Sure, you can post your TV ads to YouTube, but it won't do a lot without a media spend behind them. Even then, creative made for YouTube will always perform better than creative made for TV.

These misconceptions about YouTube mean that many marketers leave a ton of opportunity to effectively reach their audience on the table. Don't neglect YouTube and let it become a wasteland. If you have the time, you can be doing something every day to make your YouTube efforts even better than the previous day. Chapter 15 walks through the key considerations for active channel and community management.

Measuring success

Knowing what success looks like is crucial. Because YouTube offers so many options to marketers, you can easily be overwhelmed and to think you must do everything. Knowing what success looks like helps you make smart choices and get started without biting off more than you can chew.

The idea here is not to do everything possible on YouTube. The point is to make choices based on what you want to achieve for your business and use YouTube to achieve just that. I've had clients who assume that they need to make lots of videos about everything they do at their company, create playlists, work with YouTubers, come up with content series ideas. In reality, all they needed was to make some simple, effective ads to help promote a new product they were releasing that quarter.

It's easy to want to tackle everything, but instead start by asking "What does success look like?" Success may be

>> Generating leads for your business

>> Driving more clicks to your website

>> Growing your brand and product consideration

>> Growing your brand awareness and reach

Knowing what success looks like avoids the mistake that measurement is often forgotten. You've made a video, worked hard, posted it, and then you moved on to something else on your list. A few weeks go by, and you think maybe you should check to see how things are going. The best marketers make looking at the data a daily task, but more than that, they think about how they can turn that data into meaningful actions and how things like video views and subscriber rates correspond to their marketing and business goals.

WARNING

A common mistake big brands make is thinking that the important metric they should measure is how many times their video was viewed. Sure, that metric may be helpful for success, but did it drive business results? Marketers should have only one goal: drive business results. How many YouTube video views you have doesn't matter. What matters is that you drove leads or delivered to customer needs. Spending time in measurement is the key for all marketers to be truly successful at delivering results.

You should spend at least half of your time on YouTube Analytics and tools like Google Ads. Think of these tools as a mine, and every day you have the chance to uncover golden nuggets of information that can change the way you market and deliver amazing results. If you know what business success looks like and if you look every day at the data and results, you'll be able to connect these two and become a master of making YouTube work for you. Every day is an opportunity to uncover gold.

Chapter **2**

Using YouTube for Your Business

A s a marketer, a common mistake is deciding that you need a YouTube strategy, but forgetting to target a business goal it should help deliver against. In this chapter, I walk you through mapping your business challenges, deciding a campaign type, and assigning your budget.

I also explain how to create a brief, a guiding document that ensures everyone is aligned on the task at hand, breaks out all the key components that the marketing campaign must address, and ultimately helps to ensure marketing success.

Capturing All Your Business Challenges

Every marketing campaign has one thing in common: the goal of delivering to a business challenge. That goal may mean creating an awareness of a new product, getting signups for a new service, or something else altogether.

YouTube has the potential to solve any number of these business challenges, so the first step is to capture all your challenges and pick the most important challenge you'd like to solve for.

It's often helpful to use sticky notes to externalize everything you have swirling in your marketer's brain so that you can step back and make a choice about where to start. It's especially smart to start with this kind of approach so that you don't fall into the trap of thinking the challenge you need to solve for is "create YouTube strategy." That's never the thing you need to do. YouTube is a tool that can deliver to your business and marketing needs; you don't need to deliver a YouTube strategy if it doesn't help your business.

If you haven't thought through all your business challenges or you aren't sure which one YouTube should help with, grab a pad of sticky notes and a felt marker pen and work through this simple exercise:

1. **Write one business challenge per sticky-note, generating as many challenges as you possibly can.**

   Examples of challenges may be

   - Launch a new product

   - Create a new customer service tool to handle inquiries

   - Deliver a brand campaign using our new logo

   The idea is to capture as many challenges as possible

2. **Post all of these sticky-notes onto a surface where you can look at them all at once.**

   Figure 2-1 shows you what my setup looks like whenever I do this step.

3. **Move the sticky notes around so that the biggest projects are higher up on the wall.**

4. **Put the easy projects and to-do list items lower on the surface and your marketing initiatives in the middle.**

5. **Take a step back and decide which marketing initiative you think YouTube may be a fit for.**

   YouTube is great for everything from brand campaigns and sales-focused performance marketing campaigns to customer service and beyond. Pick something manageable and meaningful.

After you identify your challenge, you'll be able to set about building your brief, starting with defining what success looks like.

Don't fall into the trap of thinking you need a YouTube strategy. You need a YouTube strategy only in service of a business or marketing need.

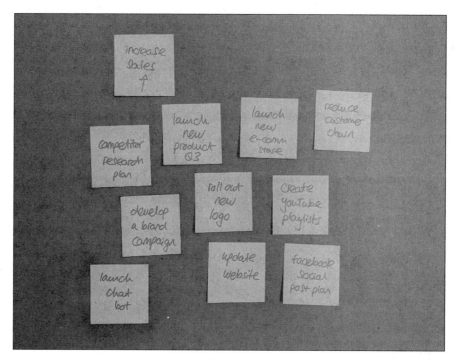

FIGURE 2-1:
Grab your sticky notes and generate all your business challenges. Pick one that you'd like.

Defining Your Campaign Type

It's important to think of what type of campaign you need in order to deliver to your business goals. A classic approach to marketing campaigns is to break them into different types connected to a well-known, somewhat traditional, and linear view of the consumer journey. Figure 2-2 explores a typical consumer journey used by marketers to think about the various stages a consumer might move through in relation to your product or service.

If you Google search (especially Google image search) things like *consumer journey* or *marketing funnel*, you can find lots of great articles that provide different ways of thinking about consumers and how you can move them with your marketing from "I don't know your product" to "I'm a fan who tells everyone they should buy your product."

While you can think about the marketing funnel in many different ways, I use a fairly traditional approach because it's an easy, clear, and commonly used way to break out the different kinds of marketing campaigns you can run on YouTube.

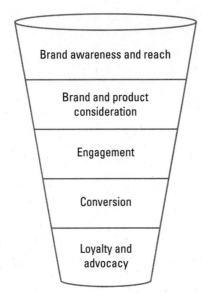

FIGURE 2-2:
A traditional
marketing funnel
showing the
consumer
journey,
commonly used
by marketers.

Whether you want people to know about your brand or product *(awareness)* or buy more of your product *(conversion)*, YouTube can deliver. Just remember that these consumer stages aren't the only ways to think about or frame your campaign efforts. However, the funnel approach is the most commonly used method. I break down each stage of the funnel and outline some common matching YouTube Key Performance Indicators (KPIs).

TECHNICAL STUFF

KPIs refer to the handful of measures of success you and your organization agree to use to evaluate whether your marketing campaign has delivered successfully. For example, your KPIs may be sales volume, number of people who saw your advertising message, and repeat purchases.

The stages of the consumer journey funnel are

>> Brand awareness and reach

>> Brand and product consideration

>> Engagement

>> Conversion

>> Loyalty & advocacy

Brand awareness and reach

Simply put, *brand awareness* is the extent to which a consumer can recognize and recall your brand. *Reach* refers to the number of people who are aware of, know about, have seen and recognize, and are able to recall the brand communicated by the campaign.

Every few years, an industry magazine or blog will publish a list of the world's most recognizable brands. These brands use marketing to maximize their awareness. The idea behind awareness is that if you know my brand and can recall it better than others, you'll be more likely to purchase it. For example, Coca-Cola is arguably the most recognized brand in the world, with its iconic red and white color and script logo. Indeed, if you were asked to name a soda, chances are you'll say Coca-Cola first. (See Chapter 7 to discover how to set up a brand awareness and reach campaign.)

REMEMBER

Metrics refers to the data you measure. A key concept of awareness marketing is the idea of *reach* and *frequency,* two simple metrics that mean "How many people did you reach with your ad?" and "How often did they see your ad during the marketing campaign?" These traditional metrics for awareness marketing assume that if you see an ad, say, five times, you're likely to be aware of the brand, product, or service.

YouTube is pretty stellar when it comes to driving awareness and reach because it offers an easy way to reach an enormous number of people on several occasions over the course of your marketing campaign.

YouTube MASTHEAD

You may be familiar with the YouTube Masthead — the large banner featuring an ad that appears on the YouTube home page. If you have a big marketing budget (and I mean big — it costs in the hundreds of thousands), you can buy the Masthead for a full 24 hours, and everyone who visits the YouTube home page will see your ad. The Masthead delivers massive awareness, reaching an audience of millions, depending on your country. The masthead is often booked far in advance, with marketers wanting to own specific days like Black Friday or Cyber Monday.

Brand and product consideration

People may be aware of your brand (see preceding section), but *consideration* is the next phase in their journey toward purchase. Consideration means that your campaign has switched something in their mind that makes them think "Yeah, this may be something for me."

Perhaps you need a marketing campaign that encourages more of your target audience to consider your product. People may know that your product exists and what it is, but it may not be on their consideration list.

Imagine this example: You're in the grocery store. You remember that you need soap, so you head over to the health and beauty aisle. Tens of different soap brands are on the shelf (I bet you can name at least five right now off the top of your head), but the brain has the capacity to process only so many choices. You may be fully aware of almost all the soap brands on the shelf — that's known as your *awareness set* —but your brain doesn't want to have to stand there and decide about each one in turn. Either consciously or subconsciously, you quickly narrow your choices down to the brands in your *consideration set,* which probably include the soap you've been using, the soap your partner likes, and maybe the soap that you recently saw on sale in a flyer.

Marketers are often concerned with how they can ensure their product is in your consideration set because if it isn't, it won't have a chance of being chosen.

YouTube published research in March 2016 that demonstrated how online video can drive consideration. YouTube already knew that its video ad offerings can drive awareness of a brand, product, or service, but the research found that the longer people watched a video, the more likely their consideration of the product would be positively impacted. In the study, YouTube looked at people who chose to watch 30 seconds or more of an ad. This group of viewers had 45 percent higher consideration than the control group that skipped after 5 seconds. The conclusion was that if you want to see your consideration metrics increase, brands should find creative ways to encourage viewers to watch more of the ad.

Chapter 7 details how to create your brand and product consideration campaign.

Engagement

In *engagement,* you create opportunities in which you involve your consumer, inviting them to be a more active participant in your marketing programs rather than a passive recipient of your advertising.

A traditional type of engagement marketing may be a special event, such as a mobile phone company creating an annual music festival, or *street marketing,* where people hand you fliers on the street or ask questions to get you to sign up for a service, such as a monthly charitable donation. Engagement on YouTube is best served through brands creating content that viewers want to watch.

TIP

YouTube has tons of options to deliver engagement-focused marketing campaigns. Even though you may think YouTube is a place to post a video to be watched at any time, it's also a social media channel and community space. The only limit to how you engage your audience in more direct and one-to-one moments is your imagination.

For example, you can start a weekly video blog *(vlog)* where you respond to consumer and viewer comments, questions, and suggestions. You can engage in text-based discussion with your audience on your Discussion or Community tab on your YouTube channel. You can stream a live video, such as an interview with someone from your company talking about a new product feature, and then post that video later to be viewed anytime. The idea here is that you're using YouTube to deliver directly engaging experiences with your audience, measuring that success by how many people watch, comment, like, and participate.

See Chapter 9 for more on developing your content strategy.

Conversion

If you're looking to drive sales of your product or service, your campaign goal may be conversion. *Conversion* is the idea that your target audience saw your video ad or piece of content and then took an action to convert — for example, to make a purchase, sign up for a test drive, or open an account online.

Conversion-focused campaigns are the focus of *performance marketers* — those marketers who are evaluating all their marketing activities based on how well they convert to a sale. You can measure the success of your conversion-focused campaign simply by the KPIs of the number of sales or conversion actions delivered by your YouTube efforts.

Chapter 7 walks through the steps to create a campaign that delivers conversions, such as website traffic and leads.

THE POWER OF INTENT SIGNALS FOR CONVERSION

YouTube uses signals of intent to determine whether someone is in the market to do something, like buying a car. The idea behind using signals of intent in your marketing is that you are delivering your ad or content to a target audience based on their signals to buy or consume your product or service, which is an incredibly effective approach for conversion campaigns.

Say, for example, that you're interested in buying a new car. You log on to Google.com on your desktop computer and search for certain makes and models of cars, watch some car review videos on YouTube, visit comparison sites, and maybe even use a car loan calculator to determine financing options. Later, you use your mobile phone to look at photos of cars on Instagram, post on Facebook to ask your friends for recommendations, and use Google Maps to search for a local dealership to visit. Perhaps you then visit that dealer's website and sign up for a test drive that coming weekend.

Marketers may use some of those signals to send you advertising messages about cars, offers and incentives, new models to consider, and more. Your digital footprints provide signals of your intent: the digital channels you visited, such as Google, YouTube, Instagram, and Facebook, now know you are in the market to buy a car, and marketers can buy advertising that will reach you based on these signals. Don't worry: They don't know it's you. All these signals are anonymous and aggregated — for example, "target people looking to buy a car."

Whether your marketing message is to let someone know about the makes and models of cars you have for sale at your dealership or to offer them a specific deal on a model you know they are searching for, YouTube can help drive intent marketing by the way in which you buy paid advertising media.

You can buy paid media on YouTube so that your ads are seen by people who search for certain things on Google.com. For example, if I search *Jeep Wrangler* on Google.com, you can buy media on YouTube that targets me with your ads for Jeep Wranglers. You can tap into a consumer's intent with Google and YouTube's advertising platform in quite a few ways — for example, by targeting people based not just on search, but by their interests, by topics they are consuming, and even by retargeting, which is the ability to show your ad to someone who, for example, visited your website. You can go even further by customizing the call to action that appears on the video ad. Perhaps you want to show a video about your car dealership to anyone in market looking to buy a car, but you change the call to action to a specific make and model based on what they've been searching for!

DOLLAR SHAVE CLUB

One of the best examples of all-time as to how YouTube videos can drive conversion comes from Dollar Shave Club. Its videos blur the line between advertising and entertaining content, with "Our Blades Are <expletive> Great," which has more than 25 million views, and its second most popular video, "The Shopping Experience," which has more than 6.8 million views. The Dollar Shave Club's videos center on its founder Mike describing the amazing features of its products and its reasonably priced subscription model, often in a comedic and absurdist style (see the figure).

When the company launched in 2012, Gillette dominated the razor market with a whopping 72 percent of the U.S. market. Entering a saturated, established category seemed like a crazy idea. However, thanks to its new model and in large part due to its success with viral video marketing on YouTube, Dollar Shave Club took off and grew. It grew so large and so fast that Unilever bought Dollar Shave Club for $1 billion in 2016. That's a pretty great conversion!

Loyalty and advocacy

While marketers are always looking to reach new audiences, they also stay mindful of existing customers who are loyal to their product or service.

Loyal customers come back to you time and again, repeatedly buying from you regardless of what competitors may be saying or doing. They're often your highest value customer.

An *advocate* is someone who will tell other people about your product or service, suggesting to them that they check it out or purchase it. Typically, advocates are telling a friend or family member, so their opinion holds weight and meaning. Just think about the last time you asked your friend for a recommendation on a place to eat or a store to buy something; you probably followed the advice.

TIP

Although loyal customers and advocates often don't require additional marketing dollars to be spent to acquire them, finding ways to keep and reaffirm their loyalty and encourage their advocacy with your marketing activities is a good idea.

Traditionally, marketers may have used incentive techniques, such as discounts, referral bonuses when a friend also purchases, or reward points programs. These programs can work very well at both keeping people loyal and giving them reasons to tell their friends about you.

YouTube can also play a role in encouraging and maintaining the loyalty of your company's biggest fans. In fact, YouTube is natively built with loyalty in mind with features like channel subscriptions.

If loyalty is your key campaign goal, a metric for success may be how many visitors to your channel have turned into subscribers. When people subscribe to your channel, they may see your newly uploaded videos in places like on their YouTube home page. A bell icon, when clicked, notifies your audience through email with a link to each new video you post. Imagine that! The moment marketers post a new video, their audience is alerted, for free, and encouraged to go watch it.

KLEENEX AND LOYALTY

In 2016, Kleenex, the brand of tissue products, made a video titled "Wrap a House in Love." The video tells the story of Nick and Shelby Nelms, who both served their country in the military and who were given a mortgage-free home by Operation Finally Home, a national, nonprofit organization dedicated to building homes for wounded, ill, or injured veterans and their families.

Kleenex "wrapped the home in love" by having friends and family members write notes of love on the walls before the drywall was put up and the home was completed. This beautiful piece of content tells both the story of hardship and of people rallying to support their loved ones, in a way that thematically connected to Kleenex's brand — that is, the idea that when someone needs a Kleenex, you hand them one, and that the tissue itself "wraps you in love."

These kinds of videos may reaffirm a sense of loyalty in Kleenex brand fans that this company is one they're happy to be loyal because they care and give back to those who are in need.

GEICO AND ADVOCACY

Marketers can create advertising campaigns and content that encourage people to advocate on their behalf. An easy way to measure your advocacy success is by the number of times someone has shared your video. Take insurance, for example. Car and home insurance isn't exactly the most exciting thing to buy, but it's a necessary expense. It's also one that takes a lot of time to shop around to get the best deal, and it usually has a deadline as to when you have to get it all sorted. It's a hassle.

I moved to Los Angeles in 2014 and needed both car and home insurance, and I'd seen Geico's commercials on YouTube. I thought they were funny and compelling, so I gave them a call and signed up. After a few years of excellent service from Geico, along with continued truly excellent advertising campaigns on YouTube, I had become not just a loyal customer, but an advocate. I was recently walking with a friend, and the topic of insurance came up. I pulled out my phone and showed him the most recent Geico commercial I'd seen (visit www.youtube.com/user/GEICO to see its videos and commercials.) I talked about how excellent I think their commercials are, how I've been really happy with their rates, and how I think their service has been truly excellent at all times. My friend messaged me a few days later to let me know he'd signed up with Geico for his new home insurance needs. In this real-world example, Geico's advertising became a tool I used in my advocacy of its service. Geico's commercials are so good I want to show my friends because I know they'll laugh. It then creates a moment where I talk about my experience and advocate to my friend to sign up for Geico's services.

TIP

If you're a marketer with customers who may be advocates, a campaign goal may be to create video content for YouTube that those advocates can then share with their friends, family and beyond. Chapter 9 outlines how to develop a content strategy.

Determining Your Budget for Media and Production

When you know the challenge your marketing brief is aiming to solve and you have a sense of what success would look like, you'll be able to set the total budget you want to assign to this campaign.

You can determine this number by looking at your total marketing budget for the year or period, such as the quarter, and deciding where else you may like to spend your money.

After you determine your budget, you need to split it into two parts: media and production.

Breaking down your annual budget

When you're planning out your marketing initiatives for the year, you'll set your total budget. For example, if you have $400,000 to spend on marketing for the year, you may break this first into quarters, assigning $100,000 per quarter.

You can then break down your budget further by geographic region, such as national versus local marketing, or by channel, assigning budgets to traditional media channels, digital channels, and other marketing initiatives like PR and events.

Taking the 70/20/10 approach

A popular approach with marketers when trying to determine the amount of money to assign to channels is the 70/20/10 approach. This model suggests that you use

>> Seventy percent of your marketing budget for your most reliable and proven marketing channels

>> Twenty percent of your budget for the channels you feel somewhat confident about but are still learning and experimenting with

>> Ten percent of your budget for testing entirely new approaches to marketing

If you're starting to use YouTube as part of your marketing for the first time, consider setting a small budget aside to experiment.

Calculating your production budget

Making video for YouTube can cost more money than making assets for other media channels. For example, Facebook and Instagram offer advertising options where all you need is an image, such as a photograph of your product, and some text with a link. Google search is even simpler, requiring just a few lines of text and a link.

YouTube, however, does require video creative. Don't worry! You don't need to make a TV-quality commercial costing millions of dollars or hire a crew of people in an exotic location. Often making video for YouTube advertising is as simple as filming using your phone's camera.

You should, however, consider whether you need to factor in the following for your production budget:

>> **Hardware:** You may need to purchase or rent a camera. Ask yourself first whether you can get away with using your mobile phone. You may also need things like lighting and microphones.

>> **People and places:** You may want to feature a person in your commercial who wants to get paid for their work. You also may need to pay rent to a location, such as a restaurant or hotel, depending on where you want to shoot your commercial.

>> **Editing and post-production:** You need to edit your video for content and length and ensure that it looks good. You can edit yourself using a laptop and freely available software, or you can find help from a professional editor. Post-production includes things like tweaking the color of the video footage and adding music.

TIP

A classic rule amongst marketers is the 80/20 rule. The idea is that your production budget should be 20 percent of your total budget. For example, if you've assigned a total budget of $20,000 to your YouTube efforts, 20 percent of this budget, or $4,000, would be set aside for the costs associated with making your video creative. The remaining 80 percent would be assigned to your media spend (see the next section).

Chapter 11 talks about how to create video, delving into topics like hardware, shooting, editing, and more in detail.

Setting your media budget

Your *media budget* is the amount of money you'll assign to buying advertising space on YouTube. If you're following the 80/20 rule (see preceding section), you'd set aside $16,000 to spend on paid advertising media.

WARNING

A common mistake with advertisers is thinking that you can upload your video to YouTube and somehow people will magically find it without any need for media spend. Unfortunately, this thinking isn't true. YouTube is a fantastic place to put your video to be found, but it's an even better place to put your video to be lost. With so many videos being uploaded to YouTube every minute of every day, videos need a media budget to ensure that the people you want to target see them.

The Google Ads solution (see Chapter 7) lets you set up your media budget and gives you an exceptional amount of control about how you spend your dollar. You can regularly check to ensure that your budget is delivering to your needs and turn your spend on or off as needed. For example:

>> You'll be able to set a maximum budget for each day, week, and month and make adjustments to the marketing spend any time.

>> You'll pay only when someone chooses to view your TrueView ad for at least 30 seconds or when they engage with your ad — like clicking on a call to action overlay, a card, or a companion banner.

>> You can set your account to bill automatically or manually; the manual option ensures you don't spend anything without confirming each time.

>> You can start with as little as $10 per day for locally focused campaigns, making YouTube a very cost-effective place to start to advertise.

Visit Chapter 7 for a detailed breakdown of how you buy and optimize paid advertising on YouTube.

The Necessary Nature of the Brief

A *brief* is very simply a document of a few pages or more, and it's where you set the challenge that your marketing campaign must solve. It delves into what is the purpose of the initiative, what success looks like, what must be delivered, budget, timelines and more.

REMEMBER

Your brief is the single most important part of a campaign because it contains all the information that lays the foundation and framework of what you'll create and deliver. If you miss something or even make a mistake in your brief, it'll affect the results of your campaign. Use the brief to

>> Capture all the relevant information needed to make decisions about your campaign.

>> Align any team members or service providers on what's required.

>> Clearly capture the mandate of your brief so that you can reflect on it and ensure that you're doing what you need and want to do.

>> Make you think thoroughly through the details and nuances and reflect back on your decisions before you start doing anything.

REMEMBER

In Chapter 1, I talk about picking a lane to help you decide whether you want to use YouTube as an advertiser, as a content marketer, or as a combination of the two. You should know your lane before you create your brief. If you don't, check out Chapter 1 and make your decision before you start writing your brief.

Developing the Key Components of a YouTube Brief

Most marketers will create their own brief template and use the same approach for each campaign they develop. A typical brief may include some or all of the following components:

>> Information about the campaign

>> Campaign or initiative's needs

>> Deliverables and considerations

REMEMBER

Even though the information described in the following sections may seem comprehensive and result in several pages, a great brief is one that is brief! It gets to the point and communicates only the most important information.

About the campaign

The section about the campaign may contain all or some of the following information:

>> **Client name:** The name of the person creating the brief, the team, and the company name

>> **Campaign name:** The working title name for the project

>> **Total budget:** The total budget assigned to the campaign

>> **Key dates:** The date the brief was written and the start and end dates of the campaign

>> **Prepared by:** The name of the person who prepared the brief

>> **Contact information:** The contact information of the person who prepared the brief

Campaign or initiative's needs

This section typically contains the following information regarding the campaign or initiative's needs:

>> Campaign overview

>> Target audience and actionable audience insights

>> Marketing messages

Campaign overview

In this section, you should provide a paragraph or two describing the campaign, providing the context as to what business challenge you're trying to solve. Consider addressing the reasons why the campaign is needed, along with any opportunities or challenges to consider.

Target audience and actionable audience insights

In this section, describe your target audience, answering who they are and where they are. (Refer to Chapter 3 for details on creating a picture of your target audience.) Also include any unique insights you may have uncovered about them.

You can attach any research you may have uncovered that provides additional information on your target audience, including their demographic profile, habits like the content they consume, where they consume it, how they spend their time, and any information about their lifestyle that is relevant. Think about how the audience thinks, feels, and behaves. You may include information on products they currently use and a brief overview of the competitive landscape, especially if your competitor is marketing a similar product.

Marketing messages

This section is your opportunity to provide specifics about the messages you'd like communicated.

A good marketing campaign usually focuses on a single message to communicate. It's the single most persuasive message that will deliver to your campaign's objective — in this case, influencing people to consider the product.

You can also include reasons to believe, which are the features of your product or service that prove it does what you say it does. These can be rational reasons — in this case, the new ingredient for effective stain fighting, as well as emotional reasons, like the fact it takes the worry out of laundry.

Include a *call to action*, the action you want people to take after they've seen your ad.

Think about the goals you'd like to achieve, such as how many video views you'd like and how many people you hope will click through to purchase. Include details on how these KPIs will be tracked, such as by using YouTube Analytics.

Deliverables and considerations

You also will want to include the following information in your brief:

>> **Creative considerations:** Call out any creative considerations that you need to address, such as any guidance as to how the ad or content should look, sound, or feel tonally. You want to give the creative a sense of the spirit.

>> **Creative requirements:** If you're creating an ad campaign to run on YouTube, you can list the ad formats you'll require creative for. Often clients writing briefs for their creative agencies won't specify the media at this stage. (Refer to Chapter 4 for an overview on the ad formats available.)

>> **Timeline:** Detail how much time is available to create the campaign, when it will go live, how long it will run for, and any special notes on media flighting. Also include when the campaign will be over.

TIP

Media flighting refers to the scheduling of your campaign's ads. Sometimes you'll have ads running; sometimes you will have them paused. You can specify start and end dates for your campaign, along with phases when your ads should be live in the market or paused.

>> **Budget breakdown:** Include a breakout of how much you'll spend on producing the creative and how much on media

>> **Any mandatories:** Include any mandatories, such as legal copy inclusion or logo usage.

>> **Additional information:** If you need to review any other resources before starting work on this campaign or add any other information to your brief, capture it here.

Chapter **3**

Targeting Your Audience

I n this chapter, you discover the power of an audience insight to form an action-able base for your ad campaigns and content initiatives on YouTube. You find out how to use powerful research tools to uncover meaningful insights about your audience and ways to use those insights to influence the creative of your ad campaign or content strategy.

Creating a Picture of Your Target Audience

Before you get started, you need to have a deep understanding of who your marketing campaign will speak to. If you know your audience, you'll be able to make choices that inform both the video creative you make and the media target-ing options you select.

You can reach just about anyone on YouTube. Google and YouTube offer lots of tools to help learn about and target your audience, ensuring that you reach only the people you want to talk to. Taking some time to think through who you'd like to target will help make your marketing campaign more manageable and focused. You'll have lots of options as to how to buy your media to reach them, but start by creating a clear picture in your head of who they are so that you know who you are talking to.

When it comes to defining an audience, marketers often break people into subgroups, which they then use to inform the development of creative, like advertisements and content, ensuring it speaks more directly to that group. For example, if you make a product that is targeted to parents, think about who those people maybe. How old are they? What are their behaviors and lives like? What challenges do they face? What do they like to watch, and where do they like to go?, These initial audience insights will inform your creative choices on how you communicate your product and ultimately how you make your YouTube video ad.

You can build a profile of your target audience by thinking through a few classic marketing dimensions:

» **Demographic:** *Demographic dimensions* are things like the audience's age, gender, parental status, or even household income. Perhaps you run a luxury stroller company, and you want to target first-time parents with a household income of $75,000 or more. Your video creative may feature parents of a similar age, dressed in a way typical of that age group that would resonate with your desired audience.

» **Geographic:** Think through where your customer is located. They could be a local audience, nationwide, or even worldwide. Ask yourself where the people most likely to be interested in hearing from you are living and keep this in mind when developing advertising creative or content that speaks to them. For example, if you run a local bakery, your video ad may feature your store and scenes of the town where it can be found. If you run an online baking supply store, featuring local imagery probably won't be as important as showcasing your supplies being used in bakeries all over the country.

» **Psychographic:** *Psychographics* deal with mindset. You can think about your audience's personality traits, including things like their value and belief systems, interests in life, political, social, and cultural attitudes, and more. When you think about your audience through a psychographic lens, you start to build a fuller picture of who they are beyond just demographic and geographic criteria. You may decide to make video creative that overtly speaks to your audience's opinions on a topic. Perhaps you're passionate about the environment and have decided to lobby for your township to change its recycling policy. In your video, you can directly appeal to your audience for support by showing a local park becoming a cleaner environment without plastic bags if a policy change was made.

» **Activities, lifestyle, and interests:** Diving deeper into building a full and complete profile of your audience members, you can think about the kinds of activities they like to engage in. Perhaps they spend their time engaged in outdoor activities, such as camping and hiking, or perhaps they prefer fine dining and wine tasting holidays. When you're creating video advertising, you can often find better performance results by including signals that resonate with your audience. For example, a Canadian-based fashion retailer made a series of advertisements promoting its men's clothing range. The retailer discovered that country music and bluegrass were popular with the desired audience, so they started to make video creative that included models with guitars and banjos. These videos performed better than the creative that didn't feature musical instruments.

» **Product usage:** What other kinds of products and services does your ideal audience use? Thinking through what else your audience may purchase and use in life can give you a sense of their expectations of other products and services. Perhaps you offer an online meal delivery service targeted to health-food fanatics and exercise fans. Understanding the other products, such as protein bars and vitamin supplements, and services, such as gym memberships and personal trainers, that they use may allow you to highlight similar features that your product or service offers. For example, if a fancy gym offers a towel service, perhaps your meal delivery includes a higher quality napkin. If a protein bar is vegan and locally sourced, highlight that your food is also sourced from local farms. You can make creative choices to highlight those connections, reaffirming in your desired audience members that what you have to offer is something that they'd like.

» **Media consumption:** Of course, media consumption is an interesting lens to think through. Your desired audience will visit certain websites, use particular apps, and be interested in topics, themes, and a variety of different types of content. The big question here to consider is whether your desired audience members use YouTube, and if they do, what do they like to watch on YouTube? You can make some creative choices based on what your audience likes to watch on YouTube.

These dimensions help you think about who you want to talk to and how to inform the video creative you make.

TIP

Jot down your thoughts about your audience for each of these dimensions so that you can use these notes to guide your choices when you're ready to buy media. YouTube offers many advanced methods of targeting the right audience. Check out Chapter 7 to find out more about buying paid media.

Gaining Insights into Your Audience

After you have a deeper picture of who you want to target (see preceding section), you can set about creating a marketing campaign that will speak to them. What you need to deliver a truly impactful marketing campaign on YouTube is a unique insight that you use to inform your creative and media that goes beyond dimensions like demographics or geography.

REMEMBER

An insight about your audience forms the basis of the messages you communicate, the video you create, the media you buy, and the actions you ask the viewer to take.

Insights

An insight is not a data point. Knowing that 55,000 people visited your website in the month of June or that 127,000 people watch your most recent quilting video are not insights. Those are interesting and potentially useful data points, but insights are more advanced than mere numbers.

An insight is

>> Based in fact, using multiple data points as supporting evidence

>> Novel and yet immediately knowable as possibly true

>> Meaningful in that you can do something with it

>> Considered by a human brain, not just pulled from a report

>> Ideally a problem your product or service can solve

Often insights are part art and part science. A great insight just feels right when you land upon it. While finding an insight can take time, when you do, it will influence your whole marketing campaign for the better.

Consider the following data points, insight, and resulting action:

>> **Fictional data point:** At Big City Bank, our reports show that people ages 34 to 54 spend more money than they save when they should be putting more money aside for retirement. When asked about their spending choices using a focus group and survey, people said they wanted things today, and that tomorrow seemed far away.

>> **Insight:** People feel that spending money is more fun than saving money for the future.

>> **YouTube Marketing campaign idea:** Video advertising creative can show people how saving can be fun today as well as a good idea for tomorrow.

OUT-OF-SIGHTS

Avinash Kaushik, a Googler who evangelizes for how marketers can use data to fundamentally reinvent their approach to digital, would often say that insights are good, but what you're really looking for is an *out-of-sight!*

I love the way Avinash thought about insights because what he's pushing for here is that the best insights really blow your mind. They can reveal truths about people that no one has addressed. If you uncover such an out-of-sight, you have found something truly magical that will transform your marketing campaign from being good to groundbreaking.

You don't need to find an out-of-sight that changes the whole world — just one that will make your marketing campaign on YouTube really stand apart.

Dove's Campaign for Real Beauty

A well-known campaign from the soap brand Dove, part of Unilever, is an excellent example of how an out-of-sight informed the creative of an advertising campaign delivered through YouTube that became one of the most watched online ads ever. Since 2004, Dove's brand campaign had been the Campaign for Real Beauty, which it created after undertaking a study that found some startling facts about how women perceive themselves.

Consider the following data point, which formed the foundation for the insight and on which the campaign was built:

- **»** **Data point:** The study found that only 4 percent of women, when asked, consider themselves beautiful.

- **»** **Insight:** The way women see themselves is not how others perceive them, and women can often be their own worst critic.

- **»** **YouTube Marketing campaign idea:** An FBI-trained forensic sketch artist draws the woman's portrait, without seeing her, based purely on her description of herself. Once the sketch is complete, the woman leaves the room. Then the same artist draws the same woman but based on the description provided by another woman, who met her earlier. When the two sketches are placed side by side, the second sketch, described by the stranger, is more beautiful — and more accurate — than the self-described sketch.

This insight informed a compelling creative idea that manifested in video creative made for YouTube, lasting more than 6 minutes, delivering over 163 million views, and becoming one of the most shared videos ever, with both metrics still growing. Dove made the video in 25 different languages and uploaded it to 46 Dove YouTube channels globally. The campaign won many advertising awards and continues to resonate with new audiences who discover it today. While the video delivered on Dove's goal of an effective brand campaign and hopefully encouraged more people to choose Dove products, it went further, giving people an important and meaningful reminder that they can be their own harshest critics.

I dare you to watch the video and not cry. Now walk over to the mirror and tell yourself you're awesome, because you are.

Developing Audience Insights

You know your campaign will be more successful if your brief contains a compelling and actionable insight, but how do you generate insights? If you want output, you need input!

Try the following approach to collect inputs and synthesize them into insights:

1. **Collect all your existing data.**

   Set about aggregating your inputs, integrating them, and looking for commonalities, patterns, trends, and themes. The more diverse the data set, often the better. Starting with what you already have is easiest — for example, grab any reports from your website, social profiles, existing videos, sales data, and more. I like to print these reports so that I can easily group them later. The idea is to gather any and all previous data, surveys, feedback from customers, and other inputs you have that may help inform your next campaign.

2. **Find more data for a fuller picture.**

   A fuller data set gives you a more accurate picture and more information to work with, so go beyond your own data and look for articles and studies from third parties. See what relevant information you can find by searching on Google. In the upcoming section "The Best Tools and Resources for Insights," I list ways to find and uncover new data points and interesting correlations, source surveys, and feedback from people, as well as how to add more data to your total data set.

3. **Sort all your data into the Four C framework.**

   Take all of these various data points and inputs and start to sort them into groups. You can use the Four C framework, described in the following section, to organize your inputs.

The Four C Framework for Insights

There's no right or wrong way to organize your data and inputs to help generate your insights. You can look for themes and commonalities or even just highlight a handful of the most interesting and useful points that you think are relevant from what you've uncovered. I like to use the Four C Framework to group things. It makes the mass of data you've assembled more manageable.

Consumer

Consumer insights deal with the individual's mindset. Think through how individuals in your target audience are feeling, what motivates them, what are they hoping to achieve, and what encourages them to act. With consumer's thoughts, feelings, and behaviors, you must look for the why behind those thoughts and actions. If behavior is functional, the insight, the why behind it, is the emotional.

Consider the following questions:

>> **What does your target audience want most in life right now?** Can you use video to explain how your offering can help them achieve something they want in life?

>> **Why would they want to choose your product or service?** Can you create video that extols the benefits of your offering in a clear and compelling way?

>> **Why might they choose a competitor's offering?** Can video combat some of the reasons why they might choose an alternative?

>> **How does your product or service make them feel?** Can you use video to tap into those positive feelings and engender more good feeling?

>> **What might stop them from buying from you?** Can you use video to address that issue? Can video convince them otherwise?

>> **How has their behavior changed over the last year?** Can you use video to speak to their changing needs, wants, and actions?

>> **What does your target audience like most about you?** Can they tell other people on your behalf about why they love you?

>> **If your customer could change one thing about your product or service, what would it be?** Perhaps you've made some tweaks that you can use video to communicate to encourage people to buy and buy again.

Category

The *category* in which you operate refers to the division of business with shared characteristics. For example, if you sell specialized sporting goods online, your categories may be sporting goods for specific sports, sporting goods in general, online retailers, clothing, ecommerce, and others. Look for insights through the category lens.

When it comes to your category:

>> **Are people's behaviors changing? Are their tastes and preferences changing?** Are there new ways to purchase or use products or services, new styles of product, or methods of service delivery in the category that may influence what you're able to sell? Can you look for videos that show indications of changing category tastes?

>> **What are the consumer's expectations of this category?** With regard to innovation, pricing, service delivery, and so on, what do they believe is standard practice? Does the consumer expect that videos about this category will be on YouTube? Do those videos exist?

>> **What other products or services are in this category?** Have any new products or services been developed? Are consumer expectations changing as a result of new developments? Can video play a role in showcasing new products or services, or can video complement or augment them?

>> **Is this category growing or shrinking?** Can you grow by reaching more people who are coming to this category, or do you need to grow by encouraging existing category customers to spend more money? Can video play a role in bringing more people to the category?

>> **How do the seasons affect this category?** Do any seasonal trends affect this category? Do people spend more or less at certain times of the year, such as during certain holidays? Would you make different YouTube video creative based on the time of the year?

>> **What trends are on the rise in this category?** Are new trends emerging in this category that may inform a change to your product or service or to your advertising creative, content, media, and ultimately your marketing campaign? Are people searching for videos related to these trends?

>> **How does this category appear on YouTube?** What videos exist on YouTube in this category? Who is making those videos, and what are the videos about? Are the videos popular? What are people commenting?

Competitor

Take a look at your *competitors*, the people who are in similar businesses as you, even if they are in different geographies, to see what they are doing. You can learn about your audience from how your competitor is talking to them and how they are reacting.

Think about the following questions:

>> **How do our competitors market to their target audience?** Does this approach tell you something about the audience you may not have considered?

>> **How is their audience different from yours?** Could you be reaching a different audience who might like to hear from you? Could you be talking to your audience in a different way?

>> **When it comes to YouTube, which of their videos performs well?** What do you think makes the video perform well? What do you like and not like about it?

>> **What are people saying in the comments and on their social sites?** Are people responding positively? Are they asking for something that's not being delivered that perhaps you can provide?

>> **What kinds of videos are they making?** Do you think these videos are of interest and helpful to the audience? What would you do differently?

>> **What do their ads look like? What's the tone and style?** Have your competitors made a creative choice that makes these ads perform well or perhaps poorly?

>> **What products or services do they offer that you don't? Are you at an advantage or a disadvantage in this regard?** Are your competitors offering something the audience wants that you don't yet offer or that you haven't yet communicated that you do offer?

Culture

Think about what may be happening at a cultural level that can affect your target audience. The cultural lens provides the context in which all other lenses are operating within and encourages you to take a wider view of what's influencing your audience. Cultural influences can inform and shape the beliefs, wants, and needs of your audience. Often, tapping into cultural insights will allow you to develop insights that inform your creative, your media, and your marketing campaign.

Use these questions to think through what's happening in culture:

>> **What is happening in the economy?** Are people employed and earning, or are times hard? Are the costs of life's essentials, such as food, accommodation, and transportation, going up or down? What videos are people making on this topic?

>> **What is the current political landscape?** How are people feeling based on the current political climate? Is it a time of prosperity or austerity? Are people feeling positive, safe, optimistic, and excited, or are they concerned about the state of the world and how it may affect them?

>> **What macro trends are occurring in culture?** Think about trends in fashion, news and media, entertainment, food, travel, consumerism, activism, the environment, and more. Can you tap in to any trends in videos on YouTube?

>> **What are the ideas that are being discussed at a cultural level?** What are the biggest issues that academics, intellectuals, pundits, and the media are discussing? What are people talking about in social media?

>> **What customs are still prevalent or are newly forming?** For example, are people communicating differently? One example is the rise of memes, emojis, and the like as valid methods of communication. How are people using video on YouTube?

>> **How are people, as a social group, behaving differently?** Are people traveling more or less? Are they spending more time at home or going out? Are more groups forming around shared interests, or are people more isolated?

>> **What are people's beliefs, feelings, and behaviors?** In general, how are people's beliefs changing? Are certain social norms or traditions being rethought? Do you have a general sense of how people are feeling about life today?

The Best Tools and Resources for Insights

Google and YouTube offer an array of incredible and freely available tools and resources that you can use to discover more about the audience you'd like to target. They can help you develop compelling insights for your marketing campaign brief.

Take a look through the following tools and resources and experiment with them:

>> The Trending Video page on YouTube and the YouTube Trends blog

>> The Google Trends tool

>> The Google Surveys tool

>> Social media and comments

Trending on YouTube

Trends can be helpful indicators of what people are responding to and watching at any given time. A few resources are available to help you track trends:

>> Trending videos on YouTube (www.youtube.com/feed/trending)

>> YouTube trends blog (http://youtube-trends.blogspot.com)

Trending video on YouTube

The trending video page on YouTube shows you the videos that are trending around the world (see Figure 3-1). You may see some videos you'd expect, such as the latest music video from a popular artist or the summer's big blockbuster movie trailer, but you'll also find videos that will surprise you. Think of those classic videos that trended, like the Cinnamon Challenge, Harlem Shake, and even the ALS Ice Bucket Challenge. These videos are what you may call *viral videos* in that they seem to spread exponentially like a virus.

Trending videos are specific to the country you're in, but they aren't personalized to you; the videos you see are the same videos everyone else will see. YouTube updates this list every 15 minutes, so it's a super-fresh list of what's hot. Think of the trending videos page as a top chart of what's big right now on YouTube.

Trending videos aren't just based on video view count, though. In addition to how many views the video has, the trending videos page can be based on

>> How quickly these videos are garnering views, which is called *velocity*

>> Where the views are coming from

>> The age of the video

FIGURE 3-1:
The YouTube
Trending page
updates daily
showing the
latest trending
videos.

MAKING THE TRENDING VIDEOS PAGE

Whenever I give a general public talk about how to be successful on YouTube, people always ask the same question: "How do I get on the trending videos tab?" My answer is always the same: "You don't." I then go on to explain that it's a fool's errand to try and get on the trending page.

If you focus on making great content, becoming a trending video can happen, but making being a trending video your main aim is hard for two main reasons:

- A massive number of videos are competing to trend, and unless you are the latest, hottest pop sensation dropping a much-anticipated music video or a YouTuber with a massive audience, it's going to be hard to guarantee making the list.

- YouTube doesn't reveal the exact formula for how the trending list works because it doesn't want people trying to game the system. Sure, YouTube combines various signals to determine what's hot, but some magic we'll never know about is involved.

YouTube writes:

"Even if your video meets all the above criteria, it may not appear on Trending, as many other videos may also meet those criteria. The Trending system tries to choose videos that will be most relevant to our viewers and most reflective of the broad content on the platform."

— `https://support.google.com/youtube/answer/7239739?hl=en`

Oh, you can't pay to be on this page either, YouTube doesn't favor any particular people, and they don't count views you get from paid media.

TIP

When you look at the trending videos, look for creative inspiration to inform your video ad or content creative. Often, these videos have found some of the latest tips and tricks to snag those video views and shares. Think of them as a masterclass in good creative.

YouTube trends blog

Another useful resource is the YouTube trends blog at `http://youtube-trends.blogspot.com`. While the YouTube team don't post on the blog often (at the time of writing, the last post was five months old), it still appears to be an active blog with interesting content about observations and analysis of trends on YouTube.

Search for something like *#IceBucketChallenge,* and you'll find a post from 2014 that breaks down performance data of this meme or how "The Gummy Bear Song" broke 1 billion views. (I'd never heard of it either.) Think of this resource as a library of case studies of the most viral of viral videos.

Google Trends

Google Trends, shown in Figure 3-2, is gold, and time spent using this tool is never wasted. Using real-time Google and YouTube data, Google Trends lets you search for anything.

Google Trends is like the world's biggest survey, enabling you to see what people are interested in based on what they are searching for:

» You could look for spikes around things happening in the world and then make videos that tap into those interests.

» You can use the geographic data to look for regions you may like to target with your media. Perhaps more people search for your product or service in Wyoming, and so you'll buy media for your video ads targeted there.

FIGURE 3-2:
The Google
Trends tool is an
invaluable
resource to help
explore trends
and behaviors to
help develop
audience insights.

>> You can search for your brand to see whether people are searching for you, what they are searching for, and any other search terms you can tap into on YouTube.

>> You can see whether your competitor's names come up in the related search queries box to give you an idea of who you are competing with.

>> You can use Google Trends to find products and for market research, to find a niche.

Using Google Trends

If you spend time playing with Google Trends, you'll see how useful it is. Follow these steps:

1. **Visit** `http://trends.google.com` **and enter any search term you'd like and press Enter.**

   For example, enter your favorite celebrity, a product, or a sporting event. The results page, shown in Figure 3-3, displays *search interest,* or the number of people searching for that phrase, over time, showing peaks and troughs.

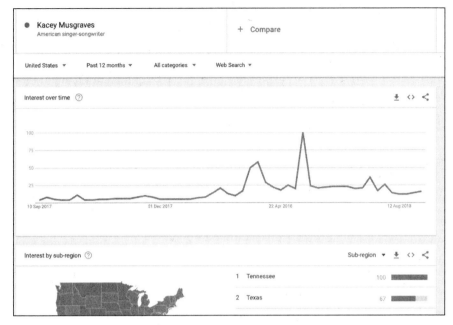

FIGURE 3-3:
My search for country singer Kacey Musgraves shows peaks in search interest, with the biggest peak in May 2018 when she appeared on the TV show SNL.

2. **(Optional) Use the drop-down menus to change the country, timeframe (going back to 2004), or category and whether you're looking for web search data or something else.**

3. **Choose YouTube Search from the drop-down menu to see how people have been searching for this phrase specifically on YouTube.**

   The menu is set to Web Search by default.

   Do you see anything revealing, such as certain times of the year when people are searching more or regions where people are searching from?

TIP

4. **Scroll down to the Related Topics and Related Queries sections to see other topics and search phrases people use similar to your search.**

   This information, shown in Figure 3-4, can be a source of inspiration to think through other angles, revealing what else is on people's minds when searching.

5. **Scroll up to the top of the Results page and add a comparison search term by clicking on + Compare.**

   You can compare two search terms against each other. You can even add more comparison terms, up to five in total (see Figure 3-5).

FIGURE 3-4:
Related topics
and related
queries let you
explore similar
search terms
people look for.

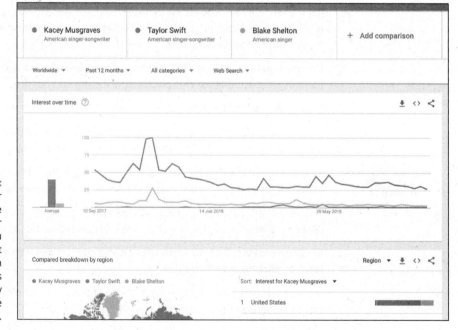

FIGURE 3-5:
I've added Taylor
Swift and Blake
Shelton for
comparison. You
can see that
search interest in
Taylor Swift is
significantly
higher than the
other two artists.

Exploring even more on Google Trends

You can explore even more on Google Trends. Use the left-hand side menu to find

» **Trending Searches:** This area shows you the break-out search terms that are trending for that particular day. You can switch to Real-Time Search Trends, shown in Figure 3-6, to see a top list of terms popular in the last 24 hours and drill down by geography and category.

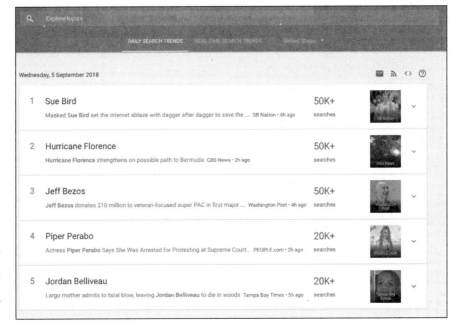

FIGURE 3-6:
At any point in time, you can check out trending searches to see what the world or a specific country is looking for.

» **Top charts:** This incredible section, shown in Figure 3-7, lets you choose a country, month, and category to see tons of top charts for the top searches for actors, animals, athletes, authors, automotive, people, politicians, TV shows, songs, musicians, and more. You can choose to see data by month or by the entire year. For example, the most popular search in 2017 in the category of calories was a Unicorn Frappuccino calories."

» **Subscriptions:** Setting up some subscriptions to search terms that are relevant to you is a good idea. Enter the search term or a topic, choose your region, and set how often you want to receive emails (weekly or monthly), and Google will send you updates about those search terms. You can choose things like the Top daily search trends or All daily search trends. Staying aware of what people are searching for can help you make decisions about the kinds of videos you may need to create.

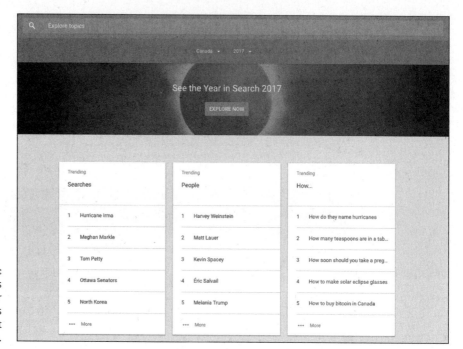

FIGURE 3-7:
Top charts breaks
out handy lists for
popular searches
into different
themed lists.

Use all of this data to think about how your videos can tap into people's intents and interests, and to uncover related topics, times of the year when you may want to run your videos, and more.

Google Surveys

One of the best ways to develop insights about your audience is to ask them questions! If you're able to hit the street, email, or call up friends, simply start asking people questions about what they like and what they want, what motivates them, what they would like to be different, and more.

If you're looking for an easier and more scalable solution to survey people, you can use Google Surveys, which is a paid service that lets you build and run your own survey, delivering it to your target audience wherever they are on the Internet.

TIP

If you don't have budget to run a paid Google Survey, you can use Google Forms to create your own questionnaire, which you can email to friends and post on social media. Visit http://docs.google.com/forms.

Google Surveys works by enabling people to answer short surveys in exchange for access to premium content. For example, imagine you want to read an article on a popular newspaper's website, but that content is behind a pay-wall. You may be given the option to answer a survey in exchange for accessing that content for free and not having to pay for the subscription. It's a win-win!

You can get results within 48 hours, and the data is presented back to you in beautiful graphs and charts, making it easy to interpret the results. Remember, real people are answering your questions, so the potential to learn is enormous.

TIP

You pay only when you're ready to send your survey. You see the confirmation screen for costs after you make your various selections as to who you want to target.

Sign into your Google account and then follow these steps the first time you run Google Surveys:

1. **Visit** `https://surveys.withgoogle.com` **and click on Run a Survey.**

2. **Choose your country.**

   Remember to choose the country where you are located. An option later allows you to change the country where the survey will run.

3. **If you're offered to opt in to email marketing communications, make your choice and click Next.**

4. **View and accept the terms of service.**

   To accept them, check the I agree box after you've read the terms and then click on Submit.

   You're then able to get started building your survey.

To create a new survey in Google Surveys:

1. **Choose + New Survey.**

2. **Click on the "+" button.**

   You see a page that allows you to build your survey.

3. **Choose who you want to target and then click on Continue.**

   You can choose options like country, age, and gender (see Figure 3-8). As you choose options, the price per completed survey will change. The more specific the audience you want to reach, the likely the higher the cost.

   After you click on Continue, you see a screen that allows you to add questions.

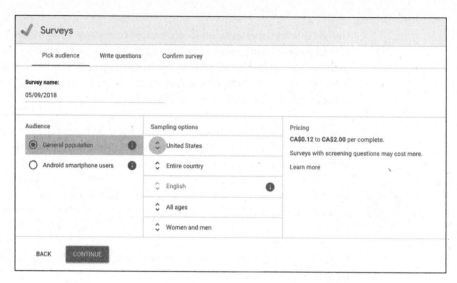

FIGURE 3-8:
Specify your
target audience.

4. **Choose the type of question you'd like to add and then click on Add Question.**

   Your choices include a single answer question, a question with multiple answers, rating scales, questions where you show an image and ask for an answer, and more.

   You return to the main survey screen.

5. **Edit the question's text and answer options.**

TIP

   When adding questions, you can set up some advanced options. For more information, see the nearby sidebar "Randomization and screener questions."

   Note that you can click on Save to save your survey's progress.

6. **Continue adding questions and editing the text and answer options; click on Confirm when you're finished.**

TIP

   To get better results, ask no more than four or five questions. While Google Surveys is a great tool to test things, it's not as useful for lengthy questionnaires.

7. **After you create all your questions, click on Confirm to proceed.**

   You see a summary Review and Purchase page, shown in Figure 3-9.

8. **Indicate how many survey responses you want to purchase and how often you want to run the survey.**

   For example, you can run the survey only once for 100 times or every month for 100 times, which is great if you want the same survey to run on a regular basis for a steady flow of market research.

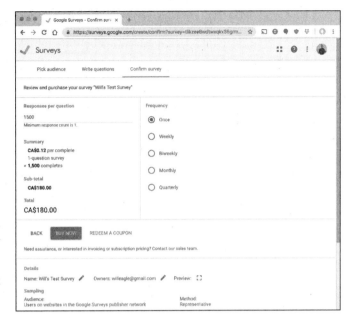

FIGURE 3-9:
Choose how many survey responses you want. Google will calculate the cost per response and give you a total.

RANDOMIZATION AND SCREENER QUESTIONS

When you're adding the text and answers for each question, you'll have some advanced options you can tweak. For example, you can randomize your answer order so that the list of answers you provide won't always appear in the same order. Randomization makes for a better testing methodology and more accurate results.

You can also add a screener question. For example, if you want to research ice cream eaters, your first question may be "Do you like to eat ice cream?" If your answer choices are yes or no, you can choose to serve your following questions only to those who answered yes.

The multiple-answers format is the best choice for screener questions because respondents can identify with more than one answer choice and select a combination of answers.

Google lets you have up to four screener questions, but keep in mind that the more specific you are, the harder it may be to get the number of respondents you want. Use screener questions only when necessary. For example, if you're surveying people about their experience owning a car, a reasonable screener question is "Are you a car owner?"

Google calculates the total cost.

TIP

Before you confirm and purchase, Google Surveys may show you a screen explaining that it can test your survey to determine the cost and the audience size. This screen typically appears when you have a screening question. Google Surveys wants to make sure that enough respondents meet your criteria. For example, if your screener questions are "Is your name John? Are you 35 years old? Do you live in Tampa?" then the screener questions may be too specific! You can edit your survey to reduce the restrictions your screener questions impose. (For more on screener questions, see the nearby sidebar.)

9. **Click on Buy Now when you're ready to proceed.**

   You may be asked to enter payment information if you don't already have that information associated with your Google account.

   Your survey will go live shortly after you've made payment.

Social media and comments

One of the easiest ways to discover insights about your audience is to look directly at what they're saying on social media, such as on your Facebook page, your Twitter, or in the YouTube comments section.

REMEMBER

People show their interest with views and likes, but they express their opinions in the comments! Spend some time on your social channels or, if you don't have any, look at your competitor's social channels. What are people saying? Do their comments give you any clues as to untapped insights that can inform your campaign?

One way to use YouTube and the comments to help mine for insights is to create a video where you simply ask people what they think! The vast majority of popular YouTubers will end their videos by asking their audience to comment, telling them what they thought of their video, of the topic, what they'd like to see next, and so on. Maybe you can make a video and post it to your YouTube channel asking people questions that you'll then use to inform your campaign.

YouTube Analytics, Google Analytics, and your Google Ads Reports are so important for mining insights that Part V is dedicated to them.

TIP

One of my favorite resources is Think With Google. Visit www.thinkwithgoogle.com for a truly amazing and comprehensive resource, direct from Google themselves, which is teeming with consumer and marketing insights, marketing resources, case studies, blog posts, and more. Check out the Tools section (found under Marketing Resources) and you'll find even more tools that can help you develop great insights.

2

Advertising Campaigns on YouTube

Chapter **4**

Advertising Formats

n this chapter, you explore a variety of YouTube ad formats. You find out the benefits of each format and the reasons to use them in a campaign. You also discover the ad policy that governs what you can and, most importantly, cannot advertise.

YouTube's Ad Format Offerings

YouTube has pioneered different ad formats and is constantly experimenting with new and compelling ways to deliver a marketer's message to the audience. YouTube always keeps in mind these two goals:

» What will be the most relevant, best possible, and most useful advertising experience for the audience without providing a negative experience of YouTube

» What will help advertisers reach the right people, at the right time, in the most effective and compelling way

Those goals are in order of priority. YouTube, and Google in general, will always put the user first.

When I worked at Google and YouTube, the company *deprecated* (meaning it stopped offering) a particular ad format that a lot of advertisers used. Why? It was simple: The ad format was too interruptive, too long, and too high a price for viewers of YouTube videos to pay (in terms of time, it took 30 seconds to watch). The ad format was no longer a good experience for the end user, and so it had to go.

YouTube's ad formats do change often, so for the latest ad format offerings, visit the official site at `https://ads.google.com`.

At the time of writing, YouTube has a simple yet comprehensive offering of ad formats that come in a variety of lengths, types, and abilities:

>> Display ads

>> Image ads

>> Skippable video ads

>> Nonskippable video ads

>> Midroll ads

>> Bumper ads

TECHNICAL STUFF

Forced versus *unforced* ads is a really important distinction to make for video ad formats. Some ad formats are forced and require you to watch to the end before your video will play. Ads that offer you a Skip Ad feature are unforced. A six-second *bumper ad* is a forced format, meaning that it plays in full before your video plays.

Display ads

You can run good old traditional display ads on YouTube. *Display ads,* sometimes known as banner ads, are ads that are static or animated image-based ads. Display ads appear on most websites next to a video that's playing on desktop and laptop computers, but not on mobile phones. On YouTube, display ads are 300 x 250 pixels or 300 x 60 pixels.

You can create your display ads in any graphics software program, such as Adobe Photoshop, and export them in formats like GIF, JPG, PNG, or HTML5.

WARNING

HTML5 ads aren't available to all advertisers. You must have an account with a history of policy compliance and good payment, and you must have spent more than $1,000 in total on advertising.

Some marketers make use of display ads on YouTube to drive clicks to their landing pages, although display ads aren't always the best type of media to deliver clicks. When was the last time you clicked on a display ad?

Think of display ads much like an outdoor billboard. Similar to someone walking by and taking in a message on a billboard, someone watching a video will likely also see the display ad and your message.

REMEMBER

Display ads are a great tool for awareness campaigns when you're trying to reach a big broad audience, but they're less useful for performance marketing campaigns where clicks and conversions are more important.

You can even run display ads in concert with your video ads, described later in this chapter, which means you have two chances on the page to communicate and reinforce your message.

TIP

If you're using a display ad to support a video ad, make sure that you keep the messaging consistent. For example, if your video ad is promoting your product's newest feature, ensure that your display ad also communicates that feature rather than a different product. Make sure that users who click on the video or display ad arrive on a landing page on your website that matches the ad's message.

Remember that display ads on YouTube are in competition with the video that's playing and all the thumbnails for other videos. Display ads, videos, and video thumbnails need to work hard to grab attention, so use animation and choose bold contrasting colors with limited text. If you're including a call to action to have people click, use something truly compelling. For example, instead of "Click here for more," you could try actions like "Sign up now" or "Donate today." The clearer and more compelling the benefit, the higher the chance for a click.

TIP

Google offers an amazing free tool named Google Web Designer that you can use to create engaging and interactive HTML5-based designs, perfect for making display ads. Google Web Designer, includes templates, which makes creating ads really easy. Visit www.google.com/webdesigner to download and install the program.

Image ads

Image ads appear across the bottom 20 percent of the video that's being played. You'll see these ads only on desktop and laptop computers. The viewer can dismiss the ad by clicking the X in the ad's upper right-hand corner. Image ads are 468 x 60 and 728 x 90 pixels and can be in JPEG, JPG, PNG, or GIF formats.

Marketers can use image ads in combination with other ads shown to the viewer in the same session. For example, a video ad may appear with a display ad to the right of the video you're watching, and an image ad may appear over the video (see Figure 4-1). Together, these ads work in concert.

TIP

If you're using image ads, make sure that you include a compelling call to action to encourage clicks.

this is a display ad

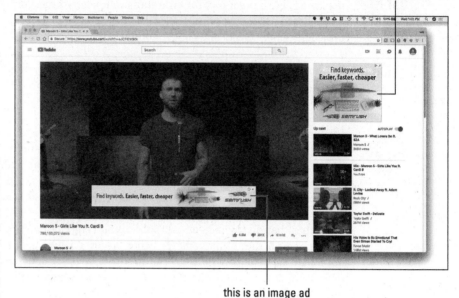

FIGURE 4-1:
While I was
watching a
Maroon 5 video,
a display ad
appeared to the
right of the video,
and an image
ad appeared
overlaying
the video.

this is an image ad

You may like this ad format because image ads

>> Are an easy ad format to create

>> Can be a cost-effective piece of your media spend

>> Complement other ad units running on the same page

WARNING

Image ads may not work for everyone. I find ads that overlay on top of the video I'm watching to be an ugly interruption, and I dismiss them immediately so they don't obscure what I'm watching. In addition, it's a small static image ad format, and the power of YouTube really exists in video.

TIP

Image ads can be confused with *in-video overlay ads.* These ads are the same as image ads in many ways but are available only in reservation sponsorship campaigns.

Skippable video ads

Possibly the ad format that makes YouTube the most incredible of platforms is the skippable video ad. *Skippable video ads* allow you to skip the ad after just five seconds of viewing.

Skippable video ads appear before, during, or after a video. The advertiser only pays when the viewer watches 30seconds or the end of the video ad, whichever comes first.

At the time of writing, Google TrueView is the name most commonly used to refer to skippable video ads on YouTube. TrueView was developed to provide a great viewing experience for the end user and to allow the advertiser to pay only for the views people watch. After all, why force someone to watch your ad when they may not be interested? Instead, TrueView encourages advertisers to make ads that people want to see. Even further, TrueView doesn't limit the length of your video ad, so you can make a 30-second ad or a 30-minute ad!

BLAH AIRLINES

In October 2014, the creative agency Eleven for the now defunct Virgin America airline created a 5 hour and 45-minute video ad. The ad features the fictional Blah Airlines flying from Newark to San Francisco. The video ad shows mannequins seated on a plane in various states of boredom, with passengers muttering, coughing, and jostling in their cramped seats and babies crying . The mind-numbingly boring video is designed to underscore just how tedious a long flight can be with standard air carriers, whereas Virgin America makes the experience an utter joy. (I always flew Virgin America and loved every minute of it. The airline doesn't exist anymore as it was bought and folded into Alaska Airlines a few years later.)

This video ad ran in TrueView on YouTube, taking advantage of the fact that you can run an ad of any length that you'd like and pay only when the viewer reaches the first 30 seconds or the end of the video, whichever comes first. I wonder how many people watched 30 seconds of it or even the entire thing! Of course, the point wasn't that people might watch the whole ad; the idea was an amazing press stunt written about on news sites and industry blogs.

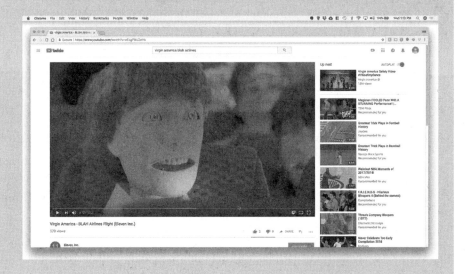

TrueView can come in two flavors:

>> **TrueView in-stream:** The TrueView in-stream ad plays before or during a video (see the nearby sidebar "Blah Airlines" for an example). You pay only when the user watches 30 seconds or to the end of the video, whichever comes first.

>> **TrueView video discovery:** This option, shown in Figure 4-2, allows your ad to appear alongside other YouTube videos in the search results page and on websites in the Google Display Network (GDN), a network of third-party websites outside of Google where your ads can also run. (For more on GDN, see the section "The Google Display Network," later in this chapter.) You pay only when the viewer chooses to watch your video by clicking on the ad.

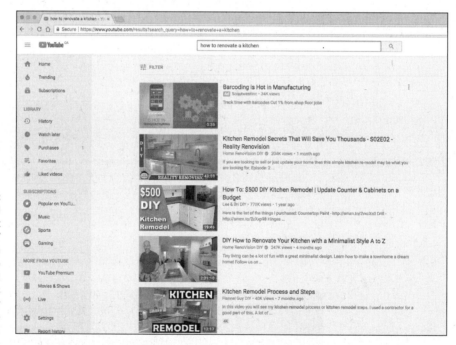

FIGURE 4-2: The ad "Barcoding is Hot in Manufacturing" appeared as a TrueView video discovery ad when I was searching for how to renovate a kitchen.

The added bonus of TrueView is that the view count of your video will be incremented each time a viewer watches 30 seconds or the full video ad, whichever comes first, or interacts with your video — for example, by clicking on the ad to visit your website. (Note that YouTube Analytics won't track video views of TrueView videos less than 10 seconds in length.)

You may like this ad format because skippable video ads

>> Have marketing power because someone is choosing to watch your ad, making it feel more like content, instead of being forced to watch it

>> Are an effective way to buy media because you're only paying when someone chooses to watch them

>> Offer up an open-ended video canvas where you're not restricted to length, unlike a TV commercial, which may limit you to 30 seconds

WARNING

Skippable video ads are more of a creative challenge because you need to make an ad that someone wants to watch. The good thing is that only lazy marketers would consider this challenge as a negative.

Nonskippable video ads

Nonskippable video ads work the same way as skippable video ads (see preceding section), except viewers do not have the option of skipping them.

YouTube is always evaluating whether nonskippable video ads provide a negative experience for the end user and will often experiment with the options available for this kind of ad format. In fact, YouTube uses a range of signals, such as how the user discovered the video, to determine when it may be okay to serve up a forced video ad.

Nonskippable video ads appear before, during, or after a video and force viewers to watch the entire ad, which are typically 15 to 20 seconds long.

Many traditional marketers like to use a nonskippable forced-view ad because that's how other media works. For example, TV commercials are forced because you can't skip ahead of them (unless you're using TiVo!) You can, of course, deliver a high-quality video ad that someone wants to watch and run it in a non-skippable ad format, but why force someone to watch your message even if they don't want to see it? Instead, make ad creative that people want to watch, run it in skippable ad formats like TrueView, and only show your ad to people who wanted to watch? (For more on skippable video ads, see the preceding section.)

You may like this ad format because nonskippable video ads

>> Guarantee someone will see your ad

>> Can work well as part of a media mix, complementing skippable formats

>> May fit the format of advertising creative already made, such as a 15-second TV ad that you can repurpose

Keep in mind that you may be forcing people to watch an ad they just don't want to see, which may mean it's not effective.

Check Google Ads (`https://ads.google.com`) for the latest options for nonskippable video ads.

Midroll ads

Midroll ads are is not so much a type of ad format, but rather a way in which your video ads may be served up. If you're watching a video that's more than 10 minutes long, a midroll ad may appear. *Midrolls ads* interrupt the video you're viewing, forcing you watch them before continuing with the video. YouTube inserts midroll ads only into longer videos, where it's not unreasonable for a viewer to complete the ad and carry on watching their video.

REMEMBER

YouTube is always running experiments to see what people will deem acceptable for their viewing experience. If YouTube finds that everyone abandons their video when a midroll ad interrupts it, it may tweak the criteria for serving up the ads — for example, only showing them in videos that last at least 20 minutes.

When popular YouTubers are uploading their longer videos, they have the option of manually inserting *ad break spaces* where their content natural pauses. They can also choose to have YouTube find the natural breaks in their video and insert midroll ad spaces automatically. For example, YouTube's machine learning is able to differentiate between moments in a video where a natural pause makes sense versus interrupting an important conversation taking place in the video.

Bumper ads

Partly thanks to the rise (and for some, fall) of platforms like SnapChat, Vine, and Instagram, shorter videos and ad formats are commonplace. A few years ago, YouTube created *bumpers,* a new ad format that is sometimes referred to as six-second ads (see Figure 4-3).

Bumper ads were developed to work especially well on mobile devices, where people don't want a long video ad to interrupt their viewing experience. The idea is that despite being a forced ad, a six-second format fits nicely with human's attention span and isn't too interruptive an experience, particularly when you're just hopping onto YouTube briefly.

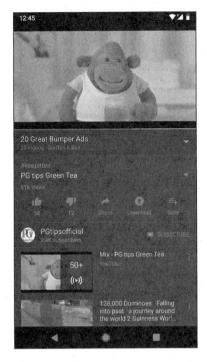

FIGURE 4-3: Bumper ads appear on mobile devices. I managed to quickly snag this screenshot before the six seconds was over.

You may be surprised at just how much you can communicate in a six-second ad and how useful they can be as part of your media mix. Six-second ads are great to

>> Complement your media, broadening your message by reaching a wider audience cost effectively, which increases your reach and frequency

>> Let you try a variety of different messages without a significant overhead of creative production

>> Add a cost-effective ad format into the mix because they're often not expensive to buy

>> Give you an ad format that works especially well on mobile devices, where the majority of people are watching YouTube and accessing the Internet

WARNING

Big marketers often take their 30-second TV commercial and cut it down into just 6 seconds. Sometimes this approach can work, but trying to force a lot of content into a short ad may not make for the best advertising creative.

You may like this ad format because bumper ads

>> Can be easier to create because they're short

>> Are great for reaching people on mobile, which is where a lot people are watching YouTube

- » Allow you to experiment with different creative approaches and messages to see what works best

- » Complement other media in the mix and can extend your reach and frequency

I can't think of any reasons why you wouldn't choose this ad format. I think bumper ads are great.

The YouTube Masthead

If you visit the YouTube home page (see Figure 4-4), you'll see the *Masthead,* a large display ad that spans across the page above the video thumbnails. The Masthead is the mother of all display ads, allowing advertisers to purchase a takeover of the YouTube home page for a full 24 hours. It's a huge canvas that you can customize by using images, text, video, and rich media.

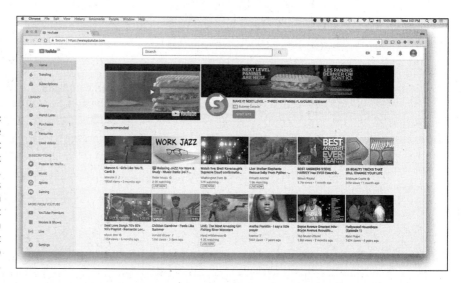

FIGURE 4-4:
Subway had the Masthead spot on the day I took this screenshot. You can see it's made up of a video that auto-played and a display ad unit with a button to visit its site.

Large-scale marketers with big budgets may buy this ad unit for a big awareness campaign because it reaches millions of people in just one day. The Masthead costs a lot of money, in the hundreds of thousands for just one day, with the price varying by country. Each time you visit the YouTube home page, see who has bought the Masthead slot that day, and think about what is being advertised and why the Masthead may be a good vehicle for it.

The Masthead

>> Is an amazing way to own a day and promote a specific event, such as a sale, or a moment in time that's happening in the world

>> Gives you access to a massive audience very quickly

>> Is a big creative canvas to play with

>> Is a PR opportunity that may get people talking.

Of course, if you don't have a few hundred thousand dollars to blow in one day, this ad format may not be for you. The Masthead is really only for the biggest of advertisers.

TIP

YouTube offers a tool that lets you see what your ad could look like in the Masthead. Visit www.youtube.com/yt/videomasthead and enter your YouTube video's link, and the tool will create a Masthead ad automatically. Just make sure that you have a few hundred thousand dollars handy if you want to buy the Masthead for a day!

Google Preferred

Google Preferred isn't an ad format but rather a way to buy media. It's predominantly for the biggest of advertisers, who spend hundreds of thousands, if not millions, of dollars per year.

YouTube has curated a collection of its top content from the most popular YouTube channels and crafted it into packages, also known as *lineups,* across a variety of categories — for example, a Beauty & Fashion package contains the top YouTubers in these categories. The top 5 percent or so of videos across all of YouTube based on quality metrics as well as popularity are *ring-fenced* (separated from the rest of YouTube's ad space inventory) into these packages, so only the advertisers with the biggest budgets can place their ads against them.

This approach is similar to how media buying occurs in the TV world, where advertisers pay larger sums upfront to buy the ad slots that run in the most popular primetime TV shows. Big advertisers are often keen to ensure that their ads run against only the best content and want to make more specific selections rather than just letting their ads run anywhere on YouTube. I suppose the idea is that ads that run against better quality content are somehow better, but that's debatable.

Google Preferred may be right for you if you're an advertiser who values the placement of your ad creative alongside premium content and don't like the idea that your ad may run against a cat video.

If you're not as concerned with which videos your ads run against or you're more interested in the most cost-effective media rather than paying a slight premium for specific placement, then Google Preferred probably isn't for you.

You can visit the U.S. lineups available through Google Preferred at `www.youtube.com/yt/lineups/united-states.html`.

The Google Display Network

If you're creating display and video ads to run on YouTube, you can use the Google Display Network (GDN), the largest advertising network in the world. All advertisers can run their ads on this ad network.

GDN reaches more than 92 percent of the Internet through a network of millions of websites that offer advertising space. Sites of any size across any topic can join the network. You can tap into these websites through a variety of targeting methods with lots of different ad formats.

Even mobile apps are in the GDN, allowing you to reach people within an app itself.

GDN allows you to reach a bigger audience and test whether different placement across the Internet can give you a more effective media buy and better results. It also lets you experiment with other ad formats not available on YouTube, such as text ads.

If you initially want to focus just on ad campaigns on YouTube, then you don't need to extend to the GDN. However, you should consider it because it may be a way to reach more people more efficiently.

GDN ad formats

Unlike YouTube, which predominantly focuses on video ads, you can run other kinds of ads on the GDN:

>> **Text ads:** While text ads don't currently run on YouTube, you may already run text ads that appear on Google Searches, and you can run these on the GDN, too. Your text ad not head, consisting of a headline and two lines of text, can run across thousands, even millions, of sites.

- » **Display ads:** The static or animated ads you create in Google Ads can run on the GDN. Indeed, the GDN offers more options for display ads than YouTube.

- » **Video ads:** Your video ads can appear when videos play on partner sites and in apps.

GDN targeting methods

GDN offers many powerful options to target people, which makes it a great complement to a YouTube-focused effort for any kind of campaign type. Targeting methods include

- » **Placement targeting:** You choose the websites where you'd like your ads to appear. For example, you may choose websites that cover special-interest areas related to your marketing campaign or that target a specific audience you'd like to reach.

- » **Contextual targeting:** You create a list of keywords that relate to your product or service and place your ads on sites that feature those terms.

- » **Topic targeting:** You choose from a list of topics, instead of specific keywords, so that your ad appears only on sites that are about that topic.

- » **Interest targeting:** This targeting method is similar to topic targeting, but instead of placing your ad on a site related to the topic, Google serves your ad to someone who is interested in that topic, regardless of the site they are on. For example, if I've been searching Google to buy a new car and then later that day I'm looking at a recipe website, I may see an ad for a car manufacturer.

- » **Remarketing:** This more advanced method of targeting people lets you show ads to people who have already been exposed to your ad or interacted with your ads or properties in some way. For example, you can show your ad to people who have visited your site, seen one of your ads but not clicked it, abandoned their shopping cart on your site or visited a product page, and more.

Being Aware of the Ad Policy

Google and YouTube are successful due in large part to their ability to create a high-quality experience across all of their products, services, apps, and sites. Delivering a high-quality experience requires having various policies in place so that their sites don't become the Wild West of the Internet, where anything goes. Imagine if you visited YouTube to search for a how-to video, and offensive adult-themed videos were served up? You may stop using YouTube altogether if it isn't a platform you can trust.

YouTube is always reviewing and improving its policies and procedures as it has the mammoth task of straddling the line between a platform for all yet needing to police content that isn't appropriate. The same is true of advertising on YouTube, in that all advertising must follow certain rules and regulations. You need to be aware of some key guidelines before you start to create your advertising creative and run your first campaign on the platform.

Prohibited content

Some of the categories listed as prohibited content may seem obvious, but people will try anything! Here are some categories that you are not allowed to advertise on Google or YouTube:

>> **Counterfeit goods:** No, you cannot sell fake Louis Vuitton and Gucci purses on any of Google and YouTube's platforms. If your product or service infringes upon the trademark or intellectual property of others, then you'll find your ads removed promptly from running.

>> **Dangerous products or services:** If you sell weapons, ammunitions, or explosive materials (including fireworks), you won't be able to advertise on Google or YouTube. You can't market tobacco products either. Drugs like marijuana also fall into this category.

>> **Anything that enables dishonest behavior:** This category includes things like hacking software or services that people use to inflate web traffic. It also includes things like academic cheating services. You won't find Will's Essay Emporium running ads on Google or YouTube!

>> **Inappropriate content:** This category is perhaps the most comprehensive and obvious of groups. Google and YouTube won't allow advertising that promotes hate speech, discrimination, violence, graphic crime scenes, cruelty, murder, self-harm, extortion, and so on.

Prohibited practices

Beyond specific prohibited content, Google and YouTube want you to be aware of the way in which they'd like advertisers to behave across their ad platforms.

NO PAY FOR PLAY

I was once at a lunch with some friends and met a charismatic entrepreneur type who wanted to connect about work in the future specifically on the topic of Google and advertising. I said sure, of course, because my job at the time was fundamentally to help people make use of Google's ad products to drive their marketing goals even though he wasn't on my client list. We met, and he intimated to me that he wanted to pay me (a lot of money) to find an internal Google mole who would approve his ad campaigns, also in exchange for a lot of money, despite the fact the ads contravened Google's policies. Google has some back-end teams in place to manually approve ad campaigns when they are so nuanced that machine learning isn't able to weed them out, and he saw this as a chance to pay to game the system. I said thank you but no and reminded him that I'd be fired for this help.

>> **Abuse of the ad network:** Google and YouTube do not want anyone to game the system including trying to trick their ad review processes (see the nearby sidebar "No pay for play"). Know that you can be banned from Google for life and have your website removed from its index for certain violations.

>> **Data collection:** It's not that data collection isn't possible because, of course, it is; it's simply that advertiser's must be responsible when collecting data. Increasingly, people are becoming aware of the importance of protecting their personal data and reviewing regularly the services they use where their data plays a role. For example, Google encourages advertisers to handle data like name, email, address, phone, mother's maiden name, and ID numbers, such as your driver's license, with care. Being irresponsible may include receiving this information over nonsecure servers.

>> **Misrepresentation:** No one wants to be misled. Any ads you make must be clear and honest, which means not intentionally excluding information or being misleading about your product or service, cost, charges, any interest rates, fees, penalties, offers, and so on. This category in the ad policy requires you to be upfront, honest, and crystal clear in all of your advertising.

Restricted content

Restricted content is the grey-area of the ad policy because it deals with content that may be legally or culturally sensitive. Google and YouTube have different policies in place depending on the country where you're advertising, and sometimes it requires advertisers promoting restricted content to complete some additional steps in order for their ads to be eligible to run. Here are some examples of what restricted content includes:

>> Adult content

>> Alcohol

>> Copyrights

>> Gambling and games

>> Healthcare and medicines

>> Political content

>> Financial services

>> Trademarks

Overall, Google and YouTube continuously review the policy in place that governs what is acceptable. They tend to take a more conservative position because they operate in so many countries, must please so many people, and ultimately are accountable to shareholders who tend not to like controversy. As long as you are an honest advertiser who is aware of the basics of the ad policy, you'll find success in using their ad platforms. If you're a nefarious marketer looking to game the system, you'd be better off going somewhere else as you'll get cracked down on pretty quickly.

Editorial and technical quality standards

Google and YouTube's ad policy has one more component piece, which covers editorial and technical requirements. Google and YouTube want to ensure that

>> You maintain a high quality editorial standard. For example, they don't want to see "BUY NOW!!!!!" with excessive capital letters and exclamation points.

>> You have a destination website or app that accurately matches your ad. For example, if your ad promotes your new health and fitness ebook, it shouldn't take you to a website packed only with shady offers for a diet pill. In addition, your destination site should be functional. Imagine if every ad you clicked on landed you on a broken site!

>> Your ads meet technical specifications, such as image size requirements, file size limits, and aspect ratios in videos, so that they run effectively. Google and YouTube want ads to be professional and high quality.

TIP

For more information on Google's ad policy, visit https://support.google.com/adspolicy

Chapter **5**

Developing Your Ad Strategy

As you build the shape of your YouTube advertising campaign, you need to think about the messages you want your audience to be exposed to and engage with. In this chapter, you find out about a framework that can help you develop your messages called micro-moments.

Developing Your Marketing Messages

A key component when a marketer is developing an advertising campaign is the creation of the messages that will be communicated through advertising creative. Simply put, the *marketing messages* are what you want to tell your target audience. You may have just one message to communicate — for example, a price promotion on a product you're selling — or you may have a variety of messages you'd like to communicate, such as the name of your brand, your product, your retail location, and a *call to action* (the action you're asking people to take.)

TIP

A general rule is to keep your messages as simple as possible. Your audience likely won't remember too many messages, and you have only so much time in a video ad, or any ad for that matter, to get across whatever you want to say.

You may have heard radio ads where the web address or phone number at the end of an ad is repeated three times. It's repeated because people need to hear things like phone numbers or offer codes more than once to remember them. This repetition, while annoying, drills the information into their heads.

As you're developing your messages, ask yourself one important question: "So what?" If your target audience sees your message and responds with "So what?" then you're not delivering the right message to them. A great marketing message may

>> Inspire a change in how they think of your brand or product

>> Tap into an insight about something they want or need

>> Speak to their beliefs, attitudes, and desires

>> Feel timely and compelling

>> Encourage them to take an action

Make sure that your marketing messages align with your campaign type (see Chapter 2) and the ad creative you want to make (see Chapter 4).

Discovering Micro-Moments

As you start to think through the various marketing messages you'd like to communicate in your advertising campaign, a helpful framework, known as *micro-moments*, can translate these messages to the YouTube platform. Google developed this framework to illustrate to marketers how technology and the daily use of devices, such as mobile phones, can reframe the way marketers develop and deliver their messages.

Think about how many times you touch your mobile phone during the course of a day. One research survey by dscout found that the typical cellphone user touches his or her phone 2,617 time every day. This study, which you can see at https://blog.dscout.com/mobile-touches, included every tap, type, swipe, and click. Those numbers broke down into 76 sessions per day, with heavier phone users averaging 132 sessions a day. That's a lot!

Every time you pick up your phone to do something, it's a *micro-moment*. A micro-moment is an instance in time where you have the intention to do something, such as watch a video or search for something. Each intent-driven micro-moment helps shape your choices and enables you to make decisions on what to watch, what to buy, where to go, and more.

REMEMBER

Each time you're using your mobile device, you're engaging in some kind of intent-driven moment. Google's micro-moments framework helps makes sense of these many moments throughout the day.

From a more strategic marketing perspective, the micro-moments framework challenges the conventional approach most marketer's take of having campaign windows with start and stop dates. Most traditional marketers will plan a campaign to launch at a certain time, with messages and media planned to run over a certain period and eventually ending. A break may occur before the next campaign begins. For more on this topic, see the upcoming section "Flighting versus always-on versus pulsing."

Instead of planning your marketing around your own calendar of product launches and events, the micro-moments framework encourages you to be always present to intercept moments when your potential consumer may want to hear from you. Your target audience is looking for things all day every day, and marketers who appear in those moments are the ones who win.

Types of micro-moments are

>> "I want to know" moments

>> "I want to do" moments

>> "I want to buy" moments

>> "I want to go" moments

I describe each of these types in the following sections.

An additional "I want to watch" micro-moment describes those times when people turn to YouTube to be inspired or entertained. Your passions and interests can be met at any time with a search on YouTube for the kinds of content you'd like to consume, and some marketers can take advantage of these moments. This moment is best met by marketers who want to use content, rather than advertising, to reach their target audience. Check out Part 3 for how to develop your content strategy, and Chapter 8 for video content formats that can meet your audience's entertainment wants.

TIP

When you've determined the most important messages you want to communicate, you can match them to the ad formats found in Chapter 4. You're looking for ad formats that will enable you to communicate your message effectively.

"I want to know" moments

The "I want to know" moments speak to those times that you are looking to learn and explore something. You may grab your phone, open up the YouTube app, and search for any number of topics that interest you.

Perhaps you're interested in what's happening in the news, recipe ideas, or gardening techniques for possible future projects. Marketers have an opportunity to be present with their messages that help people in their moments of wanting to know — for example, by offering an online cooking course or a free e-book for amateur gardeners. These want-to-know moments are a great opportunity for your awareness campaigns to let potential consumers know about your brand and product.

In Figure 5-1, I use the YouTube mobile app to search for *easy meals to make at home.* The advertiser, GayLeaFoodCoop, intercepted this moment with an ad for Nordica Smooth Dips. (This video ad is known as *TrueView video discovery.* If you'd like to run an ad like this one, see Chapter 4.)

FIGURE 5-1:
GayLeaFoodCoop intercepted a moment of wanting to know with a helpful ad that appears in the top slot of the search results.

As it relates to your marketing needs, think about what people want to know. Can you create messages and video ad creative that intercept these moments of wanting to know?

"I want to do" moments

The "I want to do" moments include all those times you're looking for a solution to a challenge, such as how to do a repair.

If your company sells lawn mowers, your video can appear in paid media when someone searches for *how to fix my <competitor brand> lawn mower when it won't start.* Perhaps your message of "Our lawn-mowers start every time" or "Our nearby location can repair your lawn-mower" can appear against those competitor-related want-to-do moments, encouraging people to switch over to your product or visit your location for service.

I searched on the YouTube app for *how to fix a cracked phone screen,* and as you can see in Figure 5-2, Samsung intercepted that moment with an ad for its Galaxy Note phone. I searched again later on that day using the same criteria, and a different advertiser intercepted that moment.

FIGURE 5-2:
Searching *how to fix a cracked phone screen* surfaced an ad from Samsung promoting a new Galaxy Note phone.

Marketers have opportunities every day to intercept these want-to-do moments with messages directed at new consumers and consumers of your competitors' products.

"I want to buy" moments

Even if you're not purchasing a product directly from YouTube, you may search for videos about products and services to help inform your decision on what to buy (see Figure 5-3).

FIGURE 5-3:
I searched for *how to buy stocks* and saw an ad entitled Volatility Trading Stocks Made Easy.

For example, if you're in the market for a new vacuum, you may look on YouTube for review videos of the models you're considering to help you decide which one is the best for you.

A marketer's video ads can appear in these moments, making these want-to-buy moments a great opportunity for your conversion-focused campaigns, encouraging people to click through to purchase.

"I want to go" moments

Although want-to-go moments are typically taking place on Google's search engine or within Google Maps, where people are searching a destination with details on how to get to a location, some want-to-go moments occur on YouTube.

For example, people may search YouTube for destination content about places they'd like to go in the future. if you're an adventure holiday company, think through whether you can intercept these want-to-go moments with your marketing messages. In Figure 5-4, I searched YouTube for Las Vegas–related phrases and saw an ad to visit Barbados. Perhaps something in their research showed people looking to travel to Las Vegas could be tempted to visit Barbados.

FIGURE 5-4: I searched YouTube for *Las Vegas travel guide* and was served an ad from Visit Barbados.

Buying Paid Media

A common misconception with YouTube is that if you upload your ad, people will see it. A lot of people assume that YouTube, along with other social media channels, are essentially free advertising channels. The reality is that uploading a video is another drop in the ocean in a sea of millions of videos already on YouTube. The only way to ensure that your video is seen by your desired target audience is to buy *paid media*. Paid media is a paid placement of your ad or content, meaning your ad or content will be surfaced to a potential viewing audience because you paid for it.

Even though buying paid media may seem unappealing, it's actually a fantastic way to reach the people you want to reach to achieve your business goals. Sure, you can make an ad that lots of people see, but if they don't convert into a purchase or another important business metric, then the video ad was a waste of time and effort. It doesn't matter if people in England love your videos if you're running a sports equipment store in Portland, Oregon. Paid media enables you to reach the people you need to reach, and it'll help you quickly learn what works and what you can tweak.

Doing it yourself

You can buy paid media yourself. You don't need any expertise. You just need a willingness to step through the process and commit to spending a little time each day looking at the results and thinking about changes you can make to ensure that the money you're spending is providing a good return.

You don't need a big budget, either. You can spend just a few hundred dollars on your advertising. When paid media works well, for every dollar you spend, you'll get more than a dollar back, giving you a positive return on your investment. When you've got a positive return, you can justify spending more money on advertising because you know it'll be driving your profits and growing your customer base.

The benefits of buying paid media yourself are

>> You can save money by not having to pay someone else to do it.

>> You learn about how paid media works and how to get more out of it.

>> You can make decisions quickly.

>> You become an expert and can take your marketing campaigns to new levels, delivering more results.

The challenges with buying paid media yourself are

>> You need to take time to set up paid media and it requires an initial learning curve.

>> You need to tend to paid media daily to ensure that everything is working and performing.

>> You may make mistakes, which can mean wasted dollars.

THAT TIME I MADE A COSTLY MISTAKE.

Do not be frightened away by this story! When I was working at MTV leading digital marketing efforts, I set up a campaign in Google Ads to run display advertising and search ads to promote a show that was about to premiere. I think it was Real World/ Road Rules Challenge. I assigned about $10,000 in budget against the campaign. I set the campaign to go live and didn't check in again until a few weeks later when the budget ran out. I went to pull my final report to see the results and noticed that I'd made a mistake in the settings, and all the ads had run in a different country. I wasted the entire budget by showing ads to people in a country where the show wasn't even airing. It was a simple mistake, and the lesson is to always check your choices before setting your campaign to go live and check your campaign daily. I never told my bosses, although I guess now they'll know.

TIP

If you have a small budget of just a few hundred dollars to a few thousand dollars, I recommend buying the media yourself. If you have a budget larger than $10,000, you may want to enlist the services of a third party to help you (see the next section).

Using a media agency

You can find an individual or a small company who specialize in buying paid media. The largest clients with the biggest budgets use large media buying agencies who have teams of people buying media across a variety of platforms. Who you work with depends on your budget.

TIP

You don't want to use up all your media budget on fees for someone to create and manage your campaign, with no money left for the actual ads themselves. Don't spend much more than 10 percent of your total media budget on fees for service providers.

The benefits of using a specialist are that

>> They can set up campaigns quickly because they know the systems well.

>> They can advise you on the best options and choices to deliver against your desired results.

>> Large agencies can often negotiate discounts on media directly with the platforms, passing those discounts on to their clients.

The drawbacks are that

>> It'll cost you some of your budget. You'll need to pay for their time and efforts, which reduces your overall media budget.

>> No one will care more about your business than you. Good media buyers and campaign managers will give you a high level of service, but not all are equal! Like any service provider, some people are better than others.

>> You need to keep an eye on their work. You want to ensure that they're spending your money well and providing the results you're looking for. Think of it as a partnership.

Exploring Pricing Models

You have quite a few *pricing models*, or methods of bidding on ads:

>> Cost per thousand (CPM)

>> Cost per view (CPV)

>> Cost per acquisition (CPA)

TIP

When you're buying types of media other than YouTube video ads, you'll come across different kinds of bidding types. The most common is CPC, cost per click, which is the default bidding type for text ads you run on Google's search engine. You may also come across cost-per-engagement (CPE), cost per lead (CPL), and cost per install (CPI) —for example, the installation of an app. There are others, too!

Sometimes you'll come across these bidding types with the letter *e* preceding them —for example, eCPM —which stands for effective. That just means you used different data to calculate the effective CPM. You can run a CPC campaign, but use your results to determine what your effective CPM cost would be. That's a handy way of comparing campaigns bought via different pricing models.

REMEMBER

Choose the pricing model that matches best to your campaign objectives.

Cost per thousand (CPM)

When you buy advertising on a cost per thousand, or CPM, basis, you pay an amount for every thousand impressions of your ad. An *impression* is a display or exposure of your ad. For example, if you are buying a radio ad on a CPM basis, you pay a set amount for each thousand listeners who are exposed to your ad.

CPM is calculated by dividing the total cost of your advertising by the number of impressions that it generates. For example, if you pay $2,000 to show your ad to 200,000 people, your CPM is $10. In other words, it cost you $10 per 1,000 impressions.

The formula to determine your CPM is Total cost of your ads / total number of impressions * 1,000.

You can set your maximum CPM bid in Google Ads (see Chapter 7).

Paying only when seen: Viewable CPM

When you're buying media on YouTube, you can buy something known as *viewable CPM*. CPM ensures that you pay only when your ads can be seen. It may seem odd to say when "your ads can be seen," as it suggests that people might pay to show their ads to people without them being seen, but the crazy thing is that's possible!

Imagine you're browsing a website that features ads throughout the site. You may click on a page but scroll only about half way down and miss an ad at the end of the page. You didn't see it, but it was technically displayed as the page loaded the ad. Advertiser's often prefer to ensure that their CPM based campaigns are viewable CPM.

An ad is counted as *viewable* when 50 percent of your ad shows on screen for one second or longer for display ads or plays continuously two seconds or longer for video ads. (In Chapter 7, you can see how you can set up a campaign and select viewable CPM as a bid strategy when you choose CPM bidding for your Display Network only campaign.)

The real benefit of buying using viewable CPM is that you're going to pay only for impressions that are measured as viewable, and that your bids will be optimized to favor ad slots that are most likely to be viewable.

TIP

Viewable CPM is a bid strategy that applies only to videos (and display ads) running on the Google Display Network. When you buy ads directly on YouTube itself, you aren't able to buy viewable CPM. That's OK because on YouTube, you can choose to pay for your video ads only when people watch them.

Using CPM

Although you can use CPM when buying YouTube ads, people commonly use it to buy display advertising on the Google Display Network.

This pricing model is often used when people are running brand awareness and reach campaigns because they're concerned primarily with reaching large numbers of people, regardless of whether they take an action or not. The act of showing the ad to as many people as possible is the focus of these awareness and reach campaigns.

Cost per view (CPV)

Cost-per-view (CPV) bidding is the default way to buy TrueView video ads in Google Ads. When you buy ads using CPV bidding, you pay only for video views or interactions, which makes it a pretty effective way to buy advertising. You're paying only for people who actually wanted to watch or interact with your ad, rather than buying on a CPM basis where you're paying to show your ad to people whether they care about it or not.

With CPV you pay when

>> A view is counted, which is when someone watches 30 seconds of your video ad or the duration if it's shorter than 30 seconds.

>> They interact with your ad – for example, by clicking on call to action overlays, cards, and companion banners.

You're charged for whichever comes first: a view or an interaction.

CPV is calculated by dividing your total ad spend by the number of total measured views. For example, if you spent $10,000 in media spend and received 25,879 views, your CPV is $0.38 per view.

Deciding your CPV

There isn't a one-size-fits-all way to decide what you think a view is worth. Advertisers in competitive spaces may pay $0.50 per view, whereas the least competitive spaces may net you CPVs of just $0.02. What constitutes a reasonable CPV is a factor of the market you're operating in. For example, if your video ads are part of your collective efforts to get people to sign up for your bank's mortgage, a high value and long-term product, then you may be prepared to pay a higher CPV.

You can set your maximum CPV, which is the most you are willing to pay for a view or interaction. Whenever possible, Google Ads aims to charge you only what was necessary for your ad to appear on the page, so you'll end up with an actual CPV that will be less than your maximum CPV. That's because Google Ads is an auction system, so you pay only as much as is needed to rank higher than the advertiser immediately below you.

Using CPV

The CPV pricing model is a great choice when you want people to actually engage with your video ad and take actions, such as clicking to visit your website. You can use this approach for your brand awareness, reach, product consideration, engagement, and driving leads campaigns.

TIP

Make the most compelling ad you possibly can so that people will want to watch it. (See Chapter 6 for more on what makes for a great YouTube ad.)

Cost per acquisition (CPA)

Cost per acquisition (CPA) is a bidding approach that is great when your campaign goals are to encourage things like sales, signups, or other actions, such as mobile app downloads. Think of *acquisition* as the moment when your target audience takes an action that brings them a step closer to you – for example, by giving you their email address or purchasing a product from your website.

These types of acquisitions are also known as *conversions* because the person converted from being a noncustomer to being a customer.

Choosing your ideal amount: Target CPA

You can set your *target CPA*, which is the ideal amount you pay to acquire or convert someone. What's great about Google Ads is that you can link your campaigns to things like your website's ecommerce storefront, enabling Google Ads to use things like conversion tracking to optimize your campaign. The system serves up your ads and monitors to see which ones perform best at converting people. It starts to tweak how and where your ads are served up so that you avoid unprofitable clicks and get conversions at the lowest possible cost. This automation by the Google system means you get more sales while paying less for the clicks that lead to those purchases.

The bidding methodology automatically finds the best cost-per-click (CPC) bid for your ad each time it's eligible to appear. It sets a higher CPC bid for more valuable clicks and lower CPC bids for less valuable clicks.

Deciding your CPA

Most marketers calculate their ideal CPA based on the cost of their product or service. Here's a simplified example. Say that you sell mobile phone chargers, which cost you $5 per unit to manufacture and ship to the end consumer, and you sell them online for $25 per unit. That means you've got $20 of profit margin to play with (just ignore things like overheads and the like for now.) You can set your CPA as high as $19, as you'd still be making $1 profit. In reality, your CPA would probably be a lot less than this amount.

Using CPA

Use the CPA pricing model when you're looking to drive sales, signups, leads, or other actions where you're converting someone from being a noncustomer to a customer.

Placing Your Media Buy

The vast majority of media bought with Google across search, display, and video is bought through *auction*, where advertisers set their bidding criteria and compete for their ads to be displayed.

However, you can also buy media through something known as *reservation*, which guarantees placements at a fixed rate cost. The approaches are different, and you may choose one over the other.

It's my opinion that almost all marketers can deliver any of their campaign goals by buying media through the auction system, and that, with a diligent approach, they'll deliver better results than through other methods of buying media. That's a pretty broad blanket rule, but I stand by it! If you're not sure which approach is right for you, go the auction route first.

Auction

In auction-bought media, you set up your campaign-making choices about the placements of your ads and the audiences you'd like to target, the pricing model, bidding choices, your budget, and timing.

The Google Ads system places your ad campaign into the auction with all the other relevant advertisers competing for similar placements and audiences. Every time someone is watching videos on YouTube, the system decides whether there's an opportunity to display an ad. Google Ads then runs an auction to see whose ad should be shown and serves up the winning advertiser's ad.

An auction is a vastly complex system, so the preceding explanation is fairly simplistic. An auction occurs each time someone searches Google, visits a website with display advertising, or watches videos on YouTube. Millions of auctions are happening every second! The good news is that these auctions happen automatically and lightning fast. Google Ads isn't like eBay, where setting up an item listing is a pretty involved process.

Buying your media through auction is a great choice because

>> **You can control things dynamically.** You can start, stop, and tweak your campaign settings at any point. This flexibility is great because you can optimize as you go, making changes to everything, including your creative, bidding, and placements.

>> **It's not a case of highest bidder wins.** Google considers various things, such as the quality of your ad creative and landing page. Google focuses on serving up ads people want, not just the ads someone paid to show, so you're rewarded by making your ads better and more relevant.

>> **You can get started with a small media budget, with no real barrier to entry.** You don't need huge budgets. You don't need to know anyone in the industry, and you don't need to negotiate deals or go for long lunches with media reps to secure media space.

>> **You can buy space almost anywhere on the Internet.** Advanced targeting options almost guarantee you'll be reaching the right person.

Auctions have some cons, however:

>> **The onus is on you, or your media agency, to constantly review and improve your campaign.** With such a powerful tool as Google Ads comes great responsibility, and you need to dedicate time to managing it.

>> **It is a more complex system than the old method of buying media.** You're not just buying space in a printed directory or on a radio station, signing a contract, and sending through your ad. With so many options, you need to make a thoughtful decision.

>> **Competitive categories have higher costs.** For example, you have to bid at much higher rates to target people interested in mortgages because mortgage providers know they can pay more and still get a return on their media investment. These highly competitive high involvement categories are more expensive auctions to participate in.

THE GOOGLE ADS AUCTION

Google is a great search engine, but what made the company truly successful was its creation of Google Ads (at the time known as Google AdWords) and its innovative use of an auction system to sell advertising space. Rather than asking clients to commit to buying advertising space upfront, Google created an auction system that let people bid to have their ad displayed. This complicated yet beautiful system looks at your bid and your *quality score*, a proprietary metric that determines how relevant and useful your ads are to the user. What's amazing about this approach is that your ad can appear above a competitor's ad (sometimes at a cheaper price) if your ad quality is better, meaning more relevant to the end user.

You can dive deep into Google's model by reading a lot online about how it all works. YouTube, for the most part, follows the same approach as Google's search engine, using an auction-based system especially for its skippable ad format TrueView, where ads are sold to the highest bidder in a marketplace of nonguaranteed inventory.

Reserve

Another method of buying media with Google is known as *reserve* or *reservation*. The key difference between this method and auctions (see preceding section) is that you're not running any auctions but you're buying media based on an agreed-upfront rate.

You buy reservation media either based on the number of impressions you'd like to purchase or based on a cost per day. For example, the YouTube Masthead is a reservation media type where you buy the space for the period of 24 hours, which is pretty cool because it's the only way you can buy advertising directly on the YouTube home page. (Chapter 4 has more details on this media option and other reservation options like Google Preferred.)

TIP

Most marketers who buy reservation are doing so because their campaign goals are to deliver brand awareness by reaching large audiences. If you've got a big budget to play with, reservation can help guarantee you'll reach a volume of audience in a certain time frame, whereas auctions require a bit more flexibility to deliver to your targets.

The pros of this approach are

>> **Reservation can provide more control in how you buy given that you're buying impressions at a fixed rate.** You may prefer this method if you want to know exactly the price you pay, such as when you buy other media in a

similar fashion or perhaps your budgets and processes work best for this approach. I once worked at a large media company where a central team controlled the budgets in a way that forbade me from using the auction until I got special permission to manage the campaigns directly.

>> **You can still buy reservation ads with Google based on topics, interests, affinity audiences, demographics, and even something known as first position.** *First position* lets you reserve the first video ad someone sees in a session. If you're buying reservation with other media companies, you'll often find you're simply buying media space on their site, without more advanced targeting options.

The cons are that

>> **In general, reservation can be more expensive.** That's mainly because you're buying such a broad audience, whereas auction allows for more specific targeting, reaching just the people you want to target. You can debate this point, but I find reservation is best when your targeting criteria is "everyone."

>> **If you want to buy reservation, you'll need to work with a Google representative.** Only the Google team can implement reservation media buys. If you don't have a Google representative, in the USA call the Google Ad's team at 1-844-201-2399 and let Google know you'd like to buy reservation media.

>> **Minimum spend requirements exist.** These requirements aren't published and vary from market to market. They also depend on the media type and its availability.

Scheduling Campaigns

You have something of a philosophical choice to make about how you'd like to market that will dictate your approach to ad media spend.

Consider the following options when you schedule your campaign to deliver media:

>> **Flighting:** Some marketers take the classic approach of *flighting* by scheduling various campaigns throughout the year), where a campaign may run with set start and end dates. A *flight* is the period when ads are running, followed by a period of no advertising, also known as a *hiatus,* followed by another flight, and so on. Sometimes your ads are running, and other times you're not communicating anything to your target audience.

This approach goes hand in hand with reservation media buying (see preceding section), where you plan chunks of campaigns and reserve the associated media, running ads intermittently throughout the year. You know when your campaigns will run and how much they'll cost. You can easily apportion your budget to each campaign, evenly or weighted.

TIP

If you're a marketer who needs to advertise only at certain times of the year, then a flight approach to your campaigns may work well.

>> **Always-on:** An alternative to flighting is *always-on*, which is somewhat self-explanatory, in that it means your campaign activity will be present in the market at all times. Always-on works well with the auction-based buying approach because you can set your total budget for the year and have the Google Ads tool evenly deliver your ads throughout that time, without running out of budget. If your budget is small, your ads may not run every day, but it does help guarantee a more even delivery and distribution of your ads ongoing.

TIP

If you're marketing a product or service that someone may be interested in any day of the year, you should be running always-on campaigns.

>> **Pulsing:** This option is a combination of both flighting and always-on. *Pulsing* is the approach where you keep an always-on campaign running, often with a low-level advertising budget, but where you heavy up your media spend at key times during the year in *pulses*. Pulsing means you're always present if someone is looking for you, but you're also taking advantage of seasonal effects, such as peak selling periods. Perhaps you spend more advertising dollars during the holidays when more people are buying products.

TIP

The best approach for marketers to enable maximum successful return on their campaign efforts is to use the pulsing approach. You flight your campaigns, run an always-on effort, and pulse your media spend at key times, which ensures that you never miss out on any opportunities to speak to or sell to your target audience.

People are always searching and watching videos, and you'll want to be there in those moments to intercept them. If you're flighting your campaigns and your target audience is watching videos on YouTube, you may miss an opportunity to show them a relevant ad, so consider using flighting, always-on, and pulsing in combination.

Chapter **6**

Ad Creative Fundamentals

I n this chapter, you explore how the most effective advertising creative on YouTube is different from the conventions of TV advertising, with different story arcs and techniques to engage the viewer. You gather the key components needed to create your advertising creative, including your marketing messages and your brand assets.

You also discover the four key guidelines to consider when making an effective YouTube ad, including how you grab the attention of your audience and ensure that they act after seeing your ad. Lastly, you explore approaches to testing your video ad creative so that you can ensure that you're constantly iterating and improving your marketing campaigns.

YouTube Is Not TV

A common misconception amongst advertisers first approaching the YouTube platform is that because it's video, it works the same as TV, and as a result, they can simply post their TV commercial on YouTube and expect it to perform effectively.

The reality is that YouTube has many things in common with TV, but it's not TV. Both allow you to

>> Sit back and be entertained

>> See advertising

>> Tune in to lots of different channels

>> Pay for premium content

With TV:

>> You can't search for a video from anywhere in the world.

>> You can't subscribe to your favorite celebrities (creators) on TV.

>> When you switch on your set, you don't get a custom page with videos customized to your interests based on what you've previously watched.

>> You typically can't easily interact with the person on TV directly.

>> You can't comment on the TV show so that everyone else watching the same show as you can see your comment and reply to you.

WARNING

YouTube is definitely not TV. Just because TV and YouTube share the content format of video doesn't mean they work at all the same, especially when it comes to marketing. YouTube is two-way communication, on-demand in a way TV is not and is accessible virtually anywhere. YouTube can be both a passive and an active viewing experience, whereas TV is almost always a passive experience. You lean back to watch TV, but you can lean back or lean forward to watch YouTube.

Marketers must recognize that YouTube is not TV and arm themselves with the knowledge to create advertising that works for YouTube.

The story arc of a TV spot

A great way to illustrate how TV and YouTube are different from a marketing perspective is to look at the typical story arc of a TV commercial and compare it with an ad made specifically for YouTube. (The *story arc* is how the story unfolds.)

TV commercials often follow a classic narrative arc of exposition, climax, and denouement (see Figure 6-1):

FIGURE 6-1:
In this TV
commercial, you
can see the stages
of exposition with
the lead-in and
build, the climax
and big reveal,
and the ending
with a call to
action and brand.

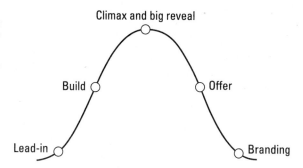

>> **Exposition:** This establishing shot, such as an aerial view of a car winding its way through the hills of an exotic location, or a medium shot of the exterior of a house, is followed by some kind of inciting incident that creates a sense of rising action. This lead-in builds to some kind of climax or reveal.

>> **Climax:** After the inciting incident, action continues to rise until you reach the peak of the action, a climax that has a big reveal, followed by a sense of falling action. The climax is where you might start to talk about your offering.

>> **Denouement:** The TV commercial ends with resolution — for example, the brand of the advertiser and a call to action as to how the offer can be unlocked. The brand's logo typically appears in the denouement.

The story arc of a YouTube ad

Video advertisements made specifically for YouTube are different than one for TV commercials, which are described in the previous section.

Video advertisements

>> **Grab attention:** Immediately grabbing the viewer's attention with an eye-catching hook is crucial. You can grab attention with an impactful visual combined with audio (see Figure 6-2).

>> **Reveal:** After you have the viewer's attention, you can start to reveal the marketing message and the brand through subtle branding cues.

>> **Keep the attention and provide direction:** Keeping the viewer's attention, provide direction on what he can do next — for example, watch another video, visit your YouTube channel or click through to your website to buy a product.

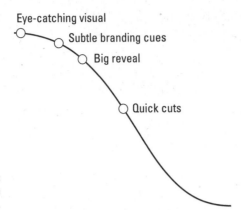

Eye-catching visual

Subtle branding cues

Big reveal

Quick cuts

FIGURE 6-2:
The story arc of a
YouTube ad.

You can see that what makes for an effective ad on YouTube is different from the traditional thinking about how to create a TV ad.

TIP

Get some inspiration from the Ads Leaderboard, a YouTube tool that helps show you the best ads out there. The YouTube Ads Leaderboard showcases the top ten ads that people choose to watch each month on YouTube. Visit `www.thinkwith google.com/advertising-channels/video/leaderboards`.

Gathering Your Marketing Essentials

Your video creative must address a few marketing essentials, such as the specific messages you want to communicate or legal disclaimers. Working through these requirements ensures that the ads you make will deliver to your campaign's needs the first time, and your ad creative won't need as many edits to go back and change things because something was omitted.

Your messages

Think through a list of all the messages you may want to communicate in your ad campaign. For example, if you're launching a new product, include the name, a visual of the product, the feature that makes it stand out from the crowd, and details on where it can be bought. If you have other messages you want to communicate, you'll need to decide whether you can communicate all of them in one video ad creative or if you need to create a few different ad creatives.

REMEMBER

Nothing is stopping you from making several video ads. Good advertising creative tends to focus on the core message you want people to remember.

Pull together a list of your messages

>> Your brand

>> The name of your product or service

>> Any price and special promotions

>> Features, especially those that set you apart from the competition

>> Testimonials from people who have used your product or service

>> Reasons why people should buy your product or service

>> Where people can buy it or other calls to action

>> Any other pertinent messages that are required to deliver against your marketing brief's needs.

TIP

Creating a matrix of your messages is an easy approach to help break out the different messages you may want to communicate in your ad campaign. You can add other variables, such as targeting different messages to different people, or different ad formats.

From that list, pick the most important message. For example, if you're a local pizza chain promoting new styles of pizza and some promotional pricing, you may want to make three video ads (see Table 6-1).

TABLE 6-1 **Possible Video Ads**

	Video Ad 1	Video Ad 2	Video Ad 3
Brand Message	The Pizza Shop	The Pizza Shop	The Pizza Shop
Product Message	New improved thick crust	Gluten-free thin crust	Classic crust
Pricing Message	Buy 2 thick crust, get 12 chicken wings	Buy a medium thin crust, get a small thin crust	Great value every day.
Call to action	Call or click to order	In store only. Click here for retail locations	Call, click, or visit

Your brand assets

When you think of Coca-Cola, you may think of the color red, a white script text, or the particular shape of a bottle, but when you think of Pepsi, you may think of blue and its circular blue, white, and red logo. When you think of McDonald's, you may think of the golden arches of the letter M that you'll see at every restaurant location, or even the audio mnemonic "I'm Lovin' It" the company uses in its commercials. These elements are examples of brand assets.

Your *brand assets* are the collection of signals that allow someone to easily recognize your brand. Brand assets can be visual, audio, or textual.

Brand assets include things like

>> The name of your brand and the name of your product or service

>> Your logo and tagline (if you have one)

>> Typography, which refers to the style of any text you include, such as font, color, and size choices

>> Shapes, images, and visuals that accompany your brand's visual treatment, such as an animated version of your logo

>> Tone or style of voice that you use for any spoken portions of the video — for example, you may be casual and friendly or more formal and academic.

>> Colors, especially if you have a bold singular color choice that appears across all your brand assets

>> Mascots, jingles or even sponsored celebrity endorsements.

When you're making video ad creative for YouTube, you'll want to gather all of your brand assets. Look at your list of these elements and decide which ones you must include in your video ad creative and whether any lend themselves particularly well to video. Gather all the files you need into one clearly organized folder, handy for when you get to the video production stage.

If you're just getting started with your marketing efforts, building all of your video ad creative to be consistent with a brand look and feel can help you grow quicker than having disconnected ad creative that looks different every time. If you're an established marketer, you probably follow a rigorous process to ensure that all your advertising follows your brand guidelines.

TIP

If you're interested in creating a consistent set of brand assets, you may want to build a *brand style guide.* A brand style guide covers everything from logos to lettering.

Existing video assets

Often in the past, I would work with advertisers to help them develop their YouTube advertising strategy, and they would assume that they needed to shoot all new video footage. Sometimes this assumption was a barrier to making

YouTube-specific advertising creative because they simply didn't have more budget available for more video shoots. However, many of these advertisers did have a library of video assets from previous shoots that could potentially be used to create their YouTube ad creative.

If you're a marketer who has existing video assets, it's well worth reviewing everything in your library to determine whether you can repurpose any of it. I've worked with clients who were able to

>> Use previously existing video footage of their product to make a simple six-second ad recut with a quick voiceover and a link.

>> Leverage b-roll content from tradeshows and retail location events.

>> Make use of footage from conferences and interviews.

Gather any existing video assets and spend some time reviewing them to see whether they apply. You'll want to ensure that the content is still accurate and that you have the necessary permissions to use the footage.

WARNING

Don't download and re-use other people's video footage unless you obtain permission first. You can reach out to people on YouTube and simply ask them for permission to use their footage.

Your mandatories

When you're creating ad creative for any marketing campaign, you need to think through what mandatories must be included. For example, certain advertisers, such as pharmaceutical companies, are required to include legal disclaimers. Mandatories can include

>> Brand assets, such as your logo at the very least

>> Additional offer information, such as redemption and expiration details

>> Legal disclaimers required by your category

>> Copyright and trademark notices

All these elements are important to include in your marketing brief. Check out Chapter 2 for how to build out a full marketing brief, which will help ensure that you make an ad campaign that is on brand and consistent with marketing campaign's needs.

Following the Rules of a Great YouTube Ad

No hard and fast rules for making the perfect video ad exist, but these guidelines can help ensure success. Remember, everything can be experimented with, but following these words of wisdom can give your YouTube ad a strong chance of performing well.

Getting attention

Your video ad creative is competing for attention with an endless number of other videos and distractions from phones and computers that can lure viewers away to other content with just a tap.

Marketers have about five seconds to capture the attention of viewers before they skip the ad, the ad ends, or they go elsewhere. Make those first five seconds count, and you'll convince them to stay to watch more of your ad. Don't snag the viewers' attention immediately, and you'll lose them the moment they can skip.

You can create impact that grabs attention with

>> **Visuals:** Try high contrasting visuals, fast pacing using techniques like *quick cuts* where you cut rapidly from scene to scene, graphic treatments, and anything that you'd consider an attention-grabbing bold visual statement.

TIP

People work better than places, and celebrities, women, children, and pets, especially dogs and cats, work better than men. Sorry, guys.

YouTube VOICE

The use of spoken voice is especially interesting in YouTube videos. While marketers often have a specific set of guidelines around the tone of voice they use in their ad creative, some tips and tricks that are unique to YouTube can help your video garner more attention.

An article in *The Atlantic* titled "The Linguistics of 'YouTube Voice'" (Dec. 7, 2015) described something known as *YouTube voice,* a variety of techniques commonly used in videos on YouTube to emphasize certain words in an effort to attract and maintain attention. While this style of voice is typically found in the vlogs of popular YouTubers, the article breaks out a few key tricks that you may want to try in your video ad creative, including overstressed vowels, extra vowels, long vowels and consonants, and *aspiration,* where more air is used to emphasize a word.

>> **Audio:** Whether it's sound effects, music, or voiceover, you can use audio to grab attention. You can experiment with the pacing of your audio — for example, the narrator may be speaking quickly or the music may be fast-paced.

>> **Super supers:** A *super* refers to something like text superimposed over a video to get attention (see Figure 6-3). You can try big bold text that flashes quickly as a technique to attract attention. Text also includes the title of your ad, which appears overlaid on your ad when the viewer mouses over the video.

FIGURE 6-3: Tom Ford leverages big bold text in this ad for lipsticks.

REMEMBER

Not all video ads are equal. A 2016 study from Nielsen Consumer Neuroscience, "U.S. Video Ad Cross-Platform Research," found that attention paid to video ads on YouTube was 1.8 times higher than on other social media platforms. The findings of this research suggest that if you're able to grab the attention of the viewer with the video ad you're running on YouTube, it'll have more attention paid to it than video ads that you run on other social media sites. (For more details on the study, go to www.thinkwithgoogle.com/data/attention-paid-youtube-ads-vs-social-media.

In other words, YouTube is a more valuable advertising platform, delivering more attention to the marketer's message. Attention is correlated with *ad recall*, which is the ability for someone who has seen your message to remember it at a later time.

THE HUMAN ATTENTION SPAN

In recent years, many articles have been published citing a research study that suggested the human attention span has shrunk from 12 seconds to around 8 seconds. (To put this in perspective, goldfish are believed to have an attention span of 9 seconds.

The cause for this decrease in the ability to focus is, of course, technology. The rise of mobile phones and social sites has meant that people are retraining their brains to focus attention for short bursts of time, limiting the ability to focus on anything longer.

Academics have subsequently debunked the idea of an average attention span and instead believe that attention is task-dependent. In March 2017, a BBC News article titled "Busting the attention span myth" quotes Dr Gemma Briggs, a psychology professor, as saying, "It's very much task-dependent. How much attention we apply to a task will vary depending on what the task demand is."

The reality for marketers on YouTube is that a lot of content is vying for focus. The viewer may have popped on to YouTube for a short viewing session or something longer, depending on their goal for that particular session. Their task may be to sit back and be entertained for an hour or to quickly find an answer on how to do something. Marketers are best off if they work hard to take every opportunity to capture viewers' attention.

The good news for goldfish is that science has also discovered that they're able to form memory and learn tasks that mammals and birds can also master!

Clearly branding

Clearly including your brand in your video is going to help people remember it. Clearly including your brand doesn't mean simply making the logo bigger or jamming as many mentions of your brand as possible into the video. Instead, think about how to brand early and often so that you immediately let people know who you are and that your brand is present throughout the video.

You can brand early and often in a variety of different ways using all your brand signals available. A *brand signal* is something that people will recognize and associate with your brand:

>> **Company name and brand logo:** These items are your most obvious brand signals, so find a way to include them. You can use audio mentions of your brand name as well as text and visual.

>> **Watermark:** A *watermark* is a semi-transparent logo or identifying image somewhere in the video, usually in the lower right-hand corner. This watermark can stay present throughout your video as a constant but subtle reminder of your brand.

>> **Actual product and its packaging:** Show the product in use and include visuals of your complete range of products to help people identify the brand behind your video ad.

>> **Primary colors and fonts:** If your brand makes use of recognizable colors and fonts including them in your visuals is a subtle signal of your brand.

>> **Brand jingles or audio mnemonics:** If your brand uses these auditory signals, include them.

Making a connection

For your ad to resonate with your audience, you'll want to make some kind of connection with the viewer. Are you making them feel or think something? Are you conveying your message in a compelling way?

Create a connection by tapping into their thoughts, feelings, and emotions with your ad creative. You can

>> **Use emotion:** Telling an emotional story that taps into how someone feels can be a great way to create a connection. An ad for an animal shelter can feature footage that tells the story of various pets available for adoption. For extra emotion, ensure that each animal is looking directly at the camera — I know, shameless but effective! Stories that invoke an emotional reaction tend to resonate with people.

» **Take a sensory approach:** Use video footage that taps into the viewer's senses, showing taste, touch, smell, sight, and sound. Perhaps you show someone tasting your restaurant's food, feeling the quality of your clothing, smelling the scent of your detergent liquid, seeing the majesty of the scenery on your adventure holiday tour, or listening to sounds of the local concert hall. Think of all the ways your brand can come to life through the senses and how you can express it in sight, sound, and motion.

» **Appeal to rationality:** A more practical route may be to demonstrate the benefits of your product or service. In your video creative, break down the reasons why viewers should consider your offering over others. Perhaps you'll make a short ad that hits viewers with the single best reason to purchase.

» **Show behavior:** Demonstrate a simple action or task that viewers can picture themselves taking. Connection is often made when people see something that they can relate to. For example, if your viewers like to travel, show video footage of people hiking and exploring.

Giving specific direction

The adage "If you don't ask, you don't get" applies to your YouTube ads. When your ad ends, make sure that you include a clear call to action. Designed to provoke an immediate response, a *call to action* is the instruction you give to your viewer. You're asking the viewer of your ad to do something. It could be to

» Click through to your website to learn more or purchase a product

» Call or visit a retail location

» Watch another video or playlist or visit your YouTube channel

» Complete an online survey or sign up for an email list

Your call to action needs to make sense in relation to your ad. Test different calls to action to see which people are most likely to take.

TIP

Make use of end screens. *End screens* show during the last 5 to 20 seconds of videos that are at least 25 seconds long. You can add up to four elements to promote your content, channel, and websites. Elements can expand to show more information when viewers hover on desktops or tap on mobile devices. See Chapter 14 for details on how you can set up end screens.

Testing Video Ad Creative

What's incredible about any digital marketing channel, especially YouTube, is that you can test different video ad creative and see which one performs best. When you're planning your campaign and creating your marketing messages, consider creating a few different versions to test. You can test a lot of different variables:

>> The **marketing message** you're communicating — for example, a product feature or price promotion

>> The **style** that you use to you creatively bring the ad to life — for example, your choices with audio, video, and text

>> The **ad format** you choose — for example, TrueView or bumper ads (see Chapter 4 for more on advertising formats)

Testing marketing messages

After you create a list of the key marketing messages you want to communicate in your campaign, you can explore how you can rewrite and tweak each message, generating a few different versions to test.

You can test your marketing messaging using the following techniques:

>> A/B testing

>> Multivariate testing

A/B testing

In *A/B testing*, you create two videos that each have a distinct message. You then run ads featuring either message A or B and see which one performs best.

For example, say that you're in the marketing team for the national chain The Pizza Shop, and you're tasked with creating video ads for its new Hawaiian pizza. You want to test which message will work best, so your short video ad's scripts may look something like

>> **Video Ad A:** Try our new and improved Hawaiian pizza. Buy one, get one free on in-store pickup.

>> **Video Ad B:** Try our new and improved Hawaiian pizza. Get a free one-topping medium pizza for in-store pickup.

In this example, you're testing which redemption offer will provide the best result. Will people prefer the "buy one, get one" offer or the "free medium pizza" offer? You'll create both video ads, run both in paid media, and then look at your redemption results to see which offer resonated best.

Multivariate testing

In *multivariate testing*, you aren't limited to testing only two messages. You can create several versions of a video ad and test them all at the same time.

You can constantly rewrite and retest your marketing messages to see which ones work best, improving your marketing campaign's results with each iteration.

TIP

For an easy option to test marketing messages, consider using Google Ad's text ads to test messages before you make your video ad creative. Google Ads offers text ads that appear when people search Google.com. For example, if people are searching for The Pizza Shop, you can show your audience text ads. Run a campaign testing your messages for a week or two, check your results, and use the best performing messages to make your video ad creative.

Testing video creative

Beyond testing your marketing messages, you can test different creative techniques to see which one yields a better result. While most marketers work within the guidelines and restrictions set out by their brand, you will still have lots of room to experiment:

>> **Video:** Try different kinds of video, using different types of people, places, pacing, and styles of visual treatment, such as animation, to test what works best.

>> **Audio:** Test to see whether different types of music, sound effects, voices, and other audio choices change how people respond to your ad.

>> **Text:** Test to see whether the inclusion of text in your video ad — for example, repeating your audio message with text, helps with the performance of your ad.

REMEMBER

You can A/B and multivariate test creative treatments (see the preceding two sections). Try something simple like using a male voiceover and a female voiceover to see which one people respond to more frequently.

See Chapter 4 to explore the different ad formats YouTube has available. You can experiment with ads of different lengths and behaviors to see which ones are most effective.

UNSKIPPABLE LABS AND DR. FORK

The charismatic and ever-inquisitive Ben Jones, the creative director of Unskippable Labs, runs a specialized team at Google. The team is constantly experimenting and testing to understand what makes for the most effective advertising possible, uncovering new learnings about consumer behaviors, busting long-held ad industry beliefs, and seeing how the YouTube platform is changing the landscape of marketing.

Ben and his team ran a video ad campaign on YouTube for a fake pizza brand called Dr. Fork. (Not The Pizza Shop. That's my fake pizza company.) They created ads using stock video footage to test 33 different ads, serving them up with 20 million YouTube views. This particular experiment was developed together with a large brand advertiser and an academic to uncover insights around the effect of sensory cues on ad effectiveness — for example, is an ad for a pizza more effective when a human is included? They uncovered all sorts of useful learnings, including that ads for food are more effective when super-close shots of the food are included. Sounds delicious!

What's crucially important here is that the biggest advertisers, academics, and special Google teams are always testing for effectiveness. Just as they are running large experiments testing nuanced and details theories, every marketer should consider some form of testing to improve marketing campaigns.

Delicious Unskippable Experiments
1,745 views

Chapter **7**

Buying Paid Ad Media

The Google Ads solution is a comprehensive tool that you can use to create your video advertising campaigns. In this chapter, you master the interface and discover its powerful advanced features. Google Ads is your key to running your paid media campaigns to deliver against your business goals.

Getting to Know Google Ads

Google Ads is the name for Google's complete advertising offering, which allows you to buy media and run advertising campaigns across Google, YouTube, and the Google Display Network, a network of millions of websites where your ads can appear. Although this deep and comprehensive tool allows for a lot of sophisticated targeting and customization options, it is easy to set up.

WARNING

Google Ads is the new name for what used to be called Google AdWords, so you may see some references online to Google AdWords. You should know that the interface can vary a bit depending on your country, but don't be too concerned if you see minor differences. The principles covered in this chapter still apply.

If for any reason you can't create video campaigns with your newly created Google Ads account, call the Google support line. You can find the relevant support number for your country in the Google Ads tool. If you're in the U.S., the number is 1-844-201-2399·

Signing up with Google Ads

Before you can access the full system and start setting up your YouTube campaign, you need to sign up for a Google account, if you don't have one, by visiting https://accounts.google.com/signup and following the steps. You also need to sign up for Google Ads with your Google account. Sign up at https://ads.google.com

In the past, Google required people signing up for the first time to create an initial campaign for text-based ads to run on Google's search engine. If you're required to do so, go ahead because you can immediately pause or delete it once done.

Getting a tour

When you first arrive at the main Google Ads interface, you may be offered a tour that walks you through key features of your account. Taking this tour is a great idea because it familiarizes you with the options available.

You also see the campaign you might have created as part of the initial setup as well as various toolbars with lots of options. Bookmark this site in your browser because you'll be visiting the tool every day when you have active campaigns.

Google Ads offers helpful guidance in a variety of different ways.

>> When you click on the question mark icon attached to a feature or section, simple definitions appear.

>> Clicking on a link to Learn More opens a help tool with an article explaining the relevant feature or section.

>> A large searchable library of content appears when you click on the upper-right corner of the question mark icon and then click on Get help.

>> Google's support team is available by phone Monday through Friday from 9 a.m. to 9 p.m. ET. You can find the relevant number listed on the Google Ad's website. If you're in the United States, you can call 1-844-201-2399.

Setting Up Video Campaigns

Google Ads has a handy flow that walks you through the best advertising options and settings to deliver to your campaign's goal. It's virtually the same for all the different campaign types you can create, with just a few different options enabled or disabled.

To set up a campaign, follow these steps:

1. **Click on All Campaigns.**

2. **Click on Campaigns.**

3. **Click the blue + button to create a new campaign and choose your campaign type.**

   Seven options appear, as shown in Figure 7-1. I list only the ones that include YouTube as an option. You can choose a campaign for

   - Leads

   - Website traffic

   - Product and brand consideration

   - Brand awareness and reach

   - Create a campaign without a goal's guidance

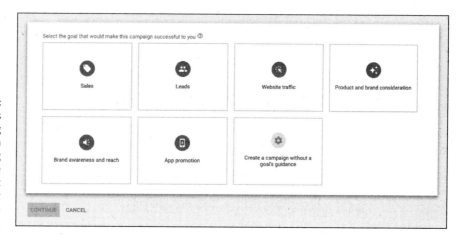

FIGURE 7-1: Google Ads offers a simple starting point to create a campaign, asking you to choose the focus of what you'd like your campaign to deliver.

4. **After you choose your campaign type, choose the Video option.**

   You may see some campaign subtype options (see details in the following campaign sections).

5. **Click on Continue.**

   The Create your campaign page appears, as shown in Figure 7-2.

6. **Enter your campaign name.**

   Choose a unique name that describes the campaign — for example, Q3 Email List Campaign.

FIGURE 7-2:
Enter your
campaign name,
set your budget,
and choose your
start and end
dates.

7. Set your budget.

You can enter a dollar amount for what you'd like to spend each day, or you can select Campaign Total from the drop-down menu to set the total amount you'd like to spend.

You may see an additional drop-down menu, which allows you to choose your delivery method. Standard mode delivers your campaign evenly over the time you allot. Accelerated mode delivers your campaign as quickly as possible while maintaining performance.

CONVERSION TRACKING

Some campaign types, such as driving leads and website traffic, require you to set up *conversion tracking*, so it's a good idea to set it up before you get started. Conversion tracking is simply a feature that helps Google know when your target audience has taken the desired action — for example, visiting your website or buying something. Conversion tracking essentially closes the loop by letting Google Ads know "Hey! They did this!" so you know what's working best.

If you haven't set up conversion tracking, you're prompted to do so when you're setting up a campaign that requires it. You can set up different conversions, such as purchases, signups, page views, and more (see figure). You can even assign a value to these conversions — for example, an email signup may be worth $1 to your business. You're given a *tag* — a little piece of code you'll add to your website that lets Google Ads know when the conversion has happened.

Create your website conversion action

Use the settings below to determine how your conversions are tracked. Learn more

Conversion name	Enter a name for this action		⌃
	0 / 100		

Category	Select the category that best describes this conversion action ⑦		⌃
	Select ▾		

Value	Select how to track the value of each conversion	The value setting lets you track how much these conversions are worth to your business.	⌃
	◯ Use the same value for each conversion	Learn more	
	◯ Use different values for each conversion		
	◯ Don't use a value		

Count	Select how many conversions to count per click or interaction	"Every" is recommended for purchases, where every conversion adds value.	⌃
	⦿ Every	Example: If someone clicks your ad, then makes 3 purchases, Google Ads will count 3 conversions.	
	◯ One	Learn more	

Conversion window	30 days	⌄

Value	Select how to track the value of each conversion	The value setting lets you track how much these conversions are worth to your business.	⌃
	◯ Use the same value for each conversion	Learn more	
	◯ Use different values for each conversion		
	◯ Don't use a value		

Count	Select how many conversions to count per click or interaction	"Every" is recommended for purchases, where every conversion adds value.	⌃
	⦿ Every	Example: If someone clicks your ad, then makes 3 purchases, Google Ads will count 3 conversions.	
	◯ One	Learn more	

Conversion window	30 days	⌄
View-through conversion window	1 day	⌄
Include in "Conversions"	Yes	⌄
Attribution model	Last click	⌄

CREATE AND CONTINUE   CANCEL

8. Choose your Start and End dates.

You can choose to have your ads start as soon as they're approved, which is usually within one business day. Google employs both machine learning and human input to ensure that all ads meet their policies.

9. Choose your networks.

Various options appear in the Networks box, shown in Figure 7-3: YouTube search results, YouTube videos, and Video partners on the Display Network.

TIP

Depending on the campaign you're setting up, some network options may not be available. For example, if you're driving leads, only YouTube videos is selected because lead-generation campaigns make use of the TrueView for Action ad format, which can run only on YouTube videos. Different flavors of TrueView run within the YouTube search results and on the Display Network.

Networks		
	☐ **YouTube search results**	
	Ads can appear next to search results on YouTube. You can use video discovery ads only.	
	☑ **YouTube videos**	
	Ads can appear on YouTube videos, channel pages, and the YouTube homepage. You can use in-stream and video discovery ads.	
	☐ Video partners on the Display Network ⓘ	

Languages	All languages
Locations	Canada (country)

Bidding	Select your bid strategy ⓘ Target CPA ▼ Target CPA $	With Target CPA (cost-per-acquisition), you set the average amount you're willing to pay for a conversion. From the Target CPA you set, we'll optimize bids to help get as many conversions as possible. Some conversions may cost more or less than your target. Learn more

FIGURE 7-3:
Depending on your campaign type, you'll have different network options available to you for where your video ad will run.

10. Choose your language, location, and bidding options.

You can target certain languages and locations — for example, Spanish speakers in the United States.

Depending on your campaign type, you see different bid strategies selected like cost per view, or cost per thousand. For example, if you're driving leads, Target CPA is selected, and the other options are greyed out. With Target CPA, you can set an average amount you're willing to pay for a *conversion* — for example, each time someone takes the desired action.

11. **In the Content Exclusions section, select where your ads can show.**

You can choose from Expanded, Standard, and Limited Inventory options. I recommend Expanded because it excludes most sensitive content, such as profanity, graphic content, and violence, but isn't overly limiting.

12. **Decide whether you want to show your video on all eligible devices.**

Unless you're concerned with reaching specific device users, choose all eligible devices.

13. **Click on Additional Settings to set your frequency capping by entering a number of how many times you want your ad shown or viewed per day.**

Frequency capping is a great option if you'd like to limit how many times your ad is shown to the same user.

For example, you can set your ad to be shown only a certain number of times per day or during the campaign.

14. **Schedule your ad to run on all days and at all times or add in time and day restrictions.**

15. **Create your ad groups.**

In a campaign, you can create more than one ad group. For example, your campaign may have five ad groups, one for each product you're promoting and each with different ad creative. Say that you're selling sports equipment online, and you're creating a campaign to promote your full range of clothing, including shoes. You can create an ad group with video ad creative that focuses just on footwear, a second ad group at a later stage that focuses on clothing, and a third ad group that focuses on accessories. These ad groups can all exist within the same campaign. Make sure that you use an ad group name that best describes the ad you'll be running in this group.

16. **In the People section, choose your target audience.**

You can target your audience using demographics, such as gender, age, parental status, and, in some countries, household income. Depending on the campaign type you're setting up, you can target by audience type based on their interests and habits (*affinity* and *custom affinity targeting*) or what they are actively researching or planning for (*in-market, life events,* and *custom intent*). You can also target your audience based on how they've previously interacted with your business, including *remarketing,* which means showing your ad to people you've previously touched somehow, such as previous website visitors, or similar audiences, which lets you upload a list of customers and find people who are similar to them.

17. **In the Content section, choose where you'd like your ads appear.**

You can have your ads run anywhere, or you can narrow the focus using certain keywords, topics, or placements.

18. Add your video ad.

Take a look at Figure 7-4 to see a video ad being added. It's a good idea to have your video already uploaded to your YouTube channel. In another browser tab, visit your video and grab the link from the browser bar so that you can copy and paste this into the input box. Google Ads pulls your video in and displays an example of how the ad will appear on the right-hand side. The Video Ad Format option is set depending on the campaign type you're creating. For example, if you're driving leads, it is set to In-Stream ad.

Chapter 11 delves into how to create your own video, and Chapter 14 walks you through the simple steps to uploading your video.

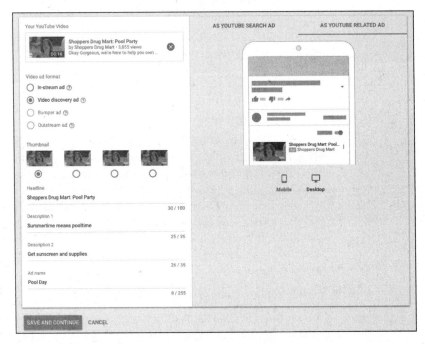

FIGURE 7-4:
Setting up your video discovery ad for your product and brand consideration campaign.

19. Enter the URL of where the ad will click through to, along with a Display URL, which is the web address that will be shown on the ad.

As you enter information, the preview ad updates.

20. Add in your call to action and your headline.

21. Preview your ad on both mobile and Desktop devices.

22. **Add a banner.**

For some campaign types, you can include a companion banner. Google Ads can automatically generate a companion banner that displays on desktop computers, or you can upload your own image. The banner, or *display ad,* is the image that appears to the right of your video. Chapter 4 has all the details on companion banners and display advertising.

23. **When you're happy with everything, click on Save and Continue.**

A final screen confirms the details.

24. **Click on Continue to Campaign.**

You return to the main Google Ads screen that shows a list of all your campaigns.

TIP

After you set up your first video campaign, the left-hand side menu lists

>> **Search campaigns,** where you can access any text or display campaigns that you're running on Google's search engine or on the Google Display Network.

>> **Video campaigns,** where all your video campaigns that run on YouTube or the Google Display Network live.

Driving leads

You can create a video campaign designed to drive leads by encouraging people to explore your product or service, sign up for an email or provide their contact information, or engage in other actions that help drive your business.

This campaign type uses an ad format known as *TrueView for Action.* This skippable video ad format runs *in-stream,* meaning that your video ad plays before, during, or after another video on YouTube. These ads give users the option to skip them after five seconds.

Along with your video, you'll be able to include a text headline and a call to action (CTA.) Headlines can contain up to 15 characters and is the primary line of text next to your video ad. Use headlines to promote your product or service. Your call to action can contain up to ten characters and appears alongside your headline. You'll use your CTA to direct people to the website you specify as your final URL.

Go to Chapter 4 to find out more about skippable ad formats and Chapter 6 to discover creative tips to ensure that your ad creative performs well.

Delivering website traffic

If you're interested in getting more traffic to your website, you can create a video campaign against this goal.

Just start by following the steps listed in "Setting up video campaigns," earlier in this chapter and choose the option Website Traffic. When you're asked to select a campaign type, choose Video.

TIP

If you haven't yet setup conversion tracking, you're asked to do so. Check out the sidebar "Conversion tracking," earlier in this chapter.

Growing product and brand consideration

Marketers looking to move people from awareness to consideration in the marketing funnel by encouraging them to explore their brand, products, and services can set up a campaign to drive product and brand consideration.

Follow the steps in the section "Setting Up Video Campaigns" earlier in this chapter, choosing product and brand consideration and then selecting video. You're offered a campaign subtype:

>> **Standard consideration,** where you can drive views of or engagement with your product or service, leading to increased consideration. This campaign type uses videos to encourage consideration by driving interactions and engagements.

>> **Shopping,** which enables you to promote relevant products alongside your video ads, encouraging people to learn about your products and services and to shop on your website.

AD SEQUENCING

Ad sequencing is an awesome feature that lets you show your video ads to people in an order you choose. It's great because you don't need to force all your messages into one ad, but can instead use several videos to communicate everything you'd like over time. Ad sequencing can be an effective way to take someone from "I don't know you" to "This might be for me" without relying on just one video to do that job. If you choose Ad Sequence when creating a new campaign, you see a blue Sequence Step link. Click that link to follow a familiar flow of creating an ad group, setting your bid, and creating your video ad. The only difference is that you can add more video ads and order them into a sequence.

>> **Ad sequence**, which lets you tell your story by showing ads in a particular sequence. It uses a mix of ad formats so that you can show a sequence of ads to people over time. See the nearby sidebar "Ad sequencing."

When it comes to creating your video ad, you have a new option available to you. You can create in-stream ads, but you can also create TrueView Discovery Ads (formerly known as TrueView in-display ads). These ads let you place your video ad in moments of discovery — for example, your video ad can appear next to related YouTube videos, as part of a YouTube search result, or even on the YouTube mobile home page.

Unlike in-stream ads, which play before, during, or after videos on YouTube, these discover ads consist of a thumbnail image taken from your video along with some text. The size and appearance of the ad can vary a bit depending on where the ad is appearing, but the idea is that discovery ads invite people to click to watch your video.

Think of it this way: Discovery ads are a bit like inserting your ad in a moment of intent, when someone has searched for something (see Chapter 5 for more on moments of intent). You're charged only when the viewer watches your ad by clicking on the thumbnail.

Adding the link to your video ad and choosing the video discovery ad option gives you some choices and some input boxes to complete. Follow these steps:

1. **Choose a thumbnail from the four that Google Ads automatically suggests.**

2. **Write a headline of under 100 characters.**

3. **Write two lines of description, both under 35 characters**

4. **Give your ad a name.**

   This name appears only in Google Ads, so viewers do not see it.

5. **Preview your ad.**

   You can toggle between As YouTube Search Ad and As YouTube Related Ad to see how your ad looks in different placements (refer to Figure 7-4). You can also see how it appears on mobile versus desktop.

Creating brand awareness and reach

You can create a brand awareness and reach campaign if you'd like to reach a big broad audience in order to create awareness of your brand, product, or service.

If you choose standard awareness when you create your video ad, you can see how your ad will appear on YouTube and on the Google Display Network. Figure 7-5 shows the different examples.

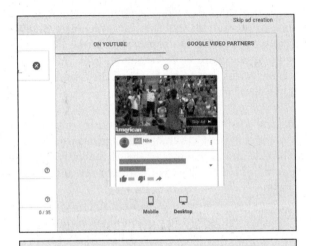

FIGURE 7-5:
An in-stream ad on YouTube on mobile devices and on video partner sites in the Google Display Network on desktop computers.

You'll have a few campaign subtype options:

>> **Standard awareness:** This subtype lets your reach viewers on YouTube and across the web. It's designed to deliver reach, impressions and views using in-stream video ads.

>> **Skippable in-stream:** This subtype lets you reach people on YouTube and across the web with skippable in-stream ads optimized for efficient impressions.

>> **Out-stream:** This subtype helps you expand your audience reach specifically with ads designed for mobile devices, reaching people on their phones and tablets.

>> **Ad sequence:** This subtype lets your drive deeper awareness or consideration by showing video ads in a specific order. Tell your story by showing ads in a particular sequence to a single user. Use in-stream or bumper ads, or a mix of both. See the nearby sidebar "Ad sequencing."

If you choose out-stream, you have some additional options to create your ad. You can include a headline of up to 80 characters, a description of up to 100 characters, and a call to action of 15 characters or less. You can upload a logo to accompany your ad and, of course, enter the URL where people will be taken if they click on your ad.

TECHNICAL STUFF

In-stream videos are what most people are familiar with. Also referred to as pre-roll, mid-roll, and post-roll, these video ads run before, during, or after a video. Simply put, in-stream video ads run when you're watching a video.

Out-stream video ads can appear in nonvideo environments. Say that you're reading an article online, and you're scrolling through the page of content. You may have seen that sometimes a page of content opens up and gives way to a video ad that's effectively been placed in the middle of the nonvideo content. That content is an out-stream ad.

TIP

If you're feeling unsure about which type of video ad is right for you, start with in-stream. In my opinion, it's the most flexible, useful format and works just as well for beginners to advanced marketers.

Designing your own custom campaign

While Google Ad's option to let you choose a goal and build a video campaign based on preselected choices makes things quick and easy to get started, sometimes you may want more control over your video campaign and the variables you'll customize. This desire is especially true if you're an advanced marketer with your own methodologies and approaches that you'd like to follow.

When you're setting up a custom campaign, all the variables are open to you. Note that some options toggle on and off as you make selections, so play around if you find something is greyed out that you want to use.

Navigating the Google Ads Interface

After you have a campaign running, you can explore the many options and features that Google Ads offers. I recommend that you check in on your campaign each day (or at the very least weekly) to see how things are performing and make tweaks as needed.

When you're viewing your video campaigns, you'll have an additional left-hand side menu with of the following sections:

- » Overview
- » Recommendations
- » Campaigns
- » Ad groups
- » Ads & extensions
- » Videos
- » Landing pages
- » Keywords
- » Audiences
- » Demographics
- » Topics
- » Placements
- » Settings

Overview

The Overview section gives you a bird's-eye view of all your campaigns, showing you data from the last seven days. You can change the date range in the upper right-hand corner. All the different data found in the Overview section has its own matching section within the left-hand menu, allowing you to dive deeper.

If you have time to check only one thing every day or so, make it the Overview section. It'll give you confidence, at a glance, that things are chugging along how you'd like.

TIP

I particularly like to look at the Biggest Changes box, which shows you the last seven days compared with the previous seven days, showing all your various campaigns listed by those who have had a large increase or a significant drop in the spending of your media budget.

Recommendations

The Recommendations section is an incredibly useful tool that takes some of the thinking out of optimizing your campaign.

After your campaigns have run for a few days or weeks, recommendations will appear in this section, advising of tweaks you can make to improve the performance of your campaigns. These recommendations will appear and refresh periodically, so check this section at least once a week.

TIP
Don't worry if you don't see any recommendations —you may not need any! All the recommendations that do appear here are customized to be relevant just to you and your campaigns; they aren't blanket messages applied to all accounts. New feature suggestions also appear here.

Campaigns

The Campaigns section provides a complete listing of all your campaigns in your account at any one time. Each campaign you have is listed with columns for budget, campaign type, summaries of the number of impressions and views delivered, the view rate, average cost per view, and total cost.

You can select one or more campaigns and

» Copy and paste the campaign to duplicate it.

» Enable, pause, or remove the campaign.

» Change your budgets or bidding strategy.

» Create automated rules that change how and when your ads appear or adjust bids based on dynamic conditions.

» Tweak your targeting criteria.

You can also search, filter, and segment your campaigns so that only certain ones appear.

TIP
As you're creating and running campaigns, compare their performance to determine why one campaign did better than the other. It may be your ad creative, your bidding or placement choices, or other variables.

Ad groups

Each campaign you create can have one or more ad groups within it. For example, you may create Cardio Classes, Strength Training, and Dance as ad groups in a Group Fitness Class campaign.

Although these ad groups are all subject to the budget set at the campaign level, they can have their own bidding strategy, targeting and placement, and video ad creative.

To create a new ad group:

1. **Choose your campaign from the left-hand side menu.**

2. **Click on Ad Groups.**

   A list of all the created ad groups for that campaign appear. (You created at least one ad group when you set up the campaign.)

3. **Click on the blue plus icon.**

   You see a screen, shown in Figure 7-6, that lets you create your new ad group.

4. **Enter a name for the ad group.**

   Choose something distinct that describes your ad group. For example, for a Group Fitness Class campaign, you might create an ad group for Cardio Classes.

5. **Set your maximum bid.**

6. **Make your selections around demographics and audience targeting and where this ad group's ads will run based on keywords, topics, or specific placements.**

7. **Paste in the URL of your video to create your video ad.**

8. **After you complete everything, click on Save and Continue.**

   A new ad group appears in the campaign.

TIP

You can pause ad groups if they aren't performing well, which directs more of your campaign's budget to the other ad groups.

Just like the Campaigns section (see the preceding section), you can view the performance of ad groups, and filter, download, and email reports.

Ads & extensions

The Ads & extensions section lets you review all the ads you have running in a campaign.

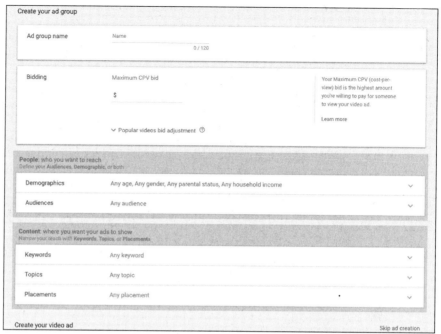

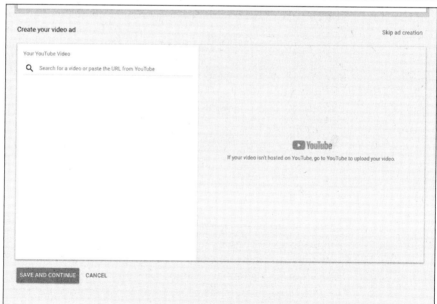

FIGURE 7-6:
You can create ad groups for each different set of ad creative you want to run.

You see a thumbnail of each video ad, the campaign and ad group that the ad lives in, whether the ad has been approved, its type, and data about how well the ad is performing. You can also see the impressions, views, view rate, average cost per click, and total cost of each ad.

If you look at Figure 7-7, you can see that the top listed ad has a cost per view of only $0.02. That amount is a really cheap cost per view and a great use of the media budget. It means that it costs only 2 cents per view of the ad. You can also see that 1,793 people have seen the ad. The ad below it has a cost per view of $0.10, which is still a great cost per view but a lot more than the ad in the top spot. The marketer behind this campaign will be considering why the first ad performed so well and whether there is anything to learn and apply to other ads moving forward.

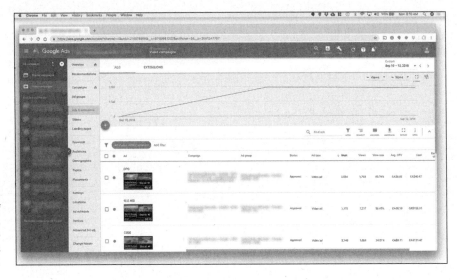

FIGURE 7-7:
A listing of the performance of all of your ads appears in the Ads & extensions section.

When you scroll to the bottom of this page, you get a summary of your Total Video Campaign results.

REMEMBER

Campaigns, ad groups, and ads all work together in a nesting hierarchy. Your campaign sets your total budget, bidding type, places your ads will run, start and end dates, and other campaign-level settings. Ad groups live within campaigns. You can create several ad groups and tweak settings for your maximum bid and your target audience and further narrow where your ads will appear. Ads live within ad groups. You can create several different video ad creatives within an ad group.

TIP

You can see extensions in the Extensions tab at the top of the page. Extensions are a powerful way to improve your ads and help potential customers find you. However these extensions typically apply only to text ads running in your campaign, not your video ads.

Videos

Clicking on the Videos section shows you a list of all the videos you've uploaded to your Google Ads account, along with how they have performed.

TIP

I like to sort video ads by average cost per view to see which ones performed the best by the dimension of cost.

Landing pages

The Landing Pages section collects a list of all the web pages where your ads click through to. A *landing page* is the page on your website that you designate as the destination for someone to click through it. It's effectively where they land after they have clicked your ad.

Keywords

When you first set up any campaign or ad groups, you can choose where your ads run and include keywords that can trigger your ad to show. For example, you can create a list of keywords that cause your ad to appear when people view content related to those keywords on YouTube, websites, and apps.

If you set up keywords, a list of them and their associated performance data appears.

To add keywords:

1. **Click on the Keywords left-hand side menu to visit the Keywords section and then click on the blue + icon.**

2. **Choose which campaign or ad group you'd like to add keywords to.**

3. **Enter keywords, one per line (see Figure 7-8).**

TIP

You can copy and paste them from a list, if you've created one. You can also enter related websites or details about your product and service, and Google will automatically generate example keywords for you.

FIGURE 7-8:
You can add keywords to your campaigns that will trigger your ad to show when people are viewing related content on YouTube, websites, or apps.

4. **Choose your Keyword setting.**

   Audience shows ads to people who are likely to be interested in these keywords. Content shows your ads on webpages and videos related to those keywords.

   TIP

   Choose Audience because you want to reach people interested in those keywords, regardless of the site they're visiting or video they're watching.

5. **Click on Save.**

   You return to the Keywords section, which now lists the keywords you added to your campaign or ad group.

Audiences

When you first set up your campaign or ad group, you chose the types of audience you'd like to reach in the People section. The Audiences section breaks out a complete list of all these people, your audiences, broken down by their type and the campaigns and ad groups where they appear.

To add audiences to your campaigns or ad groups:

1. **Click on the blue pencil icon.**

   A screen that allows you to edit audiences appears.

2. **Click on Select an ad group.**

3. **Select the ad group you'd like to edit.**

4. **Select audiences to add to your group.**

5. **After you finish making your choices, click on the Save button.**

REMEMBER

In-market audiences are the people who are actively browsing, researching, or comparing the types of products or services you sell. Based on signals of behavior and intent, you can reach these people directly. Don't worry: The people in-market are anonymous to you — you can't target a specific individual, only groups of people who appear to exhibit the behavior that suggests they're actively looking to buy.

Affinity audiences are those people you can target who have certain interests. For example, if you want to reach people with your group fitness classes, you can target people who like sports and activities, health and fitness, diet and nutrition, and other related areas of interest.

TIP

Try different audience targeting techniques to see whether you can uncover people who are more interested in seeing your video ads and taking your desired actions.

Demographics

You can use the Demographics section to see the different demographics your campaigns and ad groups are reaching.

Topics

The Topics section displays a list of all the topics your ads are running against. You can choose topics to show ads on content related to a certain subject, with the option to set up the ads when you first set up your campaign or ad group or add more topics later. For example, you can add topics to your ad group for cardio classes for Beauty & Fitness, Health, Hobbies & Leisure, and Sports.

To add topics:

1. **Click on the blue pencil icon.**

   You a screen that allows you to edit topics.

2. **Click on Select an ad group.**

3. **Select the ad group you'd like to edit.**

4. **Select topics to add to your group, as shown in Figure 7-9.**

5. **When you finish making your choices, click on the Save button.**

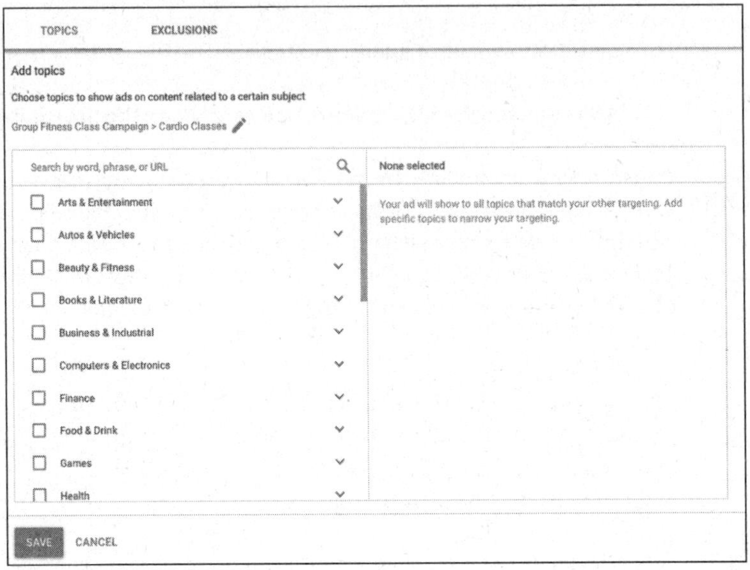

TOPICS   EXCLUSIONS

Add topics

Choose topics to show ads on content related to a certain subject

Group Fitness Class Campaign > Cardio Classes ✏

| Search by word, phrase, or URL | 🔍 | None selected |

☐ Arts & Entertainment	⌄	Your ad will show to all topics that match your other targeting. Add specific topics to narrow your targeting.
☐ Autos & Vehicles	⌄	
☐ Beauty & Fitness	⌄	
☐ Books & Literature	⌄	
☐ Business & Industrial	⌄	
☐ Computers & Electronics	⌄	
☐ Finance	⌄	
☐ Food & Drink	⌄	
☐ Games	⌄	
☐ Health	⌄	

SAVE   CANCEL

FIGURE 7-9:
You can add topics to your campaigns and ad groups.

Placements

In the Placements section, you can choose to show your ads on certain websites, apps, or videos. You can list specific YouTube channels, YouTube videos, websites, apps, or app categories.

To add placements to your ad groups:

1. **Click on the blue pencil icon.**

   You a screen that allows you to edit placements.

2. **Click on Select an ad group.**

3. **Select the ad group you'd like to edit.**

4. **Select the placements to add to your group.**

5. **When you finish making your choices, click on the Save button.**

REMEMBER

You can start your campaign running as broadly as possible, without limiting your targeting, or you can start small, being specific with who you want to reach, slowly opening up to new broader audiences. Both strategies help you find the right people.

In the Placement sections, you can also

>> **See where ads are shown:** Click on Where Ads Showed in the top horizontal menu to see a long list of every single instance of where your ad showed.

>> **Add criteria that lets you specifically exclude certain placements:** If you click on Exclusions in the top horizontal menu bar, you can add criteria so that your campaign or ad group doesn't run in excluded placements.

Settings

The Settings section lets you edit the settings applied to your campaigns and to your account as a whole so that you can make broad changes to everything in one go.

In Campaign settings, you can enable, pause, or remove your campaigns and change budgets, dates, rotation settings, and more.

The Account settings section lets you edit some advanced settings that apply at your account level. These settings are the upper-most level settings and apply to your entire account with Google Ads and all your campaigns contained within it.

Locations

The Locations section provides a list of all the locations you have chosen to either target or exclude. You can choose to see a geographic report that shows you where your customers were physically located when the ad was shown.

Ad schedule

If you've set up your campaigns to follow an ad schedule, showing ads only at certain times or on certain days, you can find details in this section. You can choose to drill down by day and hour.

Devices

The Devices section breaks out where your video ads ran for each of your campaigns. It's interesting to compare whether you get better results from one type of device over another.

Advanced bid adjustment

In the Advanced bid adjustment section, you can adjust bids. Bid adjustments allow you to show your ads more or less frequently based on where, when, and how people search. For example, sometimes a click is worth more to you if it comes from a smartphone, at a certain time of day, or from a specific location.

Change history

Given that Google Ads is such a comprehensive tool that lets you customize so many different options, the Change history section may be the best feature of all. Visit this section to see a list of all the changes you've made to your ads, bids, budgets, keywords, placements, and so on.

You can find details of your changes here, which is helpful if you find that you've made a mistake or a change you've made has negatively affected performance but you can't quite remember the change you made.

Exploring More Google Ads Features

A series of icons appear in the upper right-hand corner of Google Ads houses even more tools to help you with your campaigns. This menu bar contains

>> **Go To,** where you can search for any page and quickly navigate to that section.

>> **Reports,** where any reports you've created will live (see Chapter 16 for more on reports).

>> **Tools,** which holds a lot of special tools that I describe in the next section.

>> **Refresh,** which is a simple click to refresh your page and is helpful if something hasn't appeared to have updated.

>> **Help,** which is a deep library of help features and contact options to get more help with your campaigns.

>> **Alerts,** which displays notifications that alert you to if your campaign is ending soon or that certain settings need your attention.

>> **Your account information,** which includes your account number, name, and the email address with which you are logged in. (You can click on your profile icon and log in to a different account if you use multiple accounts for Google Ads.)

Tools

Despite being not much more than a little spanner icon in the upper right-hand menu, the Tools section contains a lot of incredibly useful and compelling tools that you can try out.

Some of the best tools for your video campaigns are

- **Keyword planner:** The Keyword planner is a cornerstone tool of the Google Ads solution. While it's primarily used to generate keywords that will trigger your text ads running on Google's search engine, you can use keywords to trigger your video ads on sites and videos that feature those keywords.

- **Audience manager:** Audience lists help you reach people who have visited your website, watched your video, engaged with your app, or shared their contact information. You can set up an audience source to reach the right people, with the right message, at the right moment.

  You can set up campaigns that remarket to people who have visited your YouTube channel. The Audiences section shows you a list of any audiences you've created. Clicking the blue pencil icon lets you ad selected audiences to campaigns or ad groups.

- **Portfolio bid strategies:** Portfolio bid strategies let you automatically set bids for multiple campaigns. Think of this tool as a way to create an overarching bidding strategy for all your campaigns rather than specifying unique bidding strategies for each campaign you're running.

- **Shared budgets:** You can apply a shared budget to any campaign or create a new one. The idea here is that you can set your overall budget available and make all your campaigns share from that pool.

Bulk actions

Bulk actions is an advanced section where you can create automated rules that do things like pause or enable your campaigns based on certain triggers.

Measurement

Measurement of your Google Ads campaigns is so important and fully featured that it has its own chapter! For details on the Measurement section, see Chapter 16.

Setup

In the Setup section, you can edit your billing and payment information and manage account access, including users, managers, and security settings, as well as your general preferences, such as language, number format, and more.

TIP

If you need help, you can call Google. You can find the telephone number for your country in the Google Ads tool. If you're in the United States. you can dial 1-844-201-2399 Monday through Friday from 9 a.m. to 9 p.m. ET.

3
Planning Your Content Strategy

IN THIS PART . . .

Explore educational, entertainment, and inspirational videos to determine which type of video you'll make.

Set the purpose of your YouTube channel.

Uncover a popular niche you'll be able to participate in.

Determine how you'll use trending versus evergreen videos.

Craft your overall video content strategy.

Follow the content creative fundamentals to ensure your videos perform.

Chapter **8**

Exploring Video Content Formats

With more than 400 hours of new video content uploaded to YouTube every minute, a number that increases every year, it's crucial to think about what people are really wanting to watch so that your video has a chance of not getting lost in the massive and ever-expanding library of videos. With so many options, if you make a video no one wants to watch, it'll flounder in the deepest darkest depths of YouTube with zero views, and all your effort will have been wasted. As a marketer, you want to make content that will need stand out against content that doesn't need to serve a marketing purpose. It's a big, but surmountable, challenge!

The good news is that there are many existing popular video formats, which are often a good place to start when thinking about the kinds of videos you might like to make and whether they'll deliver on your marketing needs. Repeatable formats are often easier to make and more accessible for the audience you're trying to reach.

In this chapter, you'll discover what people like to watch on YouTube so that you can decide which videos you should focus on making. You'll also explore the overlap between what you want to talk about as a marketer and what your audience wants to watch.

Educate, Entertain, Inspire

A framework you should consider when thinking about what content videos to make is

>> **Educate:** Marketers have an opportunity to create videos that educate the viewer on a particular task or topic.

>> **Entertain:** Marketers, especially those focused on brand marketing, can create videos that viewers watch when they want to be entertained.

>> **Inspire:** Marketers can create highly shareable videos that inspire with stories of personal triumph and emotion.

This framework broadly captures the video content formats that people might watch on YouTube and is a helpful starting point when you think about the kinds of videos you might want to make. You'll find that these content formats do overlap at times — for example, educational content can be entertaining, entertainment can be inspiring, and so on.

As you read through these different formats, think about which type may be the best vehicle for your marketing message, which type provides value to your audience, and which type you think is feasible to produce given your marketing budget restraints. Keeping these points in mind will help you narrow down your choices to the best formats to experiment with.

People Visit YouTube for Education

YouTube is one of the greatest platforms in the world simply because anyone who wants to learn has access to millions of educational videos. Educational videos are huge on YouTube. In fact, YouTube reports that educational and learning-based videos are watched four times more than animal videos. Whatever it is you want to learn about, you can find a video that will teach you, and as a marketer, this gives you an opportunity to educate people about your product, service, business, and more.

A great example of educational videos on YouTube comes from The Khan Academy (www.youtube.com/khanacademy), which provides explanations of mathematics topics like fractions, decimals, multiplication, addition, and subtraction.

The Khan Academy (see Figure 8-1) started in 2008 when a cousin of Salman Khan needed some help with tutoring. Soon after Khan started helping his cousin with math problems, other cousins also started using his tutoring services. Khan decided to post his videos on YouTube, and because of his clear and compelling style of teaching, they took off! Several of his videos have millions of views:

FIGURE 8-1:
With more than 1.5 billion views, The Khan Academy is an excellent example of educational videos on YouTube that act in part as a marketing tool for the wider organization's initiatives and programs.

FIGURE 8-1: With more than 1.5 billion views, The Khan Academy is an excellent example of educational videos on YouTube that act in part as a marketing tool for the wider organization's initiatives and programs.

» "Introduction to Limits": 3.6 million views

» "Intro to vectors and scalars": 3.6 million views

» "The beauty of algebra": 3.4 million views

Since November 2006, The Khan Academy channel has made videos totaling more than 1,546,000,000 views and has over 4 million subscribers. Who would have thought that videos that explain math topics would be so popular?

Because the response was so positive, Khan decided to quit his job and focus his time on building out The Khan Academy, which now has several YouTube channels on specialized topics and many channels in other languages. The Khan Academy has evolved into a nonprofit organization that provides education in myriad ways beyond YouTube.

The Khan Academy's content on YouTube turned from a pastime into a business, and that very same content on YouTube became part of the marketing mix that promotes The Khan Academy, its brand, and other services. Overall, The Khan Academy is a great example of education on YouTube providing detailed help on a topic many people might struggle with.

Think of the times in the recent past when you may have turned to YouTube to educate yourself. For example, I was teaching a class at the University of Toronto recently, and I asked the audience "Who here has searched YouTube for a how-to type video?" Everyone raised their hands. I asked what people had searched for, and their answers included how to

>> "Repair my dryer"

>> "Replace my car battery"

>> "Get a winged-out' eye makeup look"

>> "Get wine stains out of carpet"

>> "Open a bottle of wine when you have no bottle opener" (my favorite!)

Is an educational video the right format for your content?

You may want to make education videos when you have

>> A product to demonstrate

>> A service, process, or solution to walk people through

>> Knowledge on a topic people would like to learn about

>> A unique teaching style that people find easy to follow

>> Something you want to tell people about

>> Anything that people may be interested in learning about that somehow can further your goals as a marketer

REMEMBER

People turn to YouTube to educate themselves on all manner of topics and tasks. Chances are, if you need help learning how to do something, you'll find the answer in a video on YouTube.

Types of educational videos

If you want to make educational videos, you have lots of different subgenre styles to choose from:

>> Screencasts

>> Talking head videos

- » Listicles

- » Presentations

- » Lecture and classroom recordings

- » Interviews

- » Demonstrations

- » Illustrated explainer videos

- » Tutorials

TIP

Pick a topic and search YouTube.com to see the many different kinds of educational videos available.

The following sections describe each video style in detail.

Screencasts

A *screencast* is a recording of your computer screen's output, where activity is occurring on screen to demonstrate your topic, often with an accompanying voice-over. For example, you can record your screen showing someone how to perform a complicated task in a spreadsheet application or use an illustration or doodling tool to draw shapes to demonstrate how to draw a cartoon character. (See Figure 8-2 for an example of a screencast showing how to use Adobe Photoshop.) A screencast approach can show a potential customer how easy your tool is to use or walk existing customers through a process.

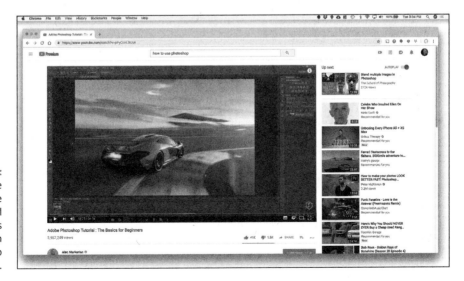

FIGURE 8-2:
Screencasts are easy-to-make educational videos, such as this video of an Adobe Photoshop tutorial.

Screencasts are a great educational tool. To create screencasts, all you need is some screen-recording software and a microphone. The one built into your computer should be sufficient.

Talking head videos

Check your teeth for spinach, turn on a good bright light, make sure the dog is in another room, sit down, turn on your webcam, and hit record— one of the easiest educational videos you can make is a *talking head video,* where you simply speak to the camera on a topic. See Figure 8-3 for an example from Warby Parker who make extensive use of this approach to provide customer service.

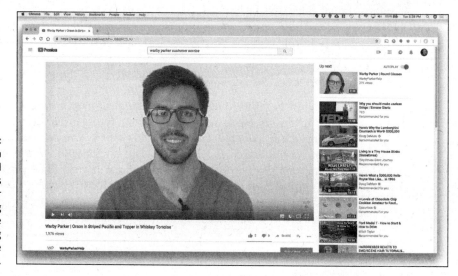

FIGURE 8-3: This example of a talking head video shows Warby Parker providing customer service by demonstrating examples of the product.

To create a talking head video, make sure that you speak clearly and confidently and stay on topic. Make a plan for the key points you need to hit and in which order.

Marketers may use talking head videos to provide customer service, such as giving an overview of an online course you offer.

Listicles

Listicle videos often take a talking-head style (see preceding section) but break the content into a set of numbered points, such as "9 Things You Didn't Know About Rhinos" or "Five Steps to Healthier Eating."

Listicles are a great format because they are an entertaining way to bring *snackable* — that is, easy to consume —., educational content. For example, if you're a marketer who is promoting a special kind of cleaning product that has many uses, you may make a listicle video that counts down the top ways to use the product — for example, "101 Ways to Use PowerBriteOut to Clean Your Home This Spring".

TIP

The YouTuber Matt Santoro (`http://bit.ly/mattsantoro`) makes awesome listicle style videos that educate people on a vast array of topics. His video "10 CREEPY URBAN LEGENDS that turned out to be TRUE!" has more than 12.5 million views. See Figure 8-4 for examples of Matt's videos.

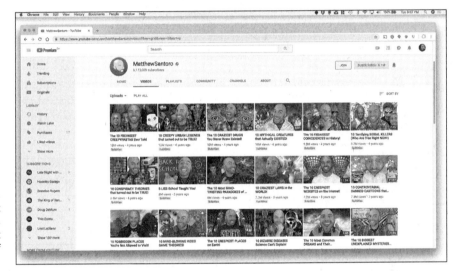

FIGURE 8-4:
YouTuber Matt Santoro has made an art form out of listicle videos.

Presentations

If you're giving a presentation, take the opportunity to capture it on camera in the form of a *presentation video*. Perhaps you're presenting at a conference or at a local school on a topic on which you're an expert, where you're standing in front of an audience either speaking or speaking in concert with a slideshow presented on a screen. See Figure 8-5 for an example from TEDTalks.

TIP

If you're presenting at a venue like a school or conference center, you'll need to work with the organizers to ensure that you capture the relevant permissions. Permission is required for both the venue and any people who may be in the video. Always ask your host first whether you're able to video the presentation. Often conferences and events are already filming the content and may be able to make the video available to you for your use.

FIGURE 8-5:
Arguably the best presentation videos on the Internet, Ted Talks are a polished presentation-style video experience.

To maximize the quality of the video recording, make sure that you set up your camera so that it's focused on where you'll be standing, the presentation screen is visible, and the audio can be captured. Also, do a test run to ensure that your camera can pick up the visuals and sound.

TIP

If you're a business-to-business (B2B) marketer, consider making presentation videos designed to train customers on your product or service.

Lecture and classroom recordings

Lecture and *classroom recordings* are perfect for teachers of all classes. In this type of video, you record the lecture or class discussion so that students can view the class content at a later date.

Unlike screencasts and talking head videos, which tend to be made with YouTube specifically in mind, lecture and classroom recordings simply capture the action.

Red Bull, the energy drink, has a YouTube channel for their Red Bull Music Academy program (www.youtube.com/user/redbullmusicacademy/videos) that features lectures and talks from artists, performers, academics, and more (see Figure 8-6). Red Bull's program is designed to foster creativity in music because music is a core part of the Red Bull brand. While the music academy is very much educational content, it helps Red Bull deliver its brand marketing goals.

You can discover more about brand marketing campaigns on YouTube in Chapter 2.

FIGURE 8-6:
Red Bull's lecture
videos make up
the content of
their Red Bull
Music Academy.

Interviews

One person interviewing another on a topic can be a great format for an educational video and tends to be entertaining. An *interview video* is a chance for the viewer to sit back and enjoy what the interviewee has to say. Ted, the nonprofit known for its Ted Talk conferences, uses the interview format for some of its content.

Interview-style videos are very popular and have spawned their own subgenres and even parodies. People in Silicon Valley love to call interviews *fireside chats* to express the idea of a casual and informal conversation between two friends, sitting by a fire (usually just a video of a fire on a tablet or screen) asking and answering questions — just in front of several hundred people!

You may be familiar with the Zach Galifianakis and the Funny or Die parody series "Between Two Ferns." In this series, Zach interviews a celebrity in a typically awkward or unprepared style, while both sit between two large ferns against a black backdrop. Zach has taken the classic features of interview-style TV shows and turned the format into a vehicle for his YouTube comedy videos. See Figure 8-7 for Zach's interview with Hillary Clinton.

This approach works well when you have an expert to interview about your product or service. For example, say that you're marketing your latest water filtration product, which you've been testing in developing countries. A potential expert to interview may be one of the on-the-ground researchers who can talk about how the product was used and how it worked in the field.

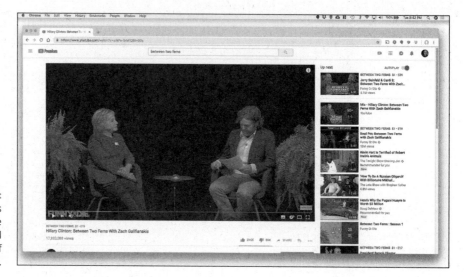

FIGURE 8-7:
Zach Galifianakis
has fun with the
stereotypical
features of
interview videos.

Demonstrations

If you have a product or a process, a step-by-step *demonstration* is a great video to make. This type of video provides the audience with a visual demonstration of the steps they need to take. For example, you can demonstrate how to dissect a frog by placing your camera directly above your lab work space and slowly walking the viewer through the process, narrating as you go.

Demonstrations may work if you're a marketer explaining how to repair the lawn mower you manufacture and sell or how to set up your new outdoor tent product available through local big box stores.

Illustrated explainer videos

A massively popular format is the *illustrated explainer* video, which is best, ahem, illustrated by the RSA Animate series (www.youtube.com/user/theRSAorg), originally conceived and executed by Andrew Park. Andrew, an illustrator based in the UK, created a cartoon series for the Royal Society of Art's YouTube channel that took content from RSA speeches (where academics and luminaries gave lectures), and turned them into illustrated, hand-drawn cartoon images to match the audio of the lecture.

Illustrated explainer videos became a popular format, with one RSA video, "RSA ANIMATE: Drive: The surprising truth about what motivates us," garnering more than 16 million views since it was posted in 2010. The video, shown in Figure 8-8, sets cartoon imagery to author Dan Pink's talk on human motivation. Later, Bill Gates chose Andrew Park to illustrate his Gates Foundation lecture on the power of vaccines.

FIGURE 8-8:
Dan Pink's talk illustrated by Andrew Park.

WARNING

While explainer videos are incredible videos to deliver a compelling visual explanation of a topic, they require skill and time. You must either be or have access to an animator and also have the patience to make the right choices of what visual to draw to best communicate the point.

Marketers can use these videos to explain how a service works — for example, if you're a member of the marketing team of a bank, you may make an explainer video that walks people through how a special mortgage product works over the span of its decades-long life.

Tutorials

Quite possibly the most popular format of all on YouTube, *tutorials* are similar to a talking head video because you're filming yourself head on, but you're providing a step-by-step tutorial for a specific task. Tutorials were originally filmed using the built-in webcam in people's laptops, which inadvertently set the style for many tutorial videos with the camera facing slightly down on the subject.

Tutorials can cover a massive array of topics, from makeup to cooking and DIY projects to giraffe doodles. Tutorials are incredibly popular, with YouTubers creating a steady stream of content explaining how to achieve a certain look or redecorate your bedroom with a new theme.

TIP

Marketers can take advantage of this format by creating tutorial videos on how your audience can use your product or by partnering with YouTubers who demonstrate how they use your product. For example, a lot of beauty bloggers and brands like Mac Cosmetics and Sephora have been able to tap into everyone from amateur

YouTubers to professional makeup artists to create video content that shows how to use their products. See Figure 8-9 for an example from Shalom Blac, a popular hair and makeup vlogger who creates tutorials. Shalom has more than 70 million video views and 1.1 million subscribers.

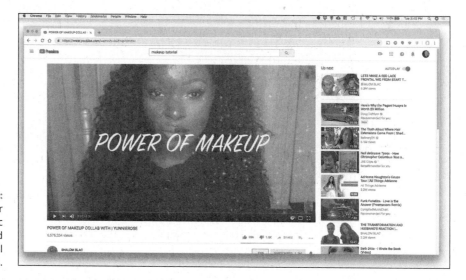

FIGURE 8-9:
Beauty vlogger
Shalom Blac
creates hair and
makeup tutorial
videos.

The distinction between edutainment and how-to

REMEMBER

A key distinction with educational videos is that they often tend to be either more *edutainment* in their style, meaning that they're entertaining content despite being educational, or more *how-to* in style, meaning that they're a more pragmatic explanation of a topic on how to do something.

Compare, for example, an interview with a celebrity on his latest charitable endeavor discussing what he learned from his recent trip to a foreign country versus a video demonstrating how to assemble an above-ground swimming pool in five easy steps. Both are educational videos, but the former leans more to entertainment, and the latter leans more to a practical "here's how you do that" style.

REMEMBER

This difference doesn't mean that a how-to video can't be compelling. It's simply that a how-to video tends to focus on just the information you need in the moment — for example, how to tie a bow tie or the best ways to clean silverware.

A checklist for making educational videos

If you're going to make educational videos, answer the following questions before you set about recording:

>> Who is the audience for your educational video?

>> Which format will your audience learn best from?

>> What content is your competition?

>> Is your credibility evident?

>> Do you have a brand?

Who is the audience for your educational video?

Think about who you are targeting with your video. Perhaps you will target the novice, with no previous knowledge on the topic, and so you'll make no assumptions and explain every concept as you go. Perhaps you are targeting experts, so you'll consider what they may already know. Maybe you're making a video for an English-speaking country, but people in other countries and languages would love to watch your video. (YouTube offers translation tools!)

Which format will your audience learn best from?

Review the different types of educational videos described earlier in this chapter and think about which format suits the audience the best. Different audiences have different learning styles. In addition, some videos, like talking heads, are easier to make than, say, illustrated explainer videos.

Further, some styles, such as a screencast, work better when scripted. Others, like a lecture, work better when informally planned. Still others, such as an interview, work best when they're delivered without too much structure, where you've planned a handful of questions but don't yet know which ones you'll ask in the moment.

TIP

The safest approach to ensure a great result is to script your video.

What content is your competition?

Search YouTube to see what content may already exist on the topic you'd like to make a video about. If you're going to make videos on learning a language, quite a few videos are already out there, so think about how you can make your video different and unique.

If you're a marketer who is the exclusive creator of a widget, then possibly no videos are already out there about the widget, which makes your job a little easier. However, someone may have bought your widget and made a how-to video explaining how to use it. Perhaps you can *curate*, or collect, the best of these videos in a playlist on your channel, without the need to make the videos yourself.

You can discover more about curation of other people's videos in Chapter 12.

Is your credibility evident?

You know you've got the credentials to speak on a topic, but viewers discovering your video for the first time may not know that you're an expert. Providing some context as to who you are will help build confidence that viewers have arrived at the right place.

REMEMBER

Tell your audience if you have a master's degree in widgets and, just like any good teacher and academic, be sure to cite your sources. Just as an endless amount of great educational content is available on YouTube and the Internet, a lot of disinformation is out there, too. If you're a credible educator and you cite your sources, then people will be able to trust that your information is true and accurate.

Do you have a brand?

If you're going to make several educational videos, you may want to create a simple consistent brand look that includes your title, description, style of video, and any logo or artwork you use.

Think about the big online educational channels, like Ted (`www.ted.com` and `www.youtube.com/user/TEDtalksDirector`) Their style is immediately recognizable, and each video starts with an intro featuring their brand logo, tagline, and music. Don't make your intro more than a few seconds because people have short attention spans and want to get right to the content.

People Visit YouTube for Entertainment

It's no surprise that people visit YouTube for entertainment. YouTube may have started as a great place for epic fail, cat videos, and epic fail cat videos, but now it's a serious entertainment destination. Content creators, including marketers of brands both new and traditional, are creating entertainment content specifically for the platform.

Take a moment to visit your recent YouTube history and see which videos you watched for purely entertainment purposes:

1. **On your computer, visit YouTube.com.**

2. **On the left-hand side menu, click History.**

   You have options to view your watch history (see Figure 8-10), your search history, the videos you may have commented on, and more.

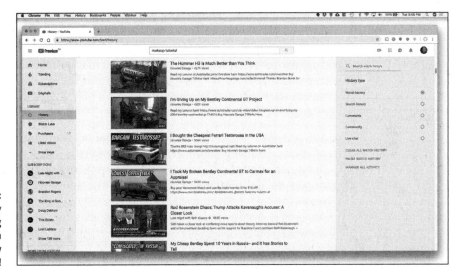

FIGURE 8-10:
An example of my YouTube viewing history. I watch a lot of car review videos!

3. **Consider which of the videos you watched were primarily entertainment videos and whether any of them were connected to a business or brand.**

   I bet it's not all cat videos, and I bet some videos served a marketing purpose.

Is an entertainment video the right format for your content?

You may want to make entertainment type videos to further your marketing goals if you firmly believe people would be interested in viewing these kinds of videos from your brand.

REMEMBER

YouTube contains a lot of competition, and many people are making entertaining video content. Viewers have plenty of choices, so if you're going to use some of your marketing budget to make a video that provides entertainment, be clear about its purpose.

For example, your brand may want to make entertainment type content if

>> **You want to show your audience things you do that they may not know about.** For example, you may create a web series featuring the community work your workforce participates in. This kind of example brings value to the audience that only your brand can uniquely can bring, and the format makes sense as a way to tell that story.

>> **Your product or service is itself connected to entertainment.** For example, a toy manufacturer may make prank or challenge videos that show the fun that can be had with its water guns. This video maybe a great way to have its message of "awesome water guns" stand out.

>> **You feel that it makes sense for your brand to participate in these kinds of videos.** An entertainment video shouldn't feel like a stretch or an awkward fit. No one wants to see comedy sketches from a bank or a makeup tutorial from an accountancy firm. Ask yourself whether picking this kind of content type is the best choice to achieve your marketing goals and whether the video you want to make is actually going to reach and connect with the desired audience.

You can find many examples of marketers using entertainment-type content on YouTube in order to achieve their marketing goals.

For example, Sony Pictures Entertainment (www.youtube.com/user/Sony Pictures), a major movie studio with more than 2.6 million subscribers to its YouTube channel, publish its movie trailers and teasers to its channel. Most movie studios publish behind-the-scenes content, bloopers, interviews, and even mini-movies and clips exclusive to YouTube. These videos meet a marketing need while also providing entertainment. What I really love about Sony Pictures Entertainment is that it creates playlists that link to other people's video content that relates to its movies, broadening the entertainment value its channel provides. For example, the playlist "Fun With Our Cast!" features clips from a variety of other media outlets, such as BBC Radio 1's interview with Tom Hardy for the movie "Venom" where kids ask difficult questions (see Figure 8-11).

Sure, movie studios are an easy example of marketers who create entertaining content on YouTube because the product they are selling is entertainment content! Other brands, whose core business isn't in content, still may create purely entertaining content.

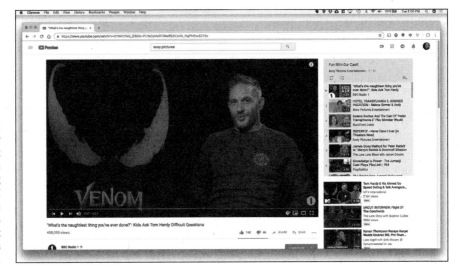

FIGURE 8-11:
Tom Hardy answers difficult questions in this entertaining video from BBC Radio 1, which Sony Pictures Entertainment links to from its channel's playlist.

Types of entertainment videos

Tons of entertainment video formats are on YouTube, and new creative approaches are being created all the time. Some of these formats may make sense for market-ers, and some may not. Here are just a few the most popular formats for enter-tainment content:

» News and celebrity entertainment shows

» Fictional shows and web series

» Short films, full-length movies, and documentaries

» Video game walk-throughs

» Unboxing, review, spree, and haul videos

» Vlogs

» Comedy, sketch, and parodies

» Pranks and challenges

» Music, dance, lip synch, and more

» Tutorials

» Super cuts

News and celebrity entertainment shows

You'll be able to find on YouTube most major news establishments, such as ABC, Fox, BBC, CBC, and CNN, as well as TV celebrity entertainment channels like E! News. These entertainment shows often feature news that's happening right now, as well as clips and content from the past.

CNN's channel features up-to-date content from the day, along with playlists, such as "Best of Van Jones," "Best of Chris Cuomo," and "Best of Jake Tapper" (see Figure 8-12). YouTube even has its own news channel, which it describes as a "destination featuring comprehensive up-to-date coverage on the latest top stories, sports, business, entertainment, politics, and more."

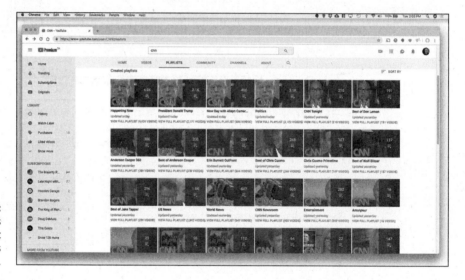

FIGURE 8-12: CNN's playlists show its "Best of . . ." news content.

Most marketers won't create news-style content, relying instead on their product or service being newsworthy and mentioned by other news creators. However, you may choose to parody the news format or perhaps create your own series of videos providing news-style updates that relate just to you. For example if you're a not-for-profit, as part of your marketing efforts, you can create news-style videos that communicate the work you're doing in various communities.

REMEMBER

News content isn't limited to the big news brands, however, as many YouTubers are creating videos in their own news-type format. YouTuber Philip DeFranco delivers news and pop culture videos five days a week (see Figure 8-13).

FIGURE 8-13:
Philip DeFranco
is a YouTuber
creating pop
culture news
content with an
audience of more
than 6.2 million
subscribers.

Fictional shows and web series

People all over the world are creating video *web series*, which are just like a TV show but without the need of a greenlight from the studio boss. The sky is the limit with creating shows.

For example, comedian Brian Jordan Alvarez created a show for YouTube entitled "The Gay and Wondrous Life of Caleb Gallo," which had five episodes of around 20 minutes length each (see Figure 8-14). The show, named IndieWire's best web series of 2016, in part helped Alvarez land representation with CAA (Creative Artists Agency) a major talent agency in Hollywood.

FIGURE 8-14:
Brian Jordan
Alvarez's web
series "The Gay
and Wondrous
Life of Caleb
Gallo."

TIP

A typical marketing approach for fictional shows and web series is to provide product integration. For example, say you're marketing a new kind of bicycle your company has manufactured, and so you reach out to a YouTuber creating a fictional web series and agree to feature your bicycle in the show. You provide the product, and the YouTuber writes a story line into the show that features the bike.

Short films, full-length movies, and documentaries

People are creating and uploading their short and full-length movies and documentaries. Plus you're able to rent mainstream movies through YouTube directly.

YouTuber Shane Dawson experiments with the documentary approach, creating long-form videos detailing the lives of other YouTubers, such as Jeffree Star. In September 2018, Dawson published a multipart documentary about the YouTuber Jake Paul.

TIP

If you're an actor, writer, or producer, making content and publishing on YouTube is a great way to market yourself and springboard into bigger projects in other channels.

Video game walk-throughs

Video gaming is a massive category on YouTube. If you're not a gamer, search for *video game walk-throughs,* and you'll come across something that may seem quite strange: People video themselves playing video games (see Figure 8-15), and millions of people watch these videos.

FIGURE 8-15:
Ninja is a popular gamer with more than 18 million subscribers. He makes videos of himself playing the game Fortnite.

TIP

Gaming is so big, YouTube created a gaming specific destination for it at `https://gaming.youtube.com`.

This format obviously presents an opportunity for marketers who are in the gaming space. Reaching out to YouTubers to play your game is an amazing way to get an audience to see the new game you've released. For marketers not in the gaming industry, companies that make merchandise can tie in related products to big game titles.

Unboxing, review, spree, and haul videos

Millions of YouTubers are creating videos daily that show them reviewing a product that they bought or that a marketer sent to them to review.

Unboxing videos are massively popular (see Figure 8-16). In an unboxing video, you provide a clear demonstration of a new still-in-the-box product that you're slowly and methodically removing from its packaging, pulling out and discussing each item in detail. Unboxing videos are sort of a product-porn approach to exciting new products like the latest gadgets and toys. You may not even talk much about the product, how it works, or what it's like, as unboxing videos are more about the experience of opening the box for the first time than anything else.

FIGURE 8-16: With more than 12 million subscribers and 2.2 billion video views, Unbox Therapy provides beautiful unboxing videos of tech gadgets and more.

In *review videos*, you might skip the unboxing and instead provide your detailed review of the features of the product. You'll walk people through a product's functions, showing how it works and providing commentary on what you think of it.

YouTubers also create a *spree* or *haul video* where a person makes a video showing the items they just purchased. In a spree or haul video, you walk through each item, where you bought it, the price, why you bought it, and so on.

Some of these videos can snag tens of millions of views and are often a great way for marketers to take advantage of showcasing their product.

REMEMBER

If you're a marketer who sends a product to a YouTuber to feature in a video, that YouTuber must disclose that she was sent this product for free by the manufacturer. In the United States, the Federal Trade Commission (FTC) enacted laws to regulate paid endorsements, requiring all content creators who accept free goods and services to ensure that they fully disclose that the items were either received for free or as part of a paid promotion.

Vlogs

Vlogs are a whole group of entertainment videos that are very much about the person simply talking about their life, their adventures, family, stories, and more. The video equivalent of writing a blog post, vlogs can be short diary entry bursts of a few minutes or longer videos of 20 minutes or more showing the events in a person's life. Vlogs tend to be popular with top YouTubers who have fan bases who love to follow along with their lives (see Figure 8-17).

FIGURE 8-17:
Jenna Marbles, a vlogger, has been posting videos on YouTube since 2010 and has more than 2.85 billion video views.

A specific kind of vlog is the *drive-with-me video*, where you place a camera on your dashboard, go pick up a friend, and record yourselves talking while driving them somewhere. A drive-with-me video is sort of a twist on the interview approach and is popular in large part due to the success of shows like "Comedians in Cars Getting Coffee" from Jerry Seinfeld and "Carpool Karaoke" from James Corden.

Ask-me-anything video are one subtype of vlogs. In this subtype, fans can ask any questions they like. Other video subtypes can show YouTubers listing their favorite things or their daily routine or reacting to things like watching a performance or trying something new.

TIP

Marketers may find opportunity in these formats by inviting YouTubers with large audiences to visit their showroom or retail store or having them talk about how they use a product or service throughout their day. For example, if you're a car dealer, you can create a drive-with-me video. Just as with product reviews and haul videos, any promotion must be declared by the content creator.

Comedy, sketch, and parodies

Whether it's a popular YouTuber or your kids filming themselves in the basement, *comedy, sketch,* and *parody videos* are big on YouTube. In a comedy video, you may simply be telling jokes stand-up style. In a sketch, you may have created a whole sketch show with some friends. In a parody video, you may parody a video that's popular in culture by remaking it. Comedy is a popular category.

Marketers may have to get creative as to how they leverage these kinds of videos. Perhaps you're a bar owner, and you decide to have an open mic. Posting the comedy routines (with permission, of course) may be a great way to promote your weekly night and general attendance at your bar.

Some years ago, an advertising agency in Canada made a parody video, shown in Figure 8-18, to promote its services by relaunching itself as a "Catvertising Agency." The video garnered 2.5 million views. You can see the video at `http://bit.ly/catvertisingexample`.

Pranks and challenges

In life, I'm not a fan of pranks, but the popularity of people pulling pranks on their friends, and even strangers, is undeniable. In *prank videos,* hidden cameras capture the creator setting up unwilling victims in any number of prank scenarios, such as walking into a room only to be slapped and sprayed with whipped cream.

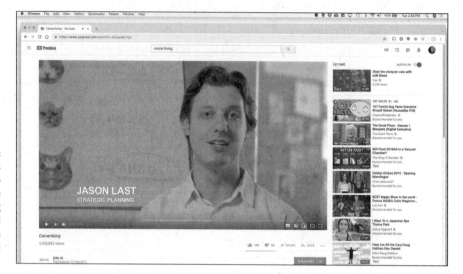

FIGURE 8-18:
John St's Catvertising video parodies the advertising industry and online video's obsession with cat videos.

Perhaps some marketers can take advantage of the prank format – for example, if you're a toy manufacturer where your product lends itself to kids playing harmless pranks on each other, you can create a series of videos of gentle pranks that kids could copy and play on their friends.

REMEMBER

Content that endangers people, especially minors, is prohibited per YouTube's content policy. Familiarize yourself with the policies by visiting www.youtube.com/yt/about/policies.

I've venture to say that *challenge videos* are a smarter option for marketers to consider. In a challenge video, people attempt a seemingly impossible challenge, with the resulting video showing just how amazingly capable humans can be when they set their mind to it.

Dude Perfect is a YouTube channel with more than 33 million subscribers, and its most popular video at the time of writing is "Ping Pong Trick Shots 3" (see Figure 8-19) with more than 155 million views. What's amazing is that the video is a partnership with Oreo, opening with a truly epic Rube Goldberg machine that incorporates Oreos and milk, with a subtle but clear message "Sponsored advertising by Oreo Dunk Challenge".

Challenge videos are a popular format, and this Oreo example is a great way to show how a marketer can take advantage of this approach. Partnering with a big YouTube channel like Dude Perfect may not be in the budget of all marketers, but I imagine the folk at Oreo were very happy with their investment and the marketing return of having such a massive volume of video views of a piece of content with great product integration.

FIGURE 8-19:
Dude Perfect's
Oreo Dunk
Challenge video.

Each year, new challenge trends emerge. For example, in 2018, a popular challenge was the "What the Fluff?" challenge. Thousands and thousands of people made videos where they hid behind a sheet in front of their dogs, quickly hiding as they dropped the sheet. Their dogs became confused and concerned by this magic trick and began searching for their owners. If people didn't have a dog, but they did have a cat, they tried the challenge on them — and quickly discovered that cats don't care where you go!

Music, dance, lip synch, and more

Of course, you'll find music videos on YouTube — just take a look at what's trending, and you'll mostly likely see the latest release from the hottest artist. You'll also find people creating their own music, music videos, and even lip synch videos thanks to platforms like TikTok (www.tiktok.com).

Typically, marketers have worked with big artists to include product integration in their videos or to sponsor the artist's wardrobe or tour.

WARNING

Smaller marketers who aren't familiar with the world of music, especially rights management and clearances, would be wise to avoid using music that they haven't secured the rights to. YouTube runs a tight ship when it comes to copyright.

See Chapter 15 on music, copyright and Content ID, YouTube's system to help content creators manage their copyright.

Tutorials

Even though tutorials are also a kind of educational video, they deserve a mention in the entertainment category, too. People may search for tutorials because they actually do want to implement the tips themselves, but a lot of people will watch videos like makeup tutorials simply for the entertainment. For example, not everyone needs to actually create a full unicorn makeup effect (see Figure 8-20) or use advanced prosthetics, but they may enjoy watching someone do just that.

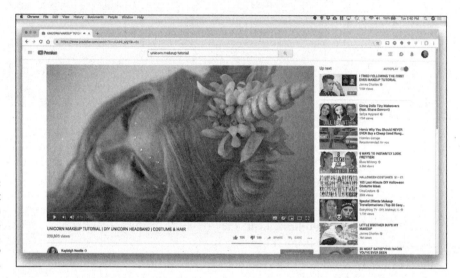

FIGURE 8-20:
Do you want
to look like a
unicorn? Well,
now you can,
thanks to
YouTube.

Fashion shows, what I'm wearing videos, outfits for the season, styling videos, interior design videos, and so many more fall into the bucket of "how I created this look." These video formats are great for marketers to tap into as integrating products and services into these videos is often straightforward. For example, perhaps you run a small chain of hardware stores in a college town. You can create tutorial videos showing how students can create a study space in their dorm room with a few simple tips, tricks, and supplies from your store.

Super cuts

Perhaps one of the simplest forms of video entertainment that YouTube is especially good at delivering are super cuts.

A *super cut* is a compilation of short video clips of the same type — for example, fail videos showing people falling or making mistakes that hurt them in quick succession.

Fail Army is a YouTube channel with 14 million subscribers, and over 4.8 billion video views. It has built a following based on its super cut videos of things like "Bark: Dog Fails" (see Figure 8-21) and "Amusement Park Fails."

FIGURE 8-21:
Fail Army makes popular super cuts of people, pets, and more making fools of themselves.

Perhaps marketers can find topical areas where it may make sense to sponsor this kind of content — for example, if you operate an amusement park or make a product that could cleverly stop a fail from happening.

If you're looking for a good laugh, just search YouTube for *vines I quote every day.* I found these kinds of videos when researching this chapter and lost 15 minutes of my life just transfixed by these dumb hilarious short videos. I laughed so hard I spat out my drink.

TIP

Marketers can make effective use of tons of entertaining video formats. As you watch videos on YouTube, make a note of the videos your audience may like and think about how you can integrate your marketing efforts into that format.

Lean in versus lean back

An interesting distinction to consider when you're thinking about entertainment videos on YouTube is the idea of leaning in versus leaning back.

Imagine these two scenarios:

> **Scenario 1:** You're visiting a friend and want to show her a video you recently found because you know it'll make her laugh. It's a short video of around 2 minutes on YouTube, so you pull out your mobile phone, find the video in your watch history, and play it for her while holding the phone. (She laughs, and you talk about where to go for dinner.)

> **Scenario 2:** You arrive home from work after a long day and plonk yourself down on the couch. You turn on your smart TV, fire up Netflix, and start the next episode of the show you're currently watching. Maybe you watch the whole episode of around 20 minutes, or perhaps you binge a few before moving to the kitchen to make dinner.

In the first scenario, your physical posture is more *leaned in* in that you're leaning toward the screen when watching the content, and you're bringing the phone closer to your face. In the second scenario, you are physically *leaned back*.

In the recent past, marketers have used this notion of lean in versus lean back to describe the idea that digital sites like YouTube and Facebook are more engaged because you are leaning in (both physically and mentally) whereas TV is a more passive content viewing environment. The idea here is that advertising on digital channels, rather than on TV, must be better because the viewer is more engaged. Whether or not this idea is true isn't super important, but the distinction is an interesting tool for when you're deciding what entertainment type content you may make.

Would you prefer shorter entertainment video content, designed more for smaller screeners like mobile phones, or would you prefer to make longer format content, perhaps better viewed on a larger screen?

The question is not whether you want more or less engagement. Rather, it's a question of what's the best kind of content to make for the viewing environment your audience will want to watch in.

TIP

Observe your own behavior this week. For example, throughout the day, when I have a few minutes to kill, I like to watch short comedy clips on my phone from late night TV show hosts doing their monologue. Later in the evening, I'll use my tablet to watch videos on YouTube when I'm eating or when I'm sitting on the couch. (Perhaps that's somewhere between lean in and lean back!)

A checklist for entertainment videos

The checklist for entertainment videos is similar to the educational checklist described in the section "A checklist for making educational videos," earlier in the chapter. However, you do need to think through some differences.

If you think entertainment-type videos are a good fit for your marketing needs, think about the following questions before you get started:

>> Who is the audience for your entertainment videos?

>> Which format will your audience like the most?

>> Which content is your competition?

>> Do you have a brand?

Who is the audience for your entertainment videos?

Think about who you want to reach with these videos. Remember, a lot of great video content is already out there, so you need to know exactly what your audience likes to watch so that you can give them a quality video that makes the cut.

Which format will your audience like the most?

Pick the format that will appeal to your audience and that makes sense for your brand to create.

For example, if you're a marketer promoting your company's new makeup range, it absolutely makes sense to make a series of makeup tutorials, and perhaps you could partner with a popular YouTuber to help you create them. If you're a fashion stylist or personal shopper, you could make a series of videos about your life, your clients, your tips and tricks, and what it takes to pull together everything needed for a magazine's editorial photoshoot. In these examples, entertainment-type content can play a role as a marketing tool.

Which content is your competition?

Don't just look for your business competitors, but search for related entertainment videos made by YouTubers. These videos will give you clues as to what makes for a great video, which will help you get started. Ideally, you'll find a way for your brand to bring something unique to the video so that you don't end up making a video that no one asked for and no one needs.

Is your credibility evident?

WARNING

Only make entertainment-type videos if it makes sense for your brand and your marketing goals. If you don't have the permission or credibility to make these videos, people won't watch.

If your company makes dog food, perhaps you can make a parody of an unboxing video where you film dogs just tearing into the packaging, which is actually quite funny.

If you're a local decorative items and souvenir store, you don't need to make a music video. (although if you search YouTube for *Selling is Service Song*, you'll find a cringeworthy but also kind of awesome video about how someone delivers customer service.)

Do you have a brand?

Find a way to integrate your brand without compromising the video and making it feel too much like an ad. However, not including your brand means that the video doesn't deliver any kind of marketing benefit.

It can be a fine balance and tricky to get right, but audio mentions, a logo in the corner, or imagery in the video itself of your logo or product can all work.

REMEMBER

Viewers are happy to see brands and products integrated when it's done well, but it sticks out like a sore thumb when done poorly.

People Visit YouTube for Inspiration

You can interpret the idea of *inspirational* video content in a few ways. For example, a video explaining how to renovate your basement can provide inspiration for your project, or a video from your favorite YouTuber talking about his gym routine may provide inspiration to take up some daily exercise.

REMEMBER

When it specifically comes to marketers, this category of video on YouTube speaks more directly to videos that make you step back and look at life and the world around you differently.

Case studies

Inspirational videos can be an effective tool for marketers as the following examples demonstrate:

>> Dove Men+Care (18 million views)

>> WestJet Christmas video (48 million views)

>> Volvo Trucks (90 million views)

Dove Men+Care

In 2015, Dove published a video titled "Dove Men+Care shares your first father-hood moments this Father's Day." With more than 18 million views, this video, shown in Figure 8-22, is a super cut of candid video clips showing men finding out that they are soon to become dads. Their partners have each found creative ways to deliver the message — for example, you see a man opening a box to find the positive pregnancy test or a gift bag containing baby clothes — and their reactions are incredible and emotional.

FIGURE 8-22:
Dove Men+Care shares your first fatherhood moments this Father's Day.

Interspersed throughout the video are messages from Dove, such as "Real strength means showing you care even from the very first moment," with the video ending with the message "Share your advice and help new dads grow stronger. #Real-Strength" and the tagline "Care makes a man stronger." Search for the long video that lasts just over a minute, watch it, and you'll cry every time.

This video doesn't feel like an advertisement, but it is part advertisement and part content. It's designed to elicit an emotional reaction in the viewer, and it's very effective at that! I've watched the video a hundred times, and it still gets me.

Marketers, like Dove, know that if they pull on your emotional heartstrings, they'll be able to communicate their message and reach a massive audience of people, many of whom will share this video with friends and family.

TIP

Shareability is a tricky thing to achieve with any video, but stories of personal triumph, emotional and relatable stories of people who fight against the odds, or stories about those who are experiencing fundamental and defining moments in life tend to be very shareable. Much like memes, inspirational videos of this sort are essentially built to encourage sharing.

A *meme* is a humorous image, video, or piece of text that spreads rapidly across the Internet within culture. You can think of memes as shareable units of culture. People use memes to express jokes, opinions, thoughts, feelings, and commentary.

WestJet Christmas Miracle

One of the earliest examples of a marketer using the inspirational video approach on YouTube comes from WestJet, the airline who in 2013 published a video "West-Jet Christmas Miracle: Real-time Giving".

Set to Tchaikovsky's "Dance of the Sugar Plum Fairy", the video opens with a rewritten narrated version of "'Twas the Night Before Christmas," which tells the story of how WestJet surprised passengers in a very unexpected way. The 5:25 long video (that's a long ad!) shows Santa Claus, on a TV screen, interacting with travelers as they arrive at the airport to travel across Canada. While the passengers are on their plane heading to their destination, the WestJet team buys the gifts people had asked for. When the passengers arrive at the other end of their journey, the gifts are waiting for them on the carousel. Shocked passengers open gifts, from TV screens to socks and underwear to tablets and phones and even flights home. A lot of people cried.

This video, shown in Figure 8-23, has delivered more than 48 million views and is a wonderful brand campaign, demonstrating both WestJet's service as an airline (which you should choose when flying home at Christmas to visit family) and its brand, which aims to bring joy into people's lives throughout the year. Since the success of this video, WestJet has made videos most years at Christmas.

Volvo Trucks

Perhaps the best example of a brand creating an inspirational video to communicate a marketing message comes from Volvo.

Most people have seen the video "Volvo Trucks — The Epic Split feat. Van Damme (Live Test)" as it's now racked up more than 90 million views (see Figure 8-24). It's a beautifully orchestrated and visually stunning video set to the music of Enya that shows Jean Claude Van Damme ("The Muscles from Brussels") doing a split between two moving reversing trucks, demonstrating both his prowess as a fit and coordinated artist, and Volvo's "Dynamic Steering: technology that delivers an incredibly stable and precise ride on these largest of vehicles".

FIGURE 8-23:
The "WestJet Christmas Miracle: Real-time Giving" video, which garnered more than 48 million views.

FIGURE 8-24:
Jean Claude Van Damme performing an epic split in Volvo Truck's massively popular viral video.

This video wowed people when it came out in 2013 and is still being watched today. Comments from people include

"I think this is actually the best commercial I've seen in my life and, quite probably, the best commercial ever. Whoever came up with this idea should get an award or something."

"I watch this once every few months for motivation. Never fails."

"You know your ad rocks when people actually look for it on YouTube, not when it pops up before a video."

Who would have thought that an advertiser could make an ad longer than five minutes, have more than 90 million people watch it (some of those views were supported with paid media), and that people still want to watch it years later?

Since this video was published, Volvo Trucks has continued to make videos that aim to inspire with their sheer audacity. Search YouTube for one of their follow-up videos, "Volvo Trucks - Look Who's Driving feat. 4-year-old Sophie (Live Test)", which has more than 15 million views.

Is an inspiration video the right format for your content?

When deciding whether an inspiration video is right for your content, ask yourself two questions:

>> **Does an inspirational video make sense for your brand?** Consider the story that your brand has permission to tell. Look for the story you already have. For example, perhaps your business is a local restaurant who provides a grant to pay for tuition for a local student in need to take a cookery course. Telling that person's story is something your company has permission to do and may be a lovely way to let more people know about who you are and what you offer. (See the sidebar "The ill-advised copycat" for a video that didn't quite work out as planned.)

>> **Is your idea for a video cost-effective?** The Dove example described earlier in this chapter made use of candid footage, which a marketer can find on YouTube and simply request permission (perhaps with payment) to use from the video owner. Candid footage can be a very cost-effective way to produce the ad. The Volvo Trucks example, however, would have taken a team of people and a lot of insurance to pull off. Budget would be required for the equipment, the trucks, the rehearsals, the location, and some paid media to support the video. Look for creative ideas that are cost-effective if you're working with a smaller budget. Even Volvo Trucks had no guarantee the video will be a hit.

If you search YouTube for "Volvo Trucks Casino," you'll find some unofficial uploads of the Volvo Truck ad (which appears to be missing from its official channel) featuring a prank pulled on a valet at a casino on the Italian Riviera. The video looks like it would have been expensive to make. Although it's still pretty great, it didn't perform anywhere near the level of the Volvo Trucks Jean Claude Van Damme video.

THE ILL-ADVISED COPYCAT

I once worked with a very well-meaning client who took the WestJet Christmas Miracle example, described earlier in this chapter to heart, creating its own version of the video where it handed out cash to strangers at a mall. Despite the effort and the intent to make something good, it just didn't work out. Even though the premise of the video seemed simple and repeatable, it didn't make sense for the client's brand, as there was no real connection between what they stood for, the services they provided, and handing someone a $50 bill on the street. Combine that with the fact that the execution lacked the emotional impact that WestJet delivered so well, and the video didn't perform.

A checklist for making inspirational videos

Making big, shareable inspirational videos can be a bold approach for a marketer to tackle, so think through the following points before getting started:

>> **Audience:** The audience for these types of inspirational videos is typically broad because they tap into universal human truths, so think through how reaching that broad audience would serve your marketing needs. Perhaps you're a big brand with a nationwide operation, such as WestJet or Dove, where your audience is anyone who ever needs to travel or, um, wash themselves, which is most people.

>> **Cultural trends:** The kinds of stories that resonate with people do fluctuate over time due to trends in culture. For example, during times of political and global uncertainty, people may be more interested in videos that tell stories of individuals' personal triumph in the face of adversity, as they are a reminder that anyone can make positive change and overcome challenges despite the wider world around them. Think about what's happening in the current cultural climate and what kinds of stories are resonating with people at the time.

>> **Format:** You may be able to follow some conventions of approach to format, but the best videos will find new and compelling ways to tell these stories. Rather than copying videos that have worked in the past, marketers must find new ways to tell inspiring stories. Using the principles of good storytelling to guide your video creation is easier than copying the approaches of other videos.

>> **Credibility:** Audiences won't respond to your video if you, as the marketer, don't have permission to tell the story you're telling. If you're going to tell a story of inspiration, make sure that you have permission in the eyes of the audience to be the one who tells it.

>> **Brand:** While including your brand may seem counter to the idea of an inspirational storytelling video, you need to find ways to incorporate your

brand into the video. Otherwise, you may get millions of views, but no one will know it was for your brand, product, or service. Brand elements go beyond just your logo or tagline and include visual clues of colors, people using the product or service, the places where your brand may appear, and more.

Connecting Formats to a Content Strategy

Marketers need to have a clear and considered content strategy to apply to the myriad options for great content formats. One approach may be to use your instincts to simply pick a style of video to make — for example, an educational video that shows how your product helps with a DIY task or an inspirational video that shows your company's community work. However, creating a strategic approach to content will typically serve most marketers better, ensuring that they don't waste time and money creating the wrong video.

You can use the worksheet in Table 8-1 to generate and evaluate different ideas for the types of videos you might make. Look through this chapter and note down the video ideas you want to explore, one per worksheet. After you collect a few, evaluate which ones you think are best to pursue.

TABLE 8-1 **Video Content Format Worksheet**

Question	Your response
What do I want to accomplish with my video? (Circle the answer.)	Educate Entertain Inspire
What type of video will I make?	
What will be in the video?	
Who is this video for?	
What need does this video solve?	
Who is the competition? Can I do better?	
Do I have the credibility needed to make this video?	
How will I include my brand, product, or service?	
What business goal will this help me achieve?	
How will I measure success?	

IN THIS CHAPTER

» **Thinking through your channel's purpose**

» **Finding your niche**

» **Understanding how to leverage trending and evergreen videos**

» **Exploring all distribution channels**

» **Pulling together a complete content strategy**

Chapter **9**

Developing Your Content Strategy

I n this chapter, you find out what you need to know to put together your YouTube content strategy. You explore how your brand's purpose can guide your YouTube channel's purpose with matching themes for the content you'll create. You also discover how to find and exploit a popular niche and leverage both trending and evergreen video content types.

Having a Brand Purpose

The world's best brands stand out in the marketplace because they have a clearly articulated and regularly communicated *purpose.* Purpose is best explained by stating what your brand believes in and why you exist. For example, Nike believes that every person who has a body is an athlete, and the company exists to enable people to "Just Do It".

Your purpose will guide how you develop your YouTube content strategy and many of your other marketing decisions. If your brand doesn't have a purpose, think through what your purpose may be. Start by completing these sentences for your company or brand.

>> We believe that _____.

>> We exist to _____.

For example, the following has been Google's mission statement from its early days and expresses its purpose as a brand and company:

>> "We believe that everyone should have access to all the information that exists in the world."

>> "We exist to organize the world's information and make it universally accessible and useful."

Google wants to develop services that significantly improve the lives of as many people as possible, and this sense of purpose drives the company's business and marketing strategy.

Applying Brand Purpose to Your YouTube Channel

When you're setting about developing a video content strategy for your brand, your brand's purpose becomes your most important guiding tool.

If Nike's purpose is to empower everyone to be an athlete, the company may develop a content strategy using videos on YouTube to show how people can tackle various sports, exercises, and training programs — and Nike does!

Coca-Cola's purpose speaks to its desire to "refresh the world in mind, body and spirit . . . to inspire moments of optimism and happiness . . .," and it drives the company's content strategy to feature videos telling these types of stories. Coca-Cola's brand purpose creates a guardrail that ensures the company won't create any content that doesn't fit with its content strategy's purpose.

REMEMBER

The overlapping area between your brand purpose and your audiences needs helps you define the purpose of your YouTube channel.

With a firm sense of your purpose in mind, you are set up for success to start making choices that form your video content strategy.

TIP

Don't confuse a brand's purpose with the approach of *purpose-driven marketing,* which tends to speak more to cause-related issues. For example, a large furniture manufacturer may produce a marketing campaign showing how its supply chain and materials are sustainable and environmentally conscious. Cause marketing is important as part of the marketing mix because consumers are increasingly demanding a level of responsibility from brands. However, the idea of purpose here is that your brand exists for a reason that goes beyond "to sell people things." For more on cause marketing, see *Cause Marketing For Dummies* (Wiley Publishing, Inc.) by Joe Waters and Joanna MacDonald.

Choosing Your Themes

Video can be challenging because there's no end to how many videos you can create, except for the fact that budget and resources are finite. What helps you with this challenge in narrowing down the video content you can create by focusing on *themes* — essentially the handful of overarching subjects or topics that your videos are about.

TIP

Think of a theme as a collection of videos thematically related that make sense for your brand and your marketing goals.

Themes should align with your marketing goals. For example, if you're launching a marketing campaign with the goal of promoting awareness of your upcycled clothing brand, perhaps you'll make a shareable video of an inspirational story of how old clothes are taken, repurposed, and then donated to people in need. This theme of "stories of personal triumph" can make people feel connected to your brand.

If you're looking for a campaign that delivers sales of your new and improved tool, you'll make more performance-focused video content. For example, your video can show demonstrations of how your product or service helps someone solve a need, such as fixing a leaking tap, with a link to where your customers can buy your product. The theme of your these videos will be helpful how-to videos that solve commonly searched tasks.

Generating theme ideas

When you choose your theme, you want to generate as many themes for your content that you can and then pick the top handful that you think deliver to your marketing needs the best.

TIP

I suggest grabbing some sticky notes and a felt marker pen. Write each idea for a them on its own sticky note.

For example, if you're a nationwide manufacturer of shoes, you may generate a big list of potential topics that includes things like

- » Travel stories
- » Types of shoes
- » Shoes in history
- » Our range of products and their features
- » The people who sell our shoes
- » Famous people who wear our shoes
- » People who did amazing things in our shoes
- » Shoes we've given to people in need

Now pick the best ideas from the list. In this example, if the marketing goal is to sell more shoes, the team may decide to make videos that focus on the theme of featuring their products, famous people who wear them, and places where you can buy them.

After you choose the best ideas, match your theme ideas to what your audience is most interested in to determine the themes of your YouTube channel. You'll build video content based on these themes. Write on the sticky notes all the relevant things that you can think of that your audience cares about The shoe company in the preceding example may list the following audience interests:

- » Sports
- » Outdoors
- » Travel
- » Helping others in need
- » Running
- » Community
- » Parenting

Sure, you can make videos featuring every store that sells your shoes, but does your audience care about that? Perhaps if you tell an interesting story about each shop owner and retail outlet, but, otherwise they may not want to hear about those stores. If your audience is interested in travel, outdoor activities, and sports, you can make video content on those themes.

TIP

Find the overlap between what your brand is all about, the themes that you can make videos for, and what your audience cares about and let that drive your marketing goals so that you can make videos that people want to watch.

When it comes to how many themes you should focus on, I have no specific answer. Instead, pick the theme or themes that you think delivers the most to your marketing goal and that best matches your audience's interests.

For example, the nationwide manufacturer of shoes may choose three themes:

» Stories of how they were able to help people in need through their charitable efforts

» Stories of people who wear our shoes when they travel around the world

» Special product features that help wearers with specific sports activities

The first theme allows the shoe manufacturer to create videos throughout the year that tell a great brand story. The second theme allows them to create a series of entertaining travel vlog videos that people may like to watch over time. For the last theme, they can explain their product features and how specialist athletes may use them in how-to style videos that people may search for. These three themes deliver to a marketing and an audience need.

Lowe's Home Improvement

Lowe's Home Improvement has a clear and comprehensive YouTube content strategy that's helped the store snag more than 575,000 subscribers and 200 million video views. The store's playlists reveal its themes for video content:

» **Help beginners navigate do-it-yourself (DIY) basics:** This playlist features a series of short DIY basics videos that teach simple tasks, such as controlling sawdust when sanding, using a pressure washer, cleaning a fireplace, and removing a stripped screw. Lowe's realize that a lot of people may not be familiar with these basic tasks, so in simple under 2-minute videos with nothing more than visuals, text, and some cute music, Lowe's provides clear explanations that help people feel empowered to tackle those basics and get started with DIY projects (see Figure 9-1).

FIGURE 9-1:
This simple DIY video from Lowe's helps show people how to unclog a sink.

>> **Help more advanced DIYers tackle bigger home DIY projects with confidence:** This more involved series of how-to project playlists targets more advanced DIY projects made simple by Lowe's — for example, a playlist of videos that break down the steps required to install new flooring or build a wooden deck, as shown in Figure 9-2. The video playlist for how to install a new floor contains six videos, each around 4 minutes long, with clear instructions and narration that walks you through the steps.

>> **Inspire people to transform their spaces with simple projects that they can tackle within a budget and in only a day or two:** Lastly, Lowe's features a few different web series. One series is The Weekender, which has four seasons with episodes that are each about ten minutes (see Figure 9-3). In "The Weekender," a host tackles exactly five projects per episode that take a weekend to transform a space in need of love. This nice series shows easy, cost-effective, and inspirational projects that people can take on over the course of two days with the help of supplies from Lowe's.

FIGURE 9-2:
This playlist of videos shows the step-by-step process to build a complete deck.

FIGURE 9-3:
The Weekender is one of several show-like seasons of content, delivering inspiration for easy weekend projects.

These themes make perfect sense for a store like Lowe's that has thought through the products and services it offer, and what its customers are interested in doing, are passionate about, and search for, creating videos that live in the intersection of those two criteria. Someone watching Lowe's videos may leave feeling that the brand is one they can trust and confidently turn to for the right help. The videos may also convert people into paying customers online and in store.

Enjoying a Popular Niche

A *niche* is typically something that speaks to a smaller, specialized section of the population. YouTube is so big, though, that even niches can be quite large, hence the notion of a popular niche.

A *popular niche* refers to content that tends to be quite specific and that only a certain group of people may be interested in. However, because YouTube is massive, the number of people interested in the niche is huge! You'd be surprised how many people want to watch videos of a person, sometimes dressed as a pickle, eating pickles and various other foods (95 million views and counting -— check out the channel ASMRTheChew and Figure 9-4.) That's pretty niche, and yet it's extremely popular.

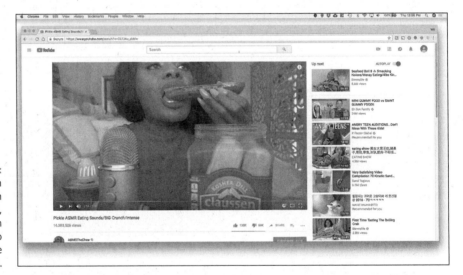

FIGURE 9-4: Spirit Payton has more than 95 million views, with 16 million for this video where she eats pickles.

Benefitting from a popular niche

A popular niche benefits anyone developing a YouTube content strategy.

TIP

The channel Primitive Technology, shown in Figure 9-5, is an excellent example of a popular niche because it's somewhat surprising that so many people (600 million-plus video views) would want to watch videos of a man quietly and patiently building things with his hands in the woods of Australia. (For more on this channel, see the nearby sidebar "Primitive Technology.")

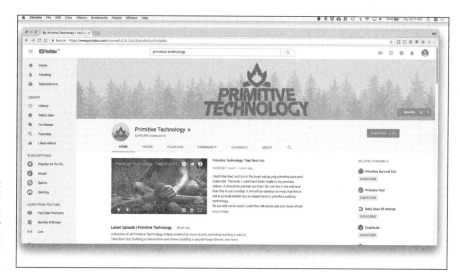

FIGURE 9-5:
The channel
Primitive
Technology
is an excellent
example of a
popular niche.

Another excellent example of a popular niche is Hydraulic Press, shown in Figure 9-6, where someone with access to a press and endless curiosity found that millions of people love watching videos of things being crushed. (See the nearby sidebar for more on Hydraulic Press.)

PRIMITIVE TECHNOLOGY

One of my all-time favorite YouTubers is the channel Primitive Technology (`http://bit.ly/primitivetechnology`) where a man in the wilderness of Far North Queensland, Australia, demonstrates how to create structures using nothing but his hands or hand-created tools using the materials he finds. What's amazing is that he does this entirely in silence. All you can hear are the sounds of the animals and the forest around him, and it makes for a simple and mesmerizing approach.

The silent man featured in these videos, John, has more than 8.6 million subscribers and 600 million-plus video views. He has made more than 40 videos that show how-to tasks such as creating A-frame huts, making stoves, pottery, bricks, sandals, weapons and tools, and even cultivating cassava and yams. John's most popular video, with more than 53 million views, is how to build a tiled roof hut.

HYDRAULIC PRESS

With more than 2 million subscribers and 284 million views, the Hydraulic Press Channel features videos of a hydraulic press crushing things. That's it. For science fans and the plain old curious, the videos crush things like ball bearings, stacks of paper, diamonds, and even a motorcycle helmet. In each video, an industrial press setup is ready to crush the object of the day, while an off-screen narrator describes what's happening as cameras show the action in real-time and slow motion.

FIGURE 9-6:
Lauri, based in Finland, runs the Hydraulic Press channel with more than 284 million video views.

Both Primitive Technology and Hydraulic Press have seen lots of me-too channels copying their successful formats, often to equally great success. However, eventually a niche gets saturated, leaving not a lot of room for copy cats unless they can bring something new or fresh to the category.

Finding a popular niche

Finding a popular niche can be tricky, but it's possible. You want a balance between making videos that are too broad versus too specific. If your video is too broad, attracting an audience will be hard because a lot of video content is already out there. On the other hand, you'll struggle to find an audience if you go too niche.

Think about how to take your themes and make them more niche. Then check to see how many people are watching YouTube videos for that niche.

TIP

For example, if you're a manufacturer of high performance sports clothing and accessories and you want to make videos about people wearing your products as they take part in various activities, you can progressively add more niche to your videos by showing

» People who are into sports and adventure activities

» People who travel to take part in sports and adventure activities

» People who travel wearing your clothing taking part in sports and adventure activities

» People who travel wearing your clothes to take part in sports and adventure activities in exotic, far-flung, hard-to-reach locations

» People who travel wearing your clothes to take part in sports and adventure activities in exotic, far-flung, hard-to-reach locations who recite inspiring poetry as they rock climb

To find your own niche:

1. **Research topics related to the videos you may make.**

   Whatever you are marketing, look for all the related content on YouTube. Pick one video and then let YouTube take you on an adventure. You can watch the Up Next videos or click on tangentially related videos that appear on the right side of the screen.

   Consume as much of this content as you can. Make notes as you watch the different, interesting, unique, and unexpected angles people may have taken.

2. **Type in the search box so that its autofill feature can give you clues about popular searches.**

   For example, if I made and sold lights for bicycles, I might search *bike lights* and get autofills for

   - Bike light reviews, which shows video reviews of different types of bike lights available, helping people choose what's best for their need

   - Bike light with turn signal, which are videos that demonstrate advanced bike lights that offer a turn signal feature

   - Bike lights are important, which shows a results page of videos that explain why bike lights are important for cyclist's safety

   - Bike lights wheel, which are videos of how you can make the wheels of your bike light up with different colors and patterns (this was new to me)

- Bike light accessories, which are videos showing additional complementary accessories related to bike lights

- Bike light DIY hacks and tips, which are videos showing DIY solutions for bike lights

TIP

Google Trends and Google Search can also be helpful tools to uncover related content and niches. You can also search on Google for *YouTube keyword tool* to find a variety of free and paid third-party tools that help you explore keyword searches and popular tags on YouTube. Check out Chapter 3 for more on these tools.

3. **Check whether enough of a popular niche is available.**

   Ask yourself the following questions:

   - How many video views do these videos have?

   - Are new videos being uploaded frequently and recently?

   - How many subscribers do these channels have?

   - Are people actively commenting, and if so, what are they saying?

   - Does this niche feel saturated and competitive, with lots of people making videos on this theme?

   - Can you think of unique angles you can bring to the niche, or would you be a me-too if you took this approach?

Exploring Trending and Evergreen Videos

Video content can fall into two categories: content that is timely and trending, and content that is evergreen.

Think of *trending videos* as time-sensitive content and not just videos that appear on the YouTube Trending (www.youtube.com/feed/trending) video list. Trending videos may be shared, appear on social media sites, and appear on the You-Tube home page. Trending videos are relevant in the now and become less relevant at time goes on. For example, daily news videos are time-sensitive videos because they speak to what's happening that day. However, as time goes by, they become increasingly irrelevant. No one reads last week's newspaper!

The opposite of trending videos are evergreen videos. *Evergreen videos* are the types of videos that won't date and are primarily found through people searching YouTube's massive database.

Trending videos

Trending videos can be a great way to grab an audience for a short time. They can also be an important part of your marketing mix if part of your brand is about being the first to talk about a particular topic in culture.

The biggest problem with trending videos is that they don't have much of a long-term return. Once the trend cycle is over, people may not be searching for, discovering, and watching these videos again. As a result, trending videos tend to take a quick and easy production format approach so that they can be turned around quickly and published before the window closes.

Making trending or time-sensitive videos lets you to tap into things that are happening right now. Being the first person to create videos on current topics is hard to do, but you can find success if your video is first to meet people's watching needs. For example, if you're a news site, you'll be making videos that break stories to get the most views possible in a short space of time before all the other news channels make their own videos about the same story.

Marketers can make use of trending videos by jumping on news stories. For example, if a large cereal manufacturer recalls its product due to possible contamination, a competitor organic cereal brand can make a quickly released video about its non-GMO and healthy ingredients in the hopes of snagging some views of people searching and discovering the trending news video about the recall.

If you're going to make trending videos, you need to put in place a process that enables you to

- » Quickly identify potential topics, research them, decide whether you should make a video about them, and then choose the best angle to take

- » Have a production process that lets you quickly write the script and turn around the recording and editing of the video

- » Have the resources and a clear plan for publishing, distributing, and promoting your video that you can follow each time your newest video is released

Evergreen videos

The major benefit of time spent investing in the creation of evergreen content is that it can pay off indefinitely, with people searching for topics every day and potentially finding your video time and again.

Evergreen videos come with their own challenges, though, because their content can be quite competitive. The best videos rise to the top and can monopolize the search results page, so usurping existing videos can be difficult. You need to ensure that your evergreen content is better than any other video on the same topic.

My favorite example of an evergreen video is "How to tie a bow tie." Videos that show how to tie a bow tie will likely never date or become irrelevant (see Figure 9-7). The process of tying a bow tie is unlikely to change in the foreseeable future, and people will need to use YouTube to find out how to tie them before they are late for their event!

FIGURE 9-7:
Evergreen videos don't date and can keep accruing views over years.

REMEMBER

Especially with these kinds of how-to videos, where you are demonstrating something complicated that takes a few tries to get right, people may watch them several times, which racks up your video views.

If you're going to make evergreen videos, you'll need to

>> Develop a process to research what people are searching for to decide which is the best evergreen video to make.

>> Put in place a production process that enables you to make a volume of evergreen videos over time, such as one per week.

>> Ensure that you publish your videos with well-written titles, descriptions, and tags.

>> Find places to distribute your evergreen videos outside of YouTube, such as on blogs and websites.

If you're wondering why some videos with fewer views end up higher in the search results than those with more views, see Chapter 18.

Making the choice

Using both trending and evergreen videos in your content strategy mix is often a wise choice. Virtually all marketers have an opportunity to create evergreen videos around their brand, products, and services, but many can also keep their eye on things happening in culture that can allow them to create a timely video and capitalize on a burst of audience.

Consider the following to help you make a choice:

>> **If you're getting started,** choose evergreen videos. A handy tip is to base your evergreen content on your Frequently Asked Questions (FAQs).

>> **If your company is all about being the first to spot a trend or report something in culture or the news,** then focus more on trending videos.

>> **If you think you have the opportunity to do both types of videos,** make a plan to tackle evergreen videos on an ongoing basis, but keep your eye out for trending opportunities and have an action plan ready for when they do arise.

Distributing Content

Even though this book focuses almost exclusively on the YouTube platform, I often say to clients "The goal here is not to make a YouTube strategy, but rather to make a video strategy".

REMEMBER

Video content can be made once and can live in many places. Videos can take time and money to make, so letting them live in as many places as possible helps ensure you maximize your return on investment.

To help with developing a full video distribution strategy, I often encourage clients to think through a simple exercise:

1. **Using sticky notes and a felt marker pen, list as many distribution channels as you can think of, writing down one per sticky note.**

   YouTube, of course, is one distribution channel, but so is Facebook, Snapchat, Twitter, blogs, your website, news sites, other video platforms like Vimeo, email newsletters, screens in retail spaces, paid media syndication, and even the back of taxi cabs.

2. **After you generate as many ideas as you can, start to organize them into priority based on what you think will be easiest and have the greatest return.**

   For example, if you have a large following of fans on your Facebook page, perhaps you'll put that distribution channel toward the top of the list. If you tend not to use more outlier ideas like running your videos in taxi cabs, put those distribution channels at the bottom of the list.

3. **Choose the top three to five distribution channels.**

   The next time you make a video and post it on YouTube, also find a way to distribute your video through the channels you chose in Step 3.

Some platforms have different requirements when it comes to video, so you may want to test what works or make edits to your video for a particular channel. However, in general you should be able to post your YouTube video in many places, reaching a larger audience.

Giving Structure to Your Content Choices

When you're ready to bring your content strategy choices together, you'll have what you need to sketch out how video content will map to your marketing calendar. The key components of your content strategy are

>> Defining the overarching purpose of your YouTube channel

>> Picking the themes for your content and finding your niche

>> Choosing whether you want to make entertainment, educational, or inspirational videos and making a choice around format

>> Deciding on trending or evergreen or a combination of both

>> Thinking about where you will distribute your videos, beyond YouTube

With these choices in mind, you can use the Hero Hub Help framework to plot your videos onto a calendar, which is the last step in developing your initial content strategy.

The *Hero Hub Help framework* has consistently been one of the most popular frameworks with clients because it helps give structure to and make sense of a marketer's approach to video on YouTube. You can use this framework to bring together the types and formats of videos you want to make and how you can use paid media to bring your videos to bigger audiences (see Chapter 7).

TIP

Help videos are probably the best and easiest place for most marketers who are just getting started. If you're new to YouTube, see the section "Help videos," later in this chapter, and consider making just a few of these types of videos at first.

Hero videos

A *hero video* is a video that gets shared by millions of people. You may even call it a viral video.

Hero videos have something in common with how traditional marketers may use TV. A hero video tends to be a single piece of video creative that you publish three to four times per year as part of a campaign, supported with paid media, often in synch with a marketer's campaign schedule. For example, if you're a marketer who runs three big advertising campaigns throughout the year, you may decide to make three hero videos, one for each campaign. (Chapter 8 has great examples of hero videos.)

Although not all hero videos conform to the following criteria, a typical hero video,

>> **Usually falls into the inspiration bucket.** While not limited to this bucket, hero videos are often focused on inspiring acts and stories.

>> **Are typically a one-off video.** Although they aren't part of a series or season of a show, they tend to be made for the sole purpose of being a hero video.

>> **Have an enormous audience.** I like to say that hero videos "go off and champion on your behalf, just like a hero would." They reach audiences in the millions of views.

>> **Tend to get their audience in a shorter space of time.** Hero videos tend to have a velocity to them, in that they reach large numbers of people quite quickly. They may appear on the trending videos page, or they may come up in conversation with friends — "Did you see that video . . . ?"

- **May continue to grow in audience over time.** Even though they achieve a large share of views in a short space of time, hero videos continue to be relevant even with the passing of time and may rack up views year after year.

- **May be popular with more than your target audience.** Because hero videos have such a broad appeal, you may find that your hero video takes off in popularity around the globe.

- **Are often supported by paid media.** Viral videos are challenging to pull off, and although hero videos appear to be viral in nature, they are often supported with paid media to help them reach, or be pushed to, a big audience. Typically, an orchestrated approach to media helps hero videos reach big audiences.

- **Are often part of a brand campaign.** One of the most common uses for hero videos by marketers is to deliver to a brand campaign's objective, such as creating awareness of a brand or changing how people see the brand. A marketer can make a hero video the central star of a coordinated effort, with support from other advertising channels like offline media, social media, and influencers.

- **May be tied to a big event, important initiative, cultural moment, or universal human truth.** Successful hero videos tend to tap into moments or truths because they must resonate with a large and broad audience.

- **Tend to be very shareable thanks to use of emotion.** Taking the creative approach of telling a story of personal triumph, pride, overcoming and other emotional angles helps ensure their shareability.

- **Often require larger production budgets.** Hero videos don't have to be glossy productions in exotic locations, but often hero videos work hard to tell the stories they are telling and have a larger production effort and budget behind them.

Some or all of these things may be true. You can find examples of hero videos that don't follow all these criteria, but these features tend to be the most common elements of what makes a video a hero video.

REMEMBER

Ultimately, hero videos are an excellent choice for marketers who want to send a big bold message to a big, broad audience.

Visit Chapter 8 for examples of brands who create inspirational hero videos.

Hub videos

Hub videos are a series of episodes connected by a theme, such as a show idea or something relating to your audience's passion points. Hub videos, unlike hero videos (see preceding section), are a core grounding feature of your YouTube channel on the platform.

Hub videos are similar to a TV series in that they are episodic in nature. For example, a brand like Under Armour has made lots of playlists for its hub videos. Take a look at `www.youtube.com/user/underarmour/playlists` and see Figure 9-8.

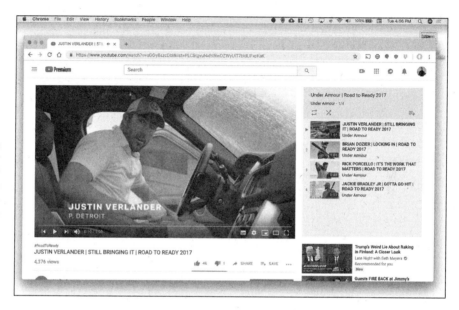

FIGURE 9-8: Under Armour makes several hub video playlists. This video features the baseball player Justin Verlander in the four-part hub video series "Road to Ready."

The following features tend to describe hub videos:

>> **Fall into the entertainment bucket.** Your hub videos may be a hosted series where the host visits families and tells how they use your product or service, or it may be a series of vlogs from your brand ambassadors.

>> **Align to your audience's passions.** Hub videos align to the interests and passions of your audiences. These videos go beyond just marketing messages or how-to videos and instead work to broaden the appeal of your brand. In this respect, hub videos are more like the videos of a YouTube creator than a marketer.

>> **Are regularly scheduled usually each week.** You can make a choice between publishing one hub video per week, or you can publish an entire season in one go. Clients always ask which approach is better. My answer is "If you're sitting on great content, waiting for all the episodes to be finished, don't. Publish what you have and let people know there will be more each week. However, don't delay in getting more episodes live. If they like episode 1, they'll want episode 2 immediately!"

>> **Are a series of episodes that follow a repeating format.** Hub videos are a series of episodes that all relate to each other and follow a consistent format, just like a TV show. You may want to choose a clear editorial voice that matches your brand.

>> **Are collected on a playlist.** The YouTube channel owner collects hub videos together by onto a playlist. That way, if your viewer finds episode 1, they can easily watch all the other episodes without hunting for them.

>> **Give viewers a reason to subscribe and build following.** Hub videos give people a reason to subscribe to your channel because they'll want to come back for more. This desire to watch more helps you build your subscriber base and keep your audience more regularly engaged.

>> **Are published consistently throughout the year.** A full hub video strategy for a marketer can feature as many as four seasons of a show or shows throughout the year. The videos are published consistently and regularly, such as weekly.

>> **Are topically related to core marketing themes but speak to the audience's interests and passions.** Hub videos live in the intersection of the topics and themes a marketer wants to create content about, but crucially tap into the interests and passions of the desired audience. If you're marketing your nationwide chain of laundromats, you don't need to make a cooking show.

>> **Can be tied to a marketer's campaign goals.** Marketers should only make hub videos if they're clear about the campaign goals they will be delivering to — for example, improving brand sentiment, encouraging consideration, or inspiring people to take on projects, tasks, adventures, and the like that make use of the brand's products or services.

>> **Have medium-sized audiences in relation to your other videos.** If hero videos have really big audiences, hub videos have a smaller, more medium-sized audience. Those numbers are relative! Success is often measured by how many subscribers join the channel and how many people watch all the episodes.

>> **Build audience over time.** Hub videos build your audience over time. They're often evergreen in nature. When people discover an episode, they'll hopefully be encouraged to watch all the other episodes in the hub series.

>> **Are great to syndicate.** Hub videos are excellent content to *syndicate*, or distribute, through your other owned channels (your website and blog), through your earned channels (your social media spaces), and through paid channels (paid syndication services that spread your content around the web).

>> **Can be large or simple production efforts.** Hub videos can have production values more akin to that of a TV show, or they may be simpler in-house studio productions. Hub videos don't have a standard quality or approach, but often they feel a bit like a TV show.

>> **Are great for your audience who want regular, engaging content from you.** Ultimately, you want to deliver hub content to your audience that they want to watch on a continuous basis. They may subscribe to your channel and choose to receive alerts when you upload new content.

Hub videos are great for marketers who want to create content that builds a relationship with their audience by tapping into their passions and interests.

WARNING

Hub videos do require some heavy lifting on the part of the marketer. For example, if you're a marketer who decides to make four seasons of a show each year, with each season featuring eight ten-minute episodes, you're committing to making 32 videos with more than five hours of video content. Even one season of a show is over an hour of content, which requires quite a bit of effort. All marketers should think carefully before committing to a strategy that features hub content. Of all components of a video strategy, hub is one of the hardest to pull off, but it can be well worth it.

Help videos

Help videos are your how-to videos. People find help videos by searching YouTube for answers to their questions. Brands have an opportunity to intercept in these moments of need with great educational content that helps them solve a challenge. Help videos can be one-offs, but typically larger brands with big marketing efforts will create a volume of help videos, sometimes numbering in the hundreds.

The following features describe a typical help video:

>> **Tend to fall into the education bucket.** If hero videos are inspirational and hub videos tend to be entertainment, help videos fall into the educational bucket. They are your how-to videos.

>> **Are found through people searching on YouTube.** Help videos are usually found when someone is searching YouTube looking for an answer to their question. Search YouTube for any question, and chances are you'll have a variety of how-to videos pop up.

>> **Answer commonly asked questions.** Help videos answer a question. If you're a marketer who wants to make help videos, look for what people search for using Google Trends (see Chapter 3). You can also talk to your customer service team or consult your customer service inbox for the

questions that are most frequently asked. Answer questions that your brand should be the one to answer; you don't need to boil the ocean by trying to answer everything that is tangentially related.

» **Are closer to the bottom of your marketing funnel.** Help videos may be closer to the bottom of your marketing funnel in that viewers are either using your product or service already, or they are looking for your product or service as a solution to the problem in front of them. Help videos can be a good converter to purchase but shouldn't feel like an ad or a sales pitch. (See Chapter 2 for more about the marketing funnel.)

» **Are informational and practical, yet entertaining.** The best help videos are short, sweet, and to the point. You can answer questions in a pragmatic way while finding simple ways to keep the videos entertaining.

» **Need to be crystal clear to beat the competition.** A client once told me that he fixed his TV over the weekend by looking for a how-to video on YouTube. In one video, the person doing the fix had large hands, which made it hard to see the fine and fiddlesome work being tackled. In another video, the person had smaller hands, which made the video clearer with its instructions on which part to replace. This simple example illustrates how the best help videos offer clear, effective explanations and are the ones that float to the top of the search results.

» **Can play a customer service role.** Help videos can often be an important part of a larger brand's customer service operations. If you're a marketer at a company where you have a customer service team, consider whether any of its members may be good on camera. With some training and a simple setup, they can set about creating videos that answer customer service queries. Not only can this approach reduce the call center and email volume of inquiries they receive, but it can build your YouTube presence. It's a win-win!

» **Can expand ideas of what people can do.** Even though a help video should focus on answering the question at hand, the end of the video may be a chance to include some "Did you also know . . .?" tips that may inspire more use of your product or service or even a purchase of another product. For example, if you make a stain-removing bar of soap and your video shows how it can remove wine from carpets, perhaps you can end the video by mentioning the myriad other uses for your product and linking to additional help videos.

» **Are always-on.** While hero videos are one-off occasions a few times a year and hub videos are seasonal or tied to marketing campaigns, help videos are always on. *Always on* means that you can create help videos all day every day. There's almost no limit to how many help videos you can make, so making a couple each week is a great idea. Over time, you'll quickly build up a big catalog of videos that will grow your overall YouTube channel.

- » **Can be collected on playlists when they're related.** If you have a few help videos that relate to each other, you can collect them together on a playlist. It almost turns your help videos into a hub series, such as "Top Ten Stain Removal Uses," "Ten Ideas to Use Widget X to Improve Your Life," or "Easy and Quick Weekend projects." As you create and publish help videos, look back to see whether you can recombine your videos into different playlists.

- » **Can be a nice entry point to the rest of your YouTube content.** People are searching YouTube every day, often for help videos, and so they are a great way for people to discover you, your brand, and your YouTube channel. Think of your help videos as your calling card or invitation to the audience to watch more of your videos. You can end your help videos by letting them know about other help videos or hub series you have on your channel.

- » **Have a long-tail audience growth.** A *long-tail audience* means that you grow a large audience of viewers by having many help videos that each have a small audience. A long-tail audience is in contrast to the large audience of a single hero video. Your many help videos grow an audience over time and collectively have a large audience, even though each video individually may have only a few thousand views.

- » **Are evergreen.** Help videos may be the best example of evergreen videos you'll find. For most marketers, the questions you're answering with your help videos will live on for a long time, making help videos a great return on your production investment. (For more on evergreen videos, see the section "Exploring Trending and Evergreen Videos," earlier in this chapter.)

- » **Can be easier to produce than hub or hero videos.** Help videos don't need to be the big glossy productions that may benefit a hero video, and they don't require the commitment of a hub series. A lot of clients I've worked with in the past have chosen to create an in-house solution, with a simple backdrop, lighting, camera, and a contract resource to help shoot and edit the videos. Sometimes they've used a smaller agency to help create their first wave of help videos as they test out whether help videos can work for them.

For all these reasons, help videos are often the best place to start for a marketer entering into video creation for the first time. You can make a few, experiment with what works, tweak and refine your production process, and generally have a greater sense for what it takes to make videos in support of marketing and brand efforts. Rather than tackling something like a hero video or hub series, you can start with just one simple video that answers a common question that your customers or potential customers are searching for.

If you want to make help videos but aren't sure where to start, create help videos for your top ten FAQs.

Mapping Video to Your Marketing Calendar

The Hero Hub Help framework, described in the preceding section, is an easy way to map all these choices onto your marketing calendar. After you step through all the facets of a content strategy, deciding things like whether you want to make one-off hero videos, seasonable hub series, always-on help videos, or all of them, you'll be ready to find the cadence of consistency that works for you and is feasible within your production budgets and resources.

If you have an existing marketing calendar that details all of your campaign efforts, grab it now and mark off places where you think video can play a role.

1. **Look for your big hero moments and consider pulsing them throughout the year for things like your brand campaigns or big tent-pole events.**

   Perhaps you have a big event in the summer, where a hero video makes sense.

2. **Look for opportunities where a hub series can support your marketing efforts.**

   You may want to make hub series for marketing campaigns, seasonal initiatives, ongoing sponsorships, or community work.

3. **Consider adding in an always-on effort to create and publish help videos.**

4. **Mark when you'll start making your videos based on search terms, FAQs, and new product launches.**

TIP

If you don't think you need to tackle a full content strategy, go to Part 2 and think about developing ads that run on YouTube. Content is a big commitment and isn't for all marketers.

IN THIS CHAPTER

» **Reaching new audiences through shareability**

» **Taking a conversational style**

» **Encouraging interactivity**

» **Keeping consistent**

» **Targeting interests**

» **Ensuring a sustainable approach**

» **Maximizing discoverability and accessibility**

» **Striving for authenticity**

Chapter **10**

Content Fundamentals

Whatever kind of video content you're making, keeping in mind certain creative considerations can give your content its best chance of performing. These creative fundamentals have been a core part of the advice YouTube provides to advertisers and creators and are based on observations of which videos from YouTubers perform well.

This chapter contains a breakdown of these core creative considerations along with examples. You don't have to ensure that every single video you make follows all these principles, but by following some of these tips, you'll be setting your video up with a fighting chance of reaching an audience of viewers.

You can see many of these principles in the videos from YouTubers who, through a process of creation, experimentation, and collaboration, have figured out how to build a loyal audience of engaged viewers. These YouTubers have in part cracked the code of what makes for successful videos on YouTube and at the same time have created a lot of the rules on how best to use the platform. Some of these principles apply specifically to YouTube, some to video, some to content, some to social media, and some to marketing in general.

Make Your Videos Shareable

Shareability is probably the highest form of praise that your video is something truly good because people share things directly with their friends only when they know they'll like it. Shareability is the holy grail for all marketers because it means you can spend less on paid media to spread your message.

WARNING

Making shareable videos can be very hard, so I caution all marketers not to set out with the intention of creating a video that will somehow magically be viewed by one person, shared to two, then four, and then exponentially grow until it has made its way all around the globe. Unfortunately, shareability doesn't really work that way.

Marketers should consider the shareability of their videos before making them. When you're thinking about an idea for a video, start by stepping back and asking yourself whether viewers will share your content. A great example comes from Rhett and Link from the channel Good Mythical Morning (www.youtube.com/user/rhettandlink2) who would say,

"When people share this, which ten words will they use to describe it to their friends?"

You can see that concept played out in Figure 10-1. The title for Rhett and Link's video "The Most Amazing Optical Illusions on the Internet" is an example of a title that is less than ten words that someone may use to describe the video as they share it with others.

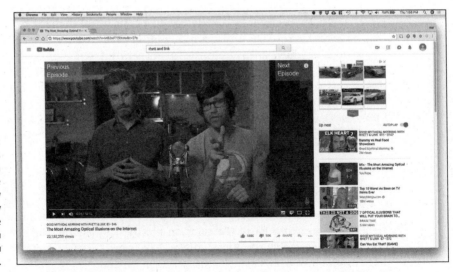

FIGURE 10-1: Rhett and Link's video title is a great example of just how someone may describe the video when sharing it with friends.

TIP

Look through your YouTube watch history to see the videos you've been watching recently. Which ones have you shared with friends? Why did you share those particular videos? I bet you'll see that some of the videos you've shared

>> **Are entertaining.** It seems obvious to say, but, you enjoyed the video and knew a friend would enjoy it, too.

>> **Speaks to a shared interest.** You knew the friend that you shared it with is also interested in this kind of content.

>> **Reaffirms something about you.** For example, it may support your beliefs or opinions.

For example, I looked back at my history just now and the last video I shared was a video by Doug DeMuro, my favorite car YouTuber, entitled "Here's why the 2018 Lincoln Navigator is worth $100,000." I shared this video with my friend Andy with the words, "I want one of these." The video was entertaining, about a shared interest and reaffirmed something I believe — that the Lincoln Navigator is a cool car.

Videos that are shareable

>> **Tell a good story.** When you get together with friends, you tell stories, and the principle applies to making videos shareable. People like to share videos that tell a good story.

>> **Are often funny or positive.** You're probably sharing a video to make a friend's day better, so videos may be more shareable if they're funny, uplifting, happy, or optimistic.

>> **Are a short, easy watch.** Very few people will share a full-length documentary (of course, you may recommend watching it), so shareable videos are often short. They're the kind of video you'd be happy to stop what you're doing to watch.

>> **Say something about the sharer.** If you look back at the videos you've shared, you may find that they say something about you. They may represent your sense of humor or a belief or that you're sharing something you thought was smart because you're also smart.

TIP

Ask people to share your video. You'll see more people share your video if you include a reminder to share it. If you don't ask, you don't get!

Take a Conversational Approach

YouTube, like other social media channels but unlike traditional media, presents a unique opportunity to converse directly with your audience. As a marketer, you can use YouTube to ask your audience what they like and don't like, what they want more of, and what they love most about you.

REMEMBER

Conversation is a key component of some of the most successful videos and uses of YouTube. One of the things you'll notice when you watch almost any video from a popular YouTuber is that they speak directly to you in a conversational style and that they ask for viewers to comment and discuss the content of their videos.

This conversation developed in part because many of today's successful YouTubers started years ago sitting in their room with the webcam on their laptop, in front of them, looking face on and directly at the camera, making content in a vlog style. The setup felt like a video chat with a friend, so YouTubers took a conversational approach.

What's interesting is that back in the day, this approach was so different from other content on TV. Rather than being a passive viewer of TV, viewers felt like a friend and celebrity was talking to them. This personal feeling is one of the main reasons YouTube and being a YouTuber really took off.

When you're making your videos, you can take the creative approach of speaking directly to your audience in a conversational style. Videos that are conversational

>> **Address the audience face on.** You can show a person facing the camera, speaking directly to the audience in a casual style and tone. In fact, a face facing forwards is better than any other angle or not using someone's face. Research has shown that videos featuring a face-forward human face are more likely to be preferred and recalled (see Figure 10-2). Humans like to see people's faces!

>> **Encourage dialogue.** Your video should specifically encourage people to use the comments to ask and answer questions. Good questions are guiding and specific — not too open-ended, broad, or vague.

REMEMBER

Make sure that you read these comments and actually respond to them either in the comments themselves or in subsequent videos. Liking or hearting the video is a simple but effective acknowledgement to the commenter.

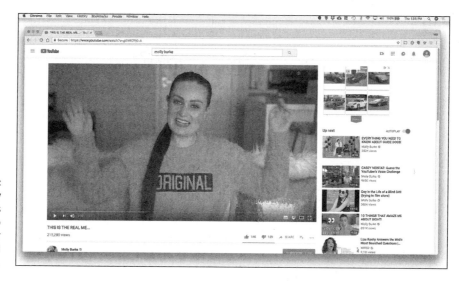

FIGURE 10-2:
YouTuber Molly
Burke speaks
directly to
camera in her
vibrant and
fun style.

>> **Make use of a light script.** If you've ever been at a party and you find yourself in conversation with someone who you'd describe as a good conversationalist, it's probably because they are telling a compelling story. It's almost like they have a clear sense of the narrative in their head — because they do! Making use of a light script, for example, that maps out a few key points you want to cover and in what order, helps provide a good conversational experience for viewers.

TIP

Watch some videos from top YouTubers and look for how they take a conversational approach to engage their viewers. Can you think of ways you can take a similar approach in your marketing videos?

TIP

Challenge yourself to find fresh ways to make your videos conversational. While simply copying a vlog style can work, you run the risk of not feeling authentic.

Involve Your Audience with Interactivity

Adding *interactivity* to your videos is a great way to engage your audience and build your viewership. Interactivity refers to any time you're soliciting your audience to engage more directly with you and your content.

For example, if you're making videos about recipes, ask viewers what they'd like to see next, such as which recipe they'd like to see you make. Do your viewers want to see the beef made in a Mexican-style recipe, or would they prefer to see beef made into a casserole? (Yeah, me, too — tacos every time!)

EPIC RAP BATTLES OF HISTORY

Epic Rap Battles of History (https://youtube.com/user/ERB) developed a simple and super compelling way to involve their audience. If you haven't seen their videos, go watch some now. You'll see they take famous people and characters from history and place them against each other in a rap battle. I'm watching one right now of James Bond versus Austin Powers, which has clocked in more than 31 million views. Each of Epic Rap Battle's videos ends the same way and involves the audience (see figure): .

"Who won?"

"Who's next?"

"You decide."

In just those six words, Epic Rap Battles asks the audience two really important questions that encourage comment.

First, they ask viewers to evaluate the video they watched and choose who they thought did the better job in the rap battle.

Second, they ask for viewer input as to which famous people or characters they should make next. This question is genius because the viewers are telling Epic Rap Battles which video to make next, which almost guarantees it's going to be massively popular.

For example, the team behind the videos may want to make a video about Martha Stewart versus Rachael Ray (I'd like to see that), but the viewer voted for Gordon Ramsay versus Julia Child.

This kind of interactivity is built right into their video concept and encourages viewers to engage and then come back for more.

If you can build in interactive ways to involve your audience, you'll learn quickly what people want to see from you. (See the nearby sidebar "Epic Rap Battles of History" for a good example of how one YouTube channel puts this concept into practice.) Interactive videos

>> **Have interactivity built into them.** The best examples of interactive videos go beyond simply asking questions of your audience and have a creative concept where interactivity is built right into them.

>> **Give the power to the audience.** Your interactive videos can allow viewers to guide which videos you make next. Sure, that's giving up some control, but you're showing your audience you're there for them, which builds loyalty.

Interactive videos can make use of native platform features. See Chapter 14 for some tools that YouTube provides that you can use to build interactivity directly into your video.

Always Be Consistent

Perhaps my favorite creative principle to follow is that of consistency, as I think it's the key to success on YouTube. Many clients with good intentions make videos and run some campaigns, but they eventually lost interest and didn't keep working toward building a successful YouTube presence that supports their marketing needs.

REMEMBER

YouTube can require more effort than other social platforms, especially when you're developing a content strategy, but the opportunity to win is there for the taking if you're prepared to commit to consistently creating quality content. Every single successful YouTube channel delivers consistently in some way.

You can be consistent by

>> **Following a regular publishing schedule.** Your audience wants to know that you'll be publishing the videos they want to see on a regular basis — for example, you upload your video every week on the same day and at the same time.

>> **Ensuring your videos are creatively consistent with brand, tone, and level of quality.** A YouTube friend recently made a video where his sound recording was a bit off, and people let him know it in the comments! They were not happy, even though it didn't really make much of a difference. Your audience on YouTube wants to see your videos following the approach they love, and they want it to be the same quality (or better) every time.

>> **Finding the format that people like the most and sticking to it.** When you develop an audience through a format they like, deviations from that format can be unpopular. You'll see this with YouTubers who became popular through consistent uploads with a format people like and then try out a different approach, finding that their viewers do not like the new format. Of course, regular experimentation is important, but don't forget to keep your core audience happy by consistently delivering the general format of videos they like so much.

Consistency is important because your viewers want to know that you'll be there when they want more content and, that they know what they're getting before they start watching.

I like my favorite car vlogger, Doug DeMuro (search him on YouTube — he's worth it), so much for a few reasons:

>> **He has a regular schedule of posting of his videos.** I know that when I visit his channel or the YouTube home page, I'll see something new from him.

>> **His personality is this awesome combination of being a deep expert, bordering on nerd, about cars, and his slightly absurdist and joyful experience of the car.** He'll make jokes about the weight of a car using animals like giraffes as a reference point, and just about every time he accelerates in a powerful car, his smile is so wide he can't help but giggle. His brand and his personality are consistent and compelling.

>> **The format is always the same.** This reason is perhaps the most important for me. I get about 20 minutes of an intro, a review of the exterior, the interior, and a driving experience, all peppered with his interesting observations and jokes (see Figure 10-3). I love watching Doug's videos just before I go to bed because I usually want about 20 minutes of content before I pass out asleep.

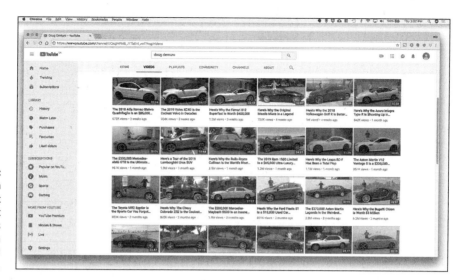

FIGURE 10-3:
You can see from his recent uploads that Doug DeMuro is consistent with his format and posting schedule.

Target Your Audience's Interests

Simply put, you want to make videos targeted to the audience you want to reach by tapping into their passions and interests. Your videos should be based on what you know about your audience and what they want to see.

The team at BuzzFeed are the masters of a content machine that aims to understand what their audience wants and targets them with content they know they will like.

Go visit BuzzFeed's website (www.buzzfeed.com), app, and YouTube channels (www.youtube.com/user/BuzzFeedVideo) right now, and you'll see just how smart they are at providing something that targets you. (For more on BuzzFeed, see the nearby sidebar.)

Videos that keep targeting in mind

>> Always keep your audience's passions and interests in mind

>> Find fresh and compelling ways to engage their needs and wants

>> Listen and respond to their feedback in the comments

>> Constantly experiment and refine what's working

See Chapter 3 for tools and tips on how to generate audience insights to inform the videos you'll create. You can use tools to learn about people's passions, interests, wants, and needs.

BUZZFEED

I was once presenting to a room full of big brand clients at the YouTube Brand Partner program. It was a week-long intensive course for clients to visit the YouTube studio in Playa Vista, California, to see expert speakers discuss YouTube and help them develop plans as to how YouTube could support their business goals.

I was about to get on stage and present on the topic of editorial calendars and scheduling. As I entered the room, I caught the last few minutes of a representative from BuzzFeed presenting. I wanted to reference BuzzFeed in my opening as a sort of segue, so I quickly popped onto the site and took the first quiz that appealed.

My opening joke "Turns out I'm a HufflePuff on the streets . . . and in the sheets . . . which, if you know me, you know to be true" half landed. I'm notorious for making jokes in the first minute that either win me the audience or make the whole presentation really difficult because everyone is thinking "Who is this idiot?" But the point here is that BuzzFeed didn't have to serve up much more than one scroll before I found something that appealed to me, a piece of content I could easily consume. BuzzFeed's marketers think deeply, using a lot of data analysis about their audience and what it likes.

Make Sure It's Sustainable

Even if you can make a great video that starts to check the boxes of lots of the content fundamentals I explain in this chapter, your efforts will be wasted if you can't make more videos. The best videos you can make are the ones that are *sustainable,* meaning that you can make more of them easily. Don't go broke making just one because it took all your time or money!

A quote from The Fine Brothers (https://youtube.com/user/TheFineBros) captures the point of sustainability perfectly:

"If we can't shoot at least three episodes in one day, we move on to the next idea."

I had a chat with Joey Helms (www.youtube.com/user/Joey2Rob) who makes beautiful videos that take him a month or more to shoot and edit together. He has made the decision that he wants to create these videos that work despite the time and effort it takes to create the beautiful result.

He has found a sustainable way to deliver the number of videos in the time period he wants, and it's a different approach from The Fine Bros, who want to shoot a volume of videos in a day and who need formats that they can turn around quickly.

TIP

The thing to think about here is "If I've made this video, can I easily make more?" Do you have the time, the money, the inclination, the resources to make more? If the answer is no, then you're making the wrong videos.

If your video content strategy is sustainable, you'll be able to

>> **Consistently and regularly deliver your popular videos.** A sustainable content strategy means you can publish a regular flow of videos without long periods of inactivity.

>> **Stay on budget and within the resources available to you.** It's a terrible situation when budgets overrun or resources get stretched thin. A sustainable content strategy is one that knows your budget and resource limit and plays within it.

>> **Deliver the quantity and quality of video you want.** It's a perfectly valid strategy to want to make one high quality video a month, but it's equally valid to find a format that you can deliver every day. A sustainable approach is making sure that you can hit the volume of videos you'd like to publish while maintaining their quality.

Maximize Your Chances of Discoverability

YouTube is a search engine. Sure, sometimes people visit YouTube and immediately find something on its home page that kicks off their viewing session. Other times, people start their YouTube session with a search. People may come across your video in myriad ways, such as it being embedded in a blog or shared via email by a friend. The question becomes one of how you ensure that your video is discoverable, no matter how someone is accessing YouTube or browsing the web.

Being discoverable is important but can be a real challenge given the volume of videos uploaded every day. In addition, discoverability is made more complex as it's made up of a few different dimensions evaluated by the algorithm. (See Chapter 15 for more on the algorithm.)

When you upload a video, the algorithm immediately starts to evaluate it. It reviews the video to check that it meets copyright and policy guidelines. If your video passes those tests and goes live, the algorithm looks at your video's performance and decides how to serve it to potential viewers.

The algorithm is vastly complicated, but essentially, it's looking to see how many people are watching your video, whether they like it, whether they watch all of it, how many other videos they watch after yours, and so on. All these performance variables dictate the place your video finds in its index of billions of hours of video content.

You can do three things to help ensure discoverability:

>> Publish your video with accurate information that describes the video clearly and completely (see Chapter 14)

>> Use paid media to help get the video started racking up views (see Chapter 7)

>> Make videos that are either trending or evergreen (see Chapter 9)

Make Your Videos Accessible

The videos that perform the best on YouTube are the videos that you can watch in isolation, meaning you don't need to have seen other videos before or after for them to make sense.

Take an example from the 1990s TV show "Friends." The show was successful because you could watch any episode at any time, in any order, and you'd still enjoy it and get it. That accessibility makes the show perfect for endless reruns in syndication as well as one-off episodes or Netflix binging.

TIP

When you're making your videos for YouTube, make them so that viewers can enjoy them without seeing other videos.

It's not that the alternative approach can't work, because it absolutely can, but if someone wants to watch your video, you risk losing them when they find out they have to watch another one first.

Ask yourself, "Can every episode be appreciated by a brand-new viewer?"

Strive for Authenticity

Authenticity can be an abstract concept and overused in social media to the point where it becomes meaningless. However, despite its overuse, *authenticity* is about being true to one's own personality, spirit, or character. People can immediately recognize someone or something when it's inauthentic.

REMEMBER

Every video you make needs to retain authenticity. If you're true to your values and stay on brand, your videos will be authentic. You'll know immediately when you post something inauthentic — your subscribers will call you out without hesitation.

Authenticity in the context of video content can mean

» **Always staying on brand and true to your values.** The best marketers know that anything produced must remain on brand for the company, meaning that its creative choices of tone, look and feel, and more all feel like they are representative of the brand and its values.

» **Making videos you uniquely can make.** Don't make videos that have nothing to do with your brand, products, or services. Sometimes people may make videos designed only to get views, but these videos won't help you drive your marketing goals. Views are never the goal, just a proxy for your business goals!

» **Striving for originality.** If you're really good, you'll find ways to make your videos feel original and fresh rather than being me-too copycats of other videos. Viewers will just go watch those videos instead.

» **Listening to constructive feedback in the comments.** Even though comments can sometimes be unhelpful and misguided, look for the gems of constructive feedback and use them to keep your authenticity on track.

For creative tips on how to make video advertising that performs, see Chapter 6.

4

Making Videos for Ad Campaigns and Content

IN THIS CHAPTER

» **Making equipment decisions**

» **Planning your shoot in preproduction**

» **Shooting video in the production phase**

» **Editing your video in post-production**

» **Exploring advanced video types**

Chapter **11**

Creating Video

C reating great-looking videos yourself has never been easier as most people have a powerful camera in their pocket already. Whether you're making ads or content, keeping a few considerations in mind can set you up for video production success.

In this chapter, I walk you through the gear you need and describe the decisions you need to make about the script and shots. I also cover shooting and editing the video, as well as what you need to do to polish it for publishing.

Gathering Your Gear

Gear refers to the hardware and equipment used to create your video. Before you hit record, take inventory of the gear you have access to. Thinking through some choices and potentially upgrading components of your gear with cost-effective options can make for a much better quality video result. Some simple and smart choices with gear can ensure that the visual and audio quality of your end product are where you want them to be.

Cameras

You have a few options when it comes to cameras, ranging from the phone that is probably already in your pocket to high-end cameras used for top-quality production needs.

The two main recording qualities are 1080p HD and 4k UHD:

>> **1080p HD** (High Definition) has long been the standard for high definition and delivers high quality video up to 1920 x 1080 pixels in size. This quality is perfectly acceptable. It is lighter on memory storage space and works well for YouTube.

>> **4k UHD** (Ultra High Definition) delivers almost four times the number of pixels on a screen compared with 1080p, and more people are using this resolution. The quality is exceptional, but it does take up more memory storage space. If you're making video advertising, use this format.

TIP

At the very least, ensure that your camera of choice shoots in 1080p HD at a rate of 30 frames per second (fps). However, consider shooting in 4K. The biggest benefit of 4K beyond the fact that it is an ultra-high definition level of quality that is good enough for movies in the theater is that you can scale down your video to lower resolutions. Think of it this way: If you shoot your video in 4K, you can play it on the largest screens and scale it down to the smallest of screens. If you shoot in 1080p, you won't be able to scale it up to a quality suitable for the movie theater, and hey, there's always a chance your video could make it to the big screen!

Your phone camera

Don't think that the camera that's built into your phone isn't up to the job just because it's part of your phone. If you have an Apple iPhone 6S or above or are an Android user with a phone such as the Google Nexus 5 or any of the Google Pixel range, you'll be able to shoot in 4K. Take a look at your phone's tech specs in the manual or online to see what your camera is capable of.

TIP

If you're not sure whether your phone shoots in 4K, search for its technical specifications online. You may need to go into your phone's settings to tweak your video recording resolution because it may be set at something like 1080p by default. The camera on your phone is typically more than enough for most people's needs when it comes to creating video for YouTube. Because you probably already have one, your phone's camera is a cost-effective camera option to start out with.

Assuming that you have a phone that can shoot 4K, you may want to use the camera on your phone because

>> You already have one and don't need to buy more equipment.

>> It'll shoot in a quality more than you need.

>> You can buy accessories like tripods to help with shooting.

>> It's incredibly easy to record and upload footage to edit later.

>> You can start recording something immediately.

DSLR

DSLR stands for digital single-lens reflex, which refers to the way in which the camera's mechanism works. Inside the camera, a mirror reflects light from the lens into the viewfinder, through a prism or mirrors, which allows you to see exactly what you're capturing in real-time. This mechanism is a more accurate way to capture exactly the shot you want.

DSLRs have some major benefits over the camera built into your phone — for example, they can typically autofocus a lot better. When you're moving around or shooting yourself, the camera is better able to keep everything in focus, whereas phones tend not to be as good at this task.

DSLRs have a flip-out screen that you can turn to face you so that you can see yourself as you record. This feature makes these cameras especially popular with vloggers.

Some DSLRs have a remote-control app that you can add to your phone, which easily lets you start and stop recording even when the camera is set up on a tripod across the room from you.

DSLRs allow for interchangeable lenses so that you can shoot different kinds of videos in various situations. The lens that comes with your DSLR is a great general-purpose lens suitable for all kinds of video shooting, but you can try out many other lenses, such as a macro lens that lets you do super close-up shots.

DSLRs also offer better memory options, with a memory card slot that you can switch out quickly rather than having to wait for your phone to upload to the cloud.

All in all, the DSLR is your professional solution for video capture. Most people won't need a top of the range DSLR, and many excellent mid-range options are available, such as the Canon T7i, which starts at $700, or the Canon 70D, which starts at around $1,000.

You may want to choose a DSLR if you

>> Want more options for greater image resolution quality

>> Like the idea of an easier shooting solution

>> Use different lenses for different situations

>> Want something that is faster to start up and focus

>> Like having a more expandable memory storage option

>> Want the freedom to tweak with manual controls

>> Don't mind spending the money

TIP

Look out for deals on second-hand DSLRs. Lots of people buy equipment thinking they'll use it and then sell it after they find they've not really made much use of it at all. Make sure to check that everything is in working order before purchasing and consider buying from a trusted second-hand retailer or camera specialist.

Memory

Video footage takes up a lot of memory storage space and you don't want to run out of space when shooting.

If you're shooting with your phone, delete old apps that you no longer use and archive things like photos to clear up memory space. Check how much storage you have available and test how much space a 10-minute video takes up. Make sure that you've got enough space available in your phone's memory to shoot the videos you want. Some phones have slots for memory expansion.

TIP

If you're using a DSLR, you'll be able to purchase memory cards that you can swap out as you're shooting. If you have two cards, you can use one to shoot, while the other uploads its files to a hard drive ready to be cleared out and swapped back in. For more on memory cards, see the nearby sidebar.

Audio

Without good audio, people will turn off your video. If you think the audio you've recorded isn't great but is acceptable, it's not; it has to be really good every time. This may not seem super important, but if your audio is bad, people will almost always immediately click away. You must nail the audio.

SHOPPING FOR MEMORY CARDS

The most popular types of memory cards are the microSD and SD memory cards. The key difference between the two is their physical size, with SD cards being slightly larger in dimension. Check your phone or DSLR camera for the type of card they accept. When you're shopping around look for

- **Capacity:** Cards are available in many different capacities, with microSD cards up to 512GB and SD cards up to 1TB. These capacities are growing constantly.

- **Speed:** The speed of the memory card is the rate at which it can receive and store the content you're capturing on your camera. Some cards are slower and may not be suitable for recording higher definition video or specialized recordings like 360-degree videos.

As with most things in technology, get the most capacity and the fastest speed that your budget will allow.

The main kinds of microphones for shooting video are

TIP

>> **Built-in microphones:** Your phone has a microphone built right in, but you can also buy external microphones, for as little as $10, that connect to your phone through a cord.

DSLRs don't usually have a mic built in, so you need to invest in another piece of equipment to record sound. Different kinds of mics have different *pickup ranges,* meaning, the area around them where they can successfully capture audio.

>> **Shotgun microphones:** A shotgun mic sits directly on top of the camera and points right at you. These kinds of microphones are highly directional with a pickup range aimed directly at the target. They're great when you're facing the camera directly, such as when you're interviewing someone or recording yourself.

This type of mic attaches to the hot shoe of your DSLR. The *hot shoe* is the mounting point on top of your camera where you attach different accessories. It's essentially a universal bracket that lets you add different tools, such as mics, lights, and flashes. You can even get a bracket that extends your hot shoe, giving you ways to add more accessories at the same time.

>> **Lavaliers:** The lavalier, or lav for short, is the kind of microphone that clips to your clothing. It has a wire running to a transmitter that sends the audio via radio frequency to the device recording the sound. You may have seen presenters on stage giving talks wearing these little mics, which are discretely attached to the lapel of their shirt. Their pickup range allows them to capture

the sound of the speaker whilst also allowing more movement. Lavaliers are surprisingly reasonably priced.

>> **Boom mics:** A boom mic is a microphone attaches to the end of a boom, a long extendable and adjustable arm. An operator holds these mics above the sound source so that they don't appear in the shot. They may be covered in a furry cover to reduce the noise from things like wind, and they're often used when making movies.

>> **Specialist microphones:** Many kinds of microphones are used for specialist applications. If your built-in mic isn't sufficient, a shotgun mic or lavalier should work for most people. However, if you have a more sophisticated need, you should research which microphones other people recommend for those applications.

Make sure that you test your audio. For example, if you're going to record yourself unboxing products in your living room, grab your camera and make a quick video to test the audio.

To test your audio:

1. **Set up your video exactly how you would record your nontest video.**

2. **Record your video.**

3. **Upload your video to YouTube, setting the video to private so that only you can see it.**

4. **Watch the video and ask yourself "Is this sound quality sufficient?"**

    If you're not confident that the sound is good enough, consider investigating other microphone options.

Lighting

Lighting is just as important as audio because people want to see what's going on in the video clearly. You can work with the lighting you have, use one light, or use three lights.

Working with what you've got

The easiest option with lighting is to simply use what you have available. For example, if you're shooting an unboxing video in your living room, take advantage of the windows, overhead lights, and floor or table lamps around you.

You can experiment with positioning yourself and your camera setup wherever the natural light is best and augmenting it with your lights in various combinations.

TIP

You're aiming to have yourself clearly lit, not too dim and not too washed out, eliminating shadows on your face. You will probably need to take a few tests to get it right.

REMEMBER

Natural light changes throughout the day. Be cautious of consistency when using lighting sources that include the natural light of your room. If you make a video in the morning when the sun is streaming into the room and then you make another video later that evening, the sun will have shifted, and your lighting will be very different. Always strive for consistency in your videos.

One-light solutions

DSLR cameras have many options available for lights that you can attach to the hot shoe of your camera. Your lighting rig can move around with you as the camera moves, and they're convenient because they don't need any special setup. You just attach them to your camera, and you're good to go. The only con to using only one light is that it may not be as consistent because the camera can move around, which may cause shadows.

A *ring light,* a popular type of one-light solution provides a nice uniform light that comes straight from the camera's point of view. A ring light eliminates shadow and is flattering. People who create makeup tutorials often use ring lights because they enhance their facial features and clearly show the products they're using.

If you're using your camera phone, lighting accessories are available for that, too!

Three-light solutions

Three-light solutions make use of those black and silver umbrellas that are popular in photography studios. Those umbrellas give a nice wash of light, reducing the harshness of lighting without an umbrella, and add depth and definition.

While having a three-light solution may seem initially like something reserved for more professional shoots, the equipment needed is reasonably priced and can give a great result that may well make the expenditure worth it. Kits can start for as little as $100, and you may be able to find secondhand kits on local listing sites. In a classic three light solution, you'll have a

>> **Key light:** Your main light, set to the right of the subject, points directly at your subject from an angle and is positioned just slightly above your subject's eye level.

>> **Fill light:** Your fill light can be softer than the key light and is positioned on the subject on the opposite side of the key light. Your fill light helps eliminate

shadows created by the key light, hence the name fill light. It's essentially filling in the areas that the key light may make darker.

>> **Back light:** The back light creates depth by being positioned behind the subject. A back light helps separate the subject from the background. For example, if you're shooting your friend who has long dark brown hair and the background is also dark, you'll see little definition between them. Adding a back light helps cast a thin outline of light around the subject's head, helping create that depth and detail that'll look good.

REMEMBER

If you're making professional level commercials or have a shoot that requires lots of different kinds of setups, you'll need a lighting professional to advise on the needs of your shoot and to execute the lighting during the shoot.

Tripods

A *tripod* is a stabilizing device you can attach to your camera. You may not think you need a tripod or device to help stabilize your video shot, but you do. People do not want to watch shaky videos. Even the videos you may have seen on YouTube that appear to be handheld probably use a special kind of handheld stabilization device. When people start shooting video, they may prop their phone up on some books, which can work at first. However, getting the right level of adjustments for a truly great shot is hard, so look into stabilization options like tripods from the start.

Tripods come in all sizes, prices and qualities, but most people will be able to meet all their video needs with one of the following options:

>> **Classic tripod:** You can get tripods for your DSLR and your camera phone that let you position your camera to keep it stable and then adjust for height and angle. Most tripods include a spirit-level that so you can level out your shot. You can get full-length tripods that stand on the ground, as well as smaller tripods that sit on your desk or on a shelf.

>> **Monopod:** A *monopod* is just like a tripod except, as you may expect, it has only one leg instead of three. Monopods are easy and quick to set up and move around. For example, if you're making videos of birds in nature, you may need to move quickly, quietly, and easily. Although the tripod is a little cumbersome and the legs may need to be adjusted, you can pick up the monopod and hold it in place. You're effectively creating your own tripod with the monopod and both of your legs, keeping it stable. *Selfie-sticks* are a kind of handheld monopod that you can use to film yourself as you move around.

>> **GorillaPod:** The popular GorillaPod is another type of tripod and is made up of interconnected ball joints that let you bend and twist it into any shape you'd like. This flexibility results in excellent positioning on uneven surfaces and allows you to wrap it around a tree branch or hook it onto a shelf to secure your camera. If you search for ways to use a GorillaPod, you'll find many great ideas on ways to use this flexible tripod.

Preparing for Production

The *preproduction phase* is the stage before you shoot any video. It's the phase where you make all the necessary plans to ensure your success. The preproduction phase includes

>> Developing your idea

>> Storyboarding your vision

>> Crafting your script

>> Developing your shot list

>> Choosing locations

>> Creating the call sheet

>> Checking your budget

>> Tallying up costs

>> Ensuring legal compliance

REMEMBER

Time spent in the preproduction phase will save you a lot of time and potential cost down the road.

Developing your idea

Arguably the single most important stage of creating video is spending time developing your idea.

Many of the chapters in this book help you explore ideas and options. Chapter 4 details ad formats you can make videos for. For the best practices on how to create compelling video ads, see Chapter 6. Chapter 8 covers a broad range of content videos types, and Chapter 10 lists best practices for making great video content.

TIP

Spend time researching either ads or content videos, using your research to inspire your own thinking about what you want to create.

A great idea for your video

>> **Delivers to your business and marketing needs.** Check Chapter 2 for how to develop a brief, a document that helps ensure that whatever you create will deliver to your needs.

>> **Is on brand.** Your video should look, feel, and sound like it's coming from you. Avoid the temptation to copy anyone else's work too closely.

>> **Speaks to your audience.** Chapter 3 addresses how to research your audience and develop actionable insights that can inform your video ideas.

>> **Is something that you can feasibly create and deliver.** It should be something you have the ability to make without overstretching yourself, and ideally, you'll be able to make more of these videos.

>> **Inspires you!** You should be excited to make this video.

When you're thinking of ideas,

>> Generate as many as possible.

>> Think expansively, let your mind roam free, and don't limit your thinking.

>> Brainstorm with friends and colleagues to evolve and improve ideas.

>> Picking your favorites from your many ideas and further refine them.

>> Land on your best idea or two and write a one-page description of what will happen in the video.

After you choose your top ideas, wait and revisit them later, that way, you can reflect on whether you still like your idea.

Storyboarding your vision

A *storyboard* is a tool that helps you visually organize the narrative of your video. A storyboard helps create a shared understanding of your vision for the video. You can use a storyboard to make sure that all team members and stakeholders are on board with the shared vision of what will be produced.

A storyboard is a visual representation of what you'll actually shoot in the production phase (see Figure 11-1). Using a series of sketches to represent the shots you want to capture, each sketch helps you make decisions about the camera angle, lighting, and transitions and how the visuals match up with your script. You don't need to be good at drawing to create a storyboard, although it does help.

FIGURE 11-1:
A sample
storyboard.

TIP

Think of your storyboard as a dress rehearsal. When you force yourself to create a storyboard, you'll find yourself thinking through questions and challenges that may not have occurred to you. Your idea will evolve as you see it come to life in the storyboard.

Creating your storyboard

Search Google for "storyboard template," and you'll find options for lots of different storyboards. You can also use tools like Microsoft PowerPoint or Google Slides to create storyboards. When you have a template you like, follow these steps:

1. **Establish a timeline.**

   You can decide the sequence of events in the video and roughly when each one will occur.

2. **Identify your key scenes.**

   This step is where you choose what will be in the scene — for example, your product.

3. **Think through the details and action required in each scene.**

   For example, are you simply showing a close-up of your product, or are you showing someone interacting with it?

4. **Write an outline of your script.**

   Perhaps you want a voiceover describing the product's features.

5. **Sketch thumbnails to represent the visuals in each shoot.**

   Stick figures are fine!

6. **Annotate your scenes with necessary details.**

   Don't forget to think about the lighting and camera angle, the timing of cuts or transitions to other shots, and any other details related to the shooting itself.

Thinking about your video length

The single most frequent question I ever received when working at Google was "How long should my video be?" It's a great question with a frustrating answer because there is no definitive length. My answer was always that you should use as much time as you need to tell your story or deliver your message, and as long as the content is good, people will watch.

You can visit Chapter 17 to find more information on measuring the results of your videos. You're able to see when people stop watching your videos, which is a clue that maybe it was too long. Chapter 4 outlines different ad formats with set lengths, such as 6 seconds, 15 may, and longer. Chapter 8 outlines video content formats, where you might see common lengths for the video type you're creating.

TIP

If you're not sure how long your video should be, err on the side of caution and go a little shorter. This approach encourages you to keep to the best content without any unnecessary padding.

Crafting your script

In a script, you match the visuals you sketched out in your storyboard (see the preceding section) with the audio. The words you write in your script will be read as a voiceover or delivered by your on screen person. Consider the information that needs to be conveyed and the style in which the dialogue should be delivered, such as the tone of voice, emotion, and accent.

When reading your script, you or your on screen person should

>> Read your script to ensure that it matches with your storyboard and the time you've allotted for your video.

>> Aim for simplicity, removing any unnecessary information.

>> Pay attention to the *pacing,* which refers to whether the dialogue is delivered fast or slow.

>> Make space for pauses.

TIP

Use any word-processing software to create a document and make two columns. In the left column, make a note of the corresponding storyboard visual. In the right column, write the audio that will match that visual.

You and your cast can use cue cards to help deliver the script to camera, although rehearsing and delivering the script from memory is often best. You can also use teleprompting apps for your phone or tablet. A *teleprompter* is a digital screen in front of the speaker that feeds the casts their lines. (One famous president refuses to use them!)

Another option is to use the popular *quick-cut* technique, also known as *fast-cutting,* where you cut out space between what's said. That way, you can deliver your script in short bursts, cut out the space in time when you're looking at what you'll say next, and then splice things together.

Developing your shot list

With your storyboard and your script in hand, you can create your shot list. Your *shot list* is a list of every unique scene that you need to capture in video. A director may use a shot list, in concert with the storyboard and script, to ensure that all the required footage is systematically captured.

Each entry on the shot list should address the following:

>> **Shot type:** Is it a wide shot showing a larger space, or is it a closeup shot?

>> **Camera's position:** Are you placing the camera above, below, or in front the scene you want to shoot?

>> **Camera movement:** Does the camera slowly pan or zoom in?

TIP

Search YouTube for videos similar to the video you intend to make to see how other people have shot and edited their video footage. This search can help you make decisions about what you'll need to shoot, especially if you're new to making videos. Let other people's videos guide your choices; they've probably already figured out the shots that work best.

Choosing locations

Thinking through your locations and making smart choices can save you time in the production phase when you come to shoot your video. When choosing a location, think about the following questions:

>> Can you and your cast and crew easily get to the location?

>> Do you need permission to shoot at the location?

>> How much time do you need at the location to capture the required footage?

>> What will the weather most likely be on the day of your shoot?

>> Will the lighting and audio at the location be adequate, or will you need to make plans to ensure that you get clear shots and audio?

Creating the call sheet

Your *call sheet* refers to the schedule for your video shoot and informs everyone in the cast and crew where they need to be and when. Usually the director or assistant director creates a call sheet for each person and each day of the shoot, updating it as things change.

A call sheet usually includes

>> The day of the shoot

>> The person or group that the call sheet is for

>> When and where people need to report to teams

>> When and where the scene will be shot

>> Information on how to get to the location(s)

>> The weather and how to prepare for inclement weather

>> Important contact information

>> Local services, such as hospitals, restaurants, and stores.

TIP

Search Google for *call sheet template,* and you'll find lots of editable templates you can customize. You don't need to include everything if you think it's not essential. The most important thing is that people know when and where to be and that you've made a reasonable plan for how much you hope to achieve in the given time.

Tallying up costs

Take the budget you've assigned to your video's production, and tally up all the costs you think you'll incur in the production and post-production phases. This budget can include things like

>> Gear rental

>> Hiring of crew members

>> Location permits

>> Transportation

>> Meals

Ensuring legal compliance

If you're using people in your video, they'll need to sign a personal release granting permission for you to use their likeness. You'll need signed releases from everyone who is featured in your videos, including people who aren't part of your cast but who may have been included in the shot somehow, such as passersby.

You can find standard video release forms online that you can download, edit, and use. Professionals should consult a lawyer and have them draft a release form tailored to the project.

TIP

If you're casting professional actors in your videos, you'll need to determine whether they're union or non-union. If your actors are in a union, you'll need to follow specific guidelines on pay, work schedule, and usage rights for your video. Visit http://sagaftra.org, http://actra.ca, or the relevant union in your country for more information.

Shooting Your Video

The *production* phase is when you actually shoot your video. In this phase, you execute everything you planned in the preproduction phase. (See the section "Preparing for Production," earlier in this chapter, for more information.)

TIP

If you're making a simple video, such as a vlog (see Chapter 8), you won't need to worry too much about the advanced production techniques I describe in this chapter. All you'll need to do is turn on your camera and start recording.

Planning the shot

Before you pick up your camera and hit record, you have some choices to make about how you'd like to shoot your video:

>> How do you want the camera to move? It can pan from left to right, zoom in, tilt, and more.

>> What kind of shots do you want? You can have close-up shots, medium-distance shots, or wide shots.

>> What kind of angles and vantage points do you want to use? You can show the scene from different perspectives.

If you've never shot any video, practice first. A cat, dog, or willing friend are the perfect subjects to experiment with, and hone your shooting techniques.

Composition

Composition refers to how you frame the picture within each shot. When you pick up the camera and point it in the direction you'll be filming, you'll instinctively move the camera to frame the shot, which is the composition. The rule of thirds and the 180–degree rule are two rules to consider when it comes to composing your shots:

>> **The rule of thirds:** Following the *rule of thirds* places the action of your scene (such as your actors) in one-third of the total shot, meaning that the action doesn't take place in the remaining two-thirds of what's being captured. Grab your camera phone and open the settings. You'll likely have an option to turn on a grid, possibly with options for the style of grid, such as 3 x 3, 4 x 4, or the golden ratio. (I like the golden ratio grid.) These grids help you divide up your shot. To achieve a more interesting visual, place your subject one-third of the way from the edge of the frame (not the center). You can practice the rule of thirds when you're taking photographs, too.

If you're shooting a landscape, position the ground in the lower third of the frame, putting buildings, trees, and sky in the upper two thirds of the frame.

TIP

>> **The 180-degree rule:** The 180-degree rule concerns the on screen spatial relationship between a character and another character or object. When you're following the 180-degree rule, you keep the camera on one side of an imaginary axis, a line that divides two characters. Your first character is always to the right of the second character. Follow this rule to help your audience visually connect with unseen movement happening around and behind the immediate subject. If you break this rule, it can disorient viewers and confuse them as to where characters are situated.

TIP

If you're shooting using your phone, always shoot horizontally (landscape). If you shoot holding your portrait, your video will have black bars on either side to make it fit the YouTube video player.

By the way, square videos work best with sites like Facebook or Instagram. Camera phones will have a square video setting you can choose. If you're making videos for Facebook or Instagram stories, vertically shot videos work best.

B-roll

B-roll is simply extra footage that is supplemental to your main shots. Imagine that you're watching a movie set in New York City. Some footage between scenes may show the city's skyline and scenes from the street. This footage is often inserted as a cutaway to help tell the story.

TIP

Capture b-roll when you're shooting so that you can edit it into your final video to use for things like establishing where the action is taking place. It adds variety and dimension to the final video.

When shooting your video, *overshoot*, meaning shoot more video footage than you think you need. Having more footage to work with is always better than not having enough, although you don't need to go crazy. You'll likely only get one chance to shoot, so capture everything you need plus a bit more.

Continuity

Continuity is all about maintaining consistency when you're shooting. You want everything to remain the same, including the lighting, background, audio, and props. If a coffee cup moves around the scene several times, it can be an unhelpful distraction. Unexpected shifts can be jarring for the audience, so as you shoot, keep an eye on any changes and movements, especially when it comes to objects.

Editing Your Video

The post-production phase is when you edit and polish your video for publishing.

WARNING

One wrong key can delete everything you've shot and edited, so backing up is crucially important.

You may want to have your approach to backing up video ready to go before you even record a video to ensure that you don't overlook it. When you're done shooting and have your footage captured in the memory of your phone or on the memory card of your DSLR, immediately back it up. You can then back up your edits as you go and your final files when you're done editing.

A good backup solution exists in three steps:

1. **Copy your footage to the hard drive of your computer.**

   This step is the minimum required. If you lose your phone or your memory card becomes damaged, you'll have the footage available on your hard drive.

2. **Copy of your footage to an external hard drive that you then lock in a fireproof, water-resistant safe.**

   You may choose not to do this step with all your footage or every time you shoot, but at the very least, back up everything once a week or month on an external hard drive that's safe from damage and theft.

3. **Upload footage to the cloud or to an off-site storage space.**

   You can choose to upload all your footage if the files aren't too massive or just pieces of what you've captured. Keep an eye on how much bandwidth and storage space you're using so that you don't incur extra charges from your Internet service or cloud space provider. Professional production companies often send their footage to off-site services or even run their own off-site operations.

REMEMBER

Back things up. As I'm writing this book, I'm backing up my manuscript on my local hard drive, to the cloud, and to an external hard drive. Imagine the hours and money you'd waste if you lost your work.

Editing process

When you start editing, you use the storyboard you created in the preproduction phase to guide your work. (For more on creating a storyboard, see the section earlier in this chapter.) Don't worry when things don't follow the original storyboard exactly, as they rarely do. Instead, think of the storyboard as a guide-line to help you make sense of your footage.

In the editing phase, you cut up your video footage, tweak the video's color, and add effects and sound. You then prepare your video for publishing.

Offline editing is when you edit a copy of the original footage and not the original footage itself. You want to preserve your original footage so that you can always go back to it later, if needed. Instead, make a copy and edit that copy.

TIP

The approaches detailed in this section will satisfy the needs of many content and advertising shoot needs, but if you feel like any of these topics are beyond your skillset or you're going to tackle something more advanced, check out Chapter 12 for details on professionals who can help produce your video.

The rough cut

A common approach when editing is to first create your *rough cut*. Think of the rough cut as the stage when your video starts to come together and resemble the finished product, but, with errors, omissions, and so on. The rough cut gives you, and anyone you're working with, an idea of what the video will look like once finished.

EDITING SOLUTIONS

Some incredibly easy-to-use editing solutions are available for beginners and advanced users. Some of the most popular programs are

- **iMovie** comes freely pre-installed on most Apple computers. iMovie is a great place to start as it's fully featured, has lots of helpful templates, and a simple interface.

- **Adobe Premiere Pro CC**, part of Adobe's Creative Cloud offering, is used by filmmakers, YouTubers, videographers, and professionals of all sorts. This intuitive program has step-by-step tutorials and benefits from integrating with Adobe's other programs, which you may want to use as part of your creation process. You can subscribe to Adobe's Creative Cloud for a low monthly fee, in the range of $20 or so, which makes it a reasonable yet professional and fully featured option.

- **Final Cut Pro** is a professional post-production program, which costs around the $400 range, making it more of an investment and better for serious editors. Final Cut Pro has a deep set of advanced features and is best for the advanced user.

You can find lots of free to use editing applications if you search Google. If you're not comfortable editing video yourself, visit Chapter 12 for tips on outsourcing.

Making a rough cut allows you to step back and look at your video to decide if it's what you want before you spend time on more advanced editing. You can make additional changes before polishing and finalizing the video.

TIP

The rough cut is a great opportunity to create more than one version of your video, especially if you're making an ad where you'd like to test different versions. Chapter 6 covers testing methodologies for ads.

Saving and exporting

REMEMBER

Save your work regularly as you edit, saving it in the highest resolution you can in order to maintain quality.

When you're ready to export your video file, your editing software will likely give you options on file format and quality. For example, in iMovie, you can choose to share the file at theater quality, for e-mailing, and for social sites. A setting specifically for YouTube lets you upload your video directly to YouTube. I recommend sharing or exporting to a file on your computer before uploading your video to YouTube.

After you export your video and are ready to publish, refer to Chapter 14, which breaks down all the steps necessary to get your video live on YouTube.

TIP

YouTube is always innovating! YouTube maintains its position as the best video sharing platform in the world by constantly innovating, creating, and testing new technologies and formats all the time. Follow the YouTube blog to keep up to date with the latest developments: https://youtube.googleblog.com.

Exploring Advanced Video Options

All the video creation techniques described in this chapter focus on the most typical applications to create videos. However you may be interested in more advanced video creation options, such as live streaming, 360 video, and virtual reality.

Livestreaming

You can livestream with YouTube, but before you begin your first stream, you must enable your channel.

1. **Confirm that your channel is verified by following the steps at** www.youtube. com/verify.

2. **Confirm that you have no livestream restrictions in the last 90 days.**

   If you have restrictions, a message appears within the livestream section of your YouTube channel.

3. **To enable live streaming on your desktop, go to Creator Studio tools and then the Live Streaming tab.**

   Alternatively, in the YouTube app on your phone, click on the camera icon and choose Go Live.

Enabling a livestream can take up to 24 hours the first time you do it. After you complete this step, your stream can go live instantly next time.

After you complete these steps and are able to stream, you have a few options available:

» **Stream now** automatically starts and stops the stream. YouTube detects your stream's resolution and frame rate, and it automatically transcodes your stream to the rate that works best for the viewer. You can interact with the audience using live chat, you can share the link to your stream across social media, and you can see real-time analytics. After your stream is over, YouTube archives the event to your channel's video manager.

» **Events** lets you preview before you go live. You can include what's called a *backup redundancy stream,* so if your main stream stops for some reason, another stream can take its place. You can schedule your streams start time and even create multiple live events.

» **Mobile streaming** is the option to stream directly from the YouTube app on your phone. After the stream ends, an archive of the stream saves to your channel. You can edit its settings or delete it.

» **Webcam** is an easy way to go live straight from your computer without the need for an encoder. Visit http://youtube.com/webcam to get started.

360-degree video

You can watch *360-degree video* on YouTube on your computer, on your mobile device, or even using a special headset. This type of video lets you move your device around to see in every direction — for example, moving your mobile phone around moves the video around, too. The viewer can move the video left or right, or bottom to top, in a spherical space.

If you want to create 360 video, you need a special camera, but it isn't necessarily expensive. Look for cameras that have spherical capture as an option.

Virtual reality

Virtual reality (VR) is similar to 360-degree video (see preceding section) with the exception that the viewer wears a special headset and they're able to move around and interact with the environment. VR is a more immersive environment than 360-degree video because the rest of your vision is blocked out, making you feel like you're in the environment itself.

Virtual reality environments are typically computer-generated rather than being solely video based.

If you want to try out VR, Google has two headsets available for virtual reality:

» **Google Cardboard** (https://vr.google.com/cardboard)

» **Daydream** (https://vr.google.com/daydream)

Chapter **12**

Curating, Collaborating, and Outsourcing

C reating video takes some skill and quite a bit of effort and can be daunting at first if you don't have experience in video production. In this chapter, you find out how to engage video creation services, collaborate with YouTubers, and bolster your YouTube channel's video offerings through curation of other people's videos.

Getting Someone to Make Videos for You

Sometimes, you may want the outside help of professionals, such as when you want a better quality video or need to create more video than your own resources have capacity for.

If for some reason you don't have the expertise or resources available to create your own videos, don't fret, as you have several options, which I describe in the following sections.

REMEMBER

You can find options to create video that are good quality, cheap, and fast, but a rule in life is that you have to choose two of these qualities. You can have a video created that's good quality and fast, but it won't be cheap. It can be fast and cheap but it probably won't be good, and it can be cheap and good, but it won't be fast!

Advertising and marketing agencies

Advertising and marketing agencies are full-service solutions that help with not just your video creation but everything from the marketing strategy through to the analysis and measurement of your campaigns.

Advertising and marketing agencies have teams of people who work to create everything you need for your advertising campaigns. If you choose to work with an agency, you can work with them on a *project basis*, which is an agreed amount for the scope of work they'll deliver, or on a *retainer basis*, where you commit to paying a monthly fee for a set amount of resource hours per month.

The team at an agency may include

>> An **account person** who manages the relationship with you, takes your brief (see Chapter 2), lines up the right resources to deliver against its requirements, and generally ensures you're happy.

>> A **planner** who researches and creates strategies to make your campaigns effective and is responsible for making sure what you're asking to be done makes the most sense for your marketing goals.

>> A **creative team** who generate creative ideas for your advertising campaign, ensuring that they are compelling and on brand and will resonate with your audience, delivering to your campaign's brief.

>> A **production team** who transforms the creative ideas into the various ad formats you require and handles the shooting, editing, and delivery of all your final creative assets.

>> A **media buyer** who takes the creative assets and your media budget and sets up your campaign according to your criteria, making sure that your ads run and reach the right people in the most cost-effective way possible.

>> An **analyst** who takes the reports from the media buyer, analyzes the performance of your campaign, and works with the team to create recommendations for improvements.

WARNING

Working with an advertising agency will likely be the most expensive of the options available you to create your campaigns, with projects often costing in the tens of thousands of dollars and more. Agencies come in all sizes, from smaller independent shops to larger established agencies with big famous names. The largest of clients will pay their top-tier advertising agencies millions of dollars a year in retainer fees and expect their advertising campaigns to not only deliver to their business goals but also to win industry awards.

If you have the budget for an agency, research local agencies in your area who may take on clients with your size and budget of project. You can reach out to these agencies to set up a meeting to discuss your needs and determine whether you are a fit for each other.

Video production companies

If you're looking only for video creation help and don't need all the services of an advertising and marketing agency (see preceding section), you can find companies that specialize in video production.

Unlike full-service agencies that create marketing campaigns of all types, video productions companies focus only on the creation of video needed. These agencies can create anything from advertising creative to video content, such as entertainment, educational, or inspirational videos.

A video production company will have a dedicated team that includes

>> An **executive producer** who oversees the project and ensures things happen on time and in order.

>> A **supervising producer** who looks after everything on set, manages the production day to day, and keeps an eye on the details.

>> A **cinematographer** or **videographer** who frames the shot so that it looks beautiful and shoots the footage

>> An **art director** who makes sure the set looks good

>> A **sound person** who makes sure that the sound is high quality

>> An **editor** who handles all editing duties

Local freelancers

Depending on where you live, you'll likely have great local talent available to help you with creating video. Even in the smallest of towns, you can find local freelancers through online listing sites, on community pin boards in your nearby grocery store, through the recommendations of friends and family, and in local publications.

TIP

The real benefit of using a local freelancer is that you can meet them in person to explain what you're looking for and get a sense of what it'd be like working together.

Sometimes you'll need to work with a local resource, for example, if your video needs require shooting footage of your retail store, which means you'll want someone who is able to travel to your location.

If your local resource can't provide all the services you need, then consider using them in combination with other options. For example, you may find someone locally who is able to shoot video footage that you can then have edited using an online marketplace service (see the next section).

Advertising agencies, video production companies, and local freelancers will all want a clear brief from you. Check Chapter 2 for how to create your brief.

Online marketplace services

I'm a big fan of online marketplaces that let people access skilled individuals to help them in creating their video creative. I've used these marketplaces many times in the past with success.

For example, take a look at Fiverr.com, shown in Figure 12-1. On this site, people post their services available, along with their rates, timelines, examples of their work, and ratings and testimonials from people who have used them. In the Video & Animation category on Fiverr, you can find people who can create

>> Whiteboard and animated explainer videos

>> Intros and animated logos

>> Slideshows and promotional videos

>> Editing and post production services

>> Lyric and music videos

>> Spokesperson videos

>> Animated characters

>> Short video ads

>> Live action explainer videos

FIGURE 12-1:
Fiverr offers
access to
people all over
the world who
can help you
create video
content at
reasonable
prices.

To maximize your chance of success with online marketplaces, follow these tips:

>> **Work through in detail what you want before you request anyone's services.** Create a clear brief that provides all the information upfront. (See Chapter 2 for more on creating a brief.)

>> **Find a service provider whose services closely match what you're looking for.** Also, request examples of work they've previously completed that meet your criteria.

>> **Be communicative up front, taking time to clearly explain what you're looking for.** You'll be able to negotiate the final price with the service provider, especially if you're looking for something more than their standard packages. Most sellers like to discuss the project before committing to it. Continue to be communicative throughout the process, responding to questions promptly and following up with any missing information.

REMEMBER

You get what you pay for. These people are skilled creatives and should be paid accordingly for their work. Sure, they are more cost-effective than using companies because they may not have the same overhead costs, but creative work still takes time, effort, and skill, which all cost money.

The biggest pro of using online marketplace services is that you can work with anyone in the world. However, the drawback is that it's unlikely you'll find someone who is local to you who can come shoot video footage at your location. That's why these services are great for video creation for certain types, such as explainer videos, which do not require a visit to create the content.

TIP

These online marketplaces offer lots of services you might find helpful like video promotion and distribution, help with setting up video ad campaigns, digital marketing, business consulting, market research and more.

Video creation tools

As more people turn to video as a part of their marketing mix, new tools, services, apps, and programs are popping up to help meet the demand and to fill the gap of expertise by providing templated and automated options. These services are especially good for the creation of video advertising creative.

If you search Google for *video creation tools,* you'll find links to many options. These tools use templates for videos that let you drag and drop in your text, image files, video clips, and other creative assets.

Video creation tools make it easy to create marketing videos without much editing knowledge. These tools allow you to experiment with their templates to see whether they can work for you. Most video creation tools operate on a subscription service basis where you pay a monthly fee to use their tools, making them an easy and cost-effective place to start.

On the down side, the templates are more restrictive, so you'll be relying on finding a template that you can make work for the video you'd like to create.

Collaborating on Videos

Sometimes you don't need to directly create any videos yourself or use services like production companies or online marketplaces. (See the section "Getting Someone to Make Videos for You" for more on these options). You may be able to achieve your marketing goals by collaborating with YouTubers who can create videos for you that they host on their YouTube channel.

YouTubers are the video creators who have their own established brand with large audiences of people subscribed to their YouTube channel. They may also be referred to as *influencers* because they wield a certain amount of influence and credibility with their fans.

It's common for an influential YouTuber to make a video featuring a product that fans then buy because they trust and admire the opinion and choices of that YouTuber. These YouTubers already have a large and engaged audience, and they regularly make content for their own channel. Marketers can tap into their audience by working with them in collaboration to create a video that features their products or services. YouTubers work with brands on a regular basis, and it can be a lucrative revenue stream for them.

REMEMBER

YouTubers must maintain a level of authenticity at all times. Their fans don't like it when the YouTuber sells out to shill a product that doesn't make any sense for them or their audience. Any integration of product must be a good fit for the YouTuber, something they would use and can believe in.

For marketers, the pros of working with a YouTuber to create a piece of video content is that you can tap directly into an influencer who has credibility with the audience you are trying to reach. YouTubers can make a review video of your product, simply mention it, provide a tutorial or unboxing of your product, or find other methods to highlight and integrate your product in a natural, authentic way.

The pros of collaboration for marketers are that

>> You can reach a desirable target audience.

>> You benefit from the influence and credibility of the YouTuber's endorsement.

>> You help to create brand awareness and trust.

>> You potentially drive sales and usage of the product.

On the other hand, marketers must give up a certain amount of control when working with YouTubers. You can't dictate how YouTubers will make their video, and they likely won't provide any approvals on the video itself. They'll simply take your brief and integrate your product into one of their videos in the style in which you've agreed, but they won't read from a script or deliver canned marketing messages. Their fans would know that they are shilling for a product rather than delivering great content.

WARNING

The biggest challenge with working with a YouTuber as a marketer is to find someone who is the right fit for your brand, product, or service.

Here are a few options, described in the following sections, that can help you connect with the right people:

>> Email a YouTuber directly.

>> Work with a multi-channel network (MCN).

>> Use a YouTuber marketplace.

Email a YouTuber directly

Perhaps you've found someone who you think is a great fit for your brand, and you want to work with them. Look on the About tab on their YouTube channel to find their email address. Many YouTubers list a business-inquiry email address.

WARNING

This approach is typically where most marketers start when they want to work with YouTubers but I don't recommend it. There likely won't be a process in place that can help protect the marketer or the YouTuber, and it's easy for projects that take this approach to struggle through to completion while keeping both parties happy. Strong communication is required to ensure success, along with a complete and comprehensive understanding of what is being requested and what will be delivered.

Work with a multichannel network (MCN)

A *multichannel network* (MCN) is a group that represents many different YouTubers and their channels and often extends beyond YouTube into other digital and non-digital media. The MCN team represents the YouTuber talent and helps connect them with brands who want to work with them on paid marketing initiatives, sponsorships, endorsement deals, appearances, and other opportunities like TV shows and book deals. An MCN is a bit like a talent agency, a production company, and a media network combined.

Examples of MCNs include Machinima, Fullscreen, Kin Community, AwesomenessTV, and Style Haul. These teams can be a better approach for collaboration with YouTubers because they bring a level of process and professionalism to the project.

WARNING

However, MCN budget levels tend to be higher, — in the tens and hundreds of thousands of dollars — especially where their biggest YouTubers are concerned. Proceed if you have the budget to match.

Use a YouTuber marketplace

Online marketplaces help you connect with YouTubers and influencers across other platforms. They typically work by providing an interface where you create your campaign requirements, including details like what kind of videos you're looking for, the product or service that would be featured, the audience you'd like to target, and your available budget, which you then submit to the marketplace. YouTubers can respond to your campaign brief, allowing you to select people to work with.

FAMEBIT

An example of an online marketplace to find YouTubers is the Google-owned FameBit (see figure), which has tens of thousands of YouTubers that you can reach with your campaign brief. Marketers simply post their brief and make choices around the kinds of videos they'd like made, such as a review, comedy sketch, haul video, tutorial, or unboxing. YouTubers can browse briefs available, respond, and negotiate price and deliverables.

The FameBit interface helps manage the communication and process and takes a 10 percent fee from the transaction for its services. Visit https://famebit.com to learn more.

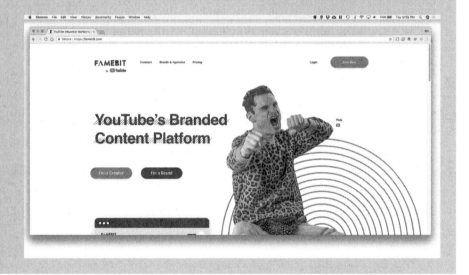

REMEMBER

If a YouTuber is paid to use or feature your product, government regulations require that they disclose the paid endorsement clearly in their video.

Curating Other People's Videos

You can add video content to your channel without actually creating any video content or breaking any laws. YouTube allows your channel to create playlists. Not only do playlists combine your own videos into themed lists, they can also include videos from other people's channels as well. This approach is known as *curation,* where you collect videos from across YouTube into themed playlists (see Figure 12-2).

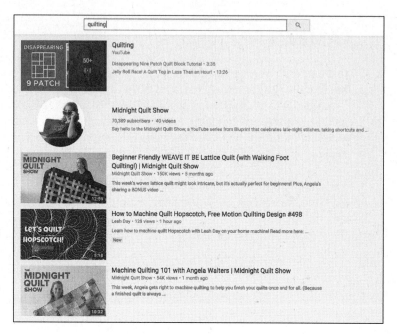

FIGURE 12-2:
The result at the top of this page is a playlist featuring more than 50 different videos from a variety of YouTube channels.

For example, if you run a quilting supply company and people make videos of the quilts they make using your patterns, materials, and equipment, you can curate a playlist of videos across YouTube from other people's channels to feature these quilts. You can call it "Our Customer's Amazing Quilting Videos" and include all the videos that specifically relate to your company's products. When people search for *quilting videos* on YouTube, your playlists can appear in the results. Playlists are a great way for marketers to collect together content that may be related to their brand, product, or service, but that isn't directly owned by them.

A healthy YouTube channel will have a combination of playlists featuring videos you've created, along with playlists of videos you've curated from across YouTube. Playlists aren't essential, but they're a great way to expand your channel's offering without having to create hundreds more videos.

5

Working with YouTube Channels

IN THIS CHAPTER

» **Setting up your YouTube channel**

» **Making your channel your own through customization**

» **Exploring ways to profit from your channel**

Chapter **13**

Launching Your YouTube Channel

B ig brands have made their home on YouTube. Take a look at the channels of GoPro (www.youtube.com/user/GoProCamera), Lowe's (www.youtube.com/user/Lowes), or Red Bull (www.youtube.com/user/redbull), and you'll see YouTube channels with millions of subscribers and even more millions of video views. Having a YouTube channel is a must for any marketer, as it will form the house for all of the content that you'll create and post on YouTube.

In this chapter, you discover how to set up and customize your own YouTube channel. You also find out how to profit from your channel.

Creating Your YouTube Channel

Your channel is your home on YouTube, a place where all your video content lives and where you can access a host of incredibly powerful features to get the most out of the platform. Spending some time setting up your channel for you, your brand, or your business will set you up for success in all you do on YouTube. After you create your channel, you'll be able to:

>> Customize your channel so that it reflects your brand identity and represents your business effectively (see Chapter 15)

>> Upload your videos ads and video content (see Chapter 14)

>> Create playlists to organize your videos (see Chapter 14)

>> Begin growing your video and subscriber count (see Chapter 10 for tips and best practices when creating your videos; see Chapter 7 on how to buy media to help boost your numbers)

Considering how valuable creating a channel can be to a marketer, it's really easy to get started. All you need is a Google account. If you don't have a Google account for your business, see the nearby sidebar.

With your Google account in hand, you're ready to fire up your YouTube channel.

WARNING

YouTube is constantly evolving and improving its platform, and features are often tweaked or moved. Despite this constant change, the principles in this section remain the same. Don't worry if a button isn't where you expect it to be; it'll likely be somewhere nearby.

Follow these steps to create your YouTube channel:

1. **Sign in to YouTube using your Google account.**

   The YouTube home page appears, and the icon in the upper-right corner changes to your account's profile picture or an icon of your name's initial.

TIP

If you have several Google accounts, make sure that you're signed in with the one you want to use for your YouTube channel.

SETTING UP A GOOGLE ACCOUNT

Before you can create a channel, you need a Google account for your business. To set up this account, go to https://accounts.google.com/signup and follow the steps to enter your information, creating an account name and password. You can even use an existing email address if you don't want a new Google email address. You'll likely be asked to verify your account through your email and your mobile phone. After you agree to the terms and conditions, you'll have a Google account.

2. **Click on the profile picture or icon and then click on Choose My Channel from the a drop-down menu that appears.**

   You see your channel, your home on YouTube.

   If this is the first time you're accessing your channel, you're asked to create a channel.

3. **Choose the name you'd like to use YouTube with.**

   You can use either your name or a name that best represents how you'll be using your channel — for example, your business or brand name. You can change this name later, but I recommend picking something that simply and clearly describes who this YouTube channel represents.

4. **Click on the Create Channel button.**

   Your brand new channel, shown in Figure 13-1, is alive. Your channel probably looks pretty empty because it's ready for you to customize it. (See the section "Customizing Your Channel," later in this chapter, for information on how to start making it your own.)

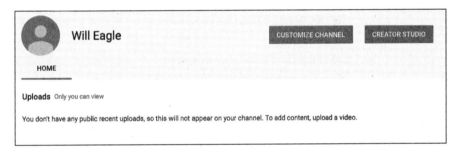

FIGURE 13-1:
A brand new
YouTube channel.

Customizing Your Channel

Figure 13-1 shows a brand new, freshly minted YouTube channel. There's not a lot to see! With no videos, no playlists, and no branding, your channel is a blank slate ready for you to customize as you see fit.

You want to customize your channel so that it is uniquely identifiable and demonstrates what can be found on it. To accomplish this goal, you should address some big items right away:

» Banner image

» Links to your banner

>> Channel icon

>> Channel description

REMEMBER

You can tweak things later as your YouTube efforts evolve. Regularly review your channel and make updates to keep things fresh.

Adding a banner image

The *banner image* is that large image spanning the top of a channel. Your banner is an opportunity to showcase your channel's identity and give it a look and feel that's unique to you.

TIP

The image you upload will be used on your channel on desktop computers, TV screens, and mobile phones, so choose an image that you think looks good across all devices.

A good image will

>> **Be a compelling representation of what your channel is about.** Choose something bold that stands out!

>> **Be on brand for your business.** It should match or be in the same family as your other brand creative, such as your website.

>> **Be as clearly visible on mobile phones as it is on desktops.** For example, if it contains text, ensure that it can be read on all devices.

REMEMBER

Whatever you choose, be sure you have the rights to the artwork you use. For example, you can use photographs you have taken yourself or illustrations you've had created. You can also find images that are available without royalty using Google Image Search.

To add a banner image to your channel:

1. **Click on the Customize Channel button.**

You will see a beautiful clean slate that is ready for your creative touch. Your Google account profile image appears in the upper-left corner of the banner, along with images of devices and the Add Channel Art button.

2. **Click on Add Channel Art.**

A box appears where you can upload photos.

3. **Select a photo from your computer to upload or choose from the images in Your Photos or Gallery.**

TIP

   Use a high resolution, large size image that is at least 2,048 x 1,152 pixels.

   A preview shows you how the image will look across devices.

4. **Click on the Adjust the Crop button to alter your image and check the check box for Auto Enhance to make changes to things like brightness.**

   Your channel art is uploaded.

TIP

YouTube offers downloadable channel art templates that you can use to design your channel art. Visit `http://bit.ly/YTchannelarttemplate` and navigate to the Image size & file guidelines section where you can find a downloadable zip file.

Adding links to your banner

On other YouTube channels, you may have noticed links to social media sites, such as Facebook, that sit on top of the channel's banner image. You can add these links to your channel's banner, too, by following these steps:

1. **Navigate to your channel and click on the About tab.**

2. **Click on the Links button (near the bottom of the page) to add up to five external website links.**

3. **Give each link a title, enter the URL, and then click on the Add button.**

   For example, you may choose to title your links as My Fan Club or My Facebook Page.

4. **Add more links until you're happy and click on the Done button.**

   These links appear on your YouTube Channel's banner.

Editing your channel icon

Your channel's icon, also known as a *profile picture,* comes from your Google account, and it'll follow you around pretty much wherever you go. The channel icon appears as the profile picture on your YouTube channel when someone visits, and it'll be the image you click to access your Google account. It will also be the image that appears next to your comments when you comment on someone else's video. It's everywhere!

TIP

Even though the image you upload for your channel icon will be square, when it's live it'll appear with a circular crop. Keep that in mind and choose a profile picture that keeps the main image in the center, and not off to the sides.

Your channel icon should complement the rest of your YouTube channel art. For example, you may want your icon to be a photo of you, your product, service, or something that represents you that is consistent with your YouTube channel overall and your banner image. Coca-Cola's channel icon, shown in Figure 13-2, is a great example because it shows its logo and product lineup, and is immediately identifiable as Coca-Cola wherever it may appear on the web.

FIGURE 13-2:
Coca-Cola's channel icon matches the channel.

To add or update your channel icon, follow these steps:

1. **Hover your mouse pointer over your channel icon and click on the pencil icon that appears.**

   An overlay message tells you that you'll be taken to your Google account to change the image.

2. **Click on the Edit button.**

   A new browser tab displays your Google About me page, with an overlay to let you upload a photo.

3. **Choose an image to upload, adjust the crop, and click on Done.**

   The image you choose is posted immediately.

4. **Return to your channel and check your channel icon.**

   Make sure that it's clear and complements your channel's banner. If you're not happy, change it!

Adding your channel description

The *channel description* is simply a few sentences describing your channel. This description appears in a few areas on YouTube, including when users mouse over your channel icon or visit the About section on your channel.

You can include links and write up to 1,000 characters in the channel description. A good channel description may say who you are and what you do, tell people what videos they can find on your channel, encourage viewers to interact with you on YouTube and your social channels, or provide links to other places where viewers may find you on the Internet, such as your website.

TIP

To get a sense of how other people have described their channels, visit other channels on YouTube and click on About to see their descriptions.

Figures 13-3 and 13-4 are two examples of great channel descriptions. In Figure 13-4, Coca-Cola gives information on who it is, the company's origin, where you can find it, and its product range. This channel description helps you know you've arrived at the right place.

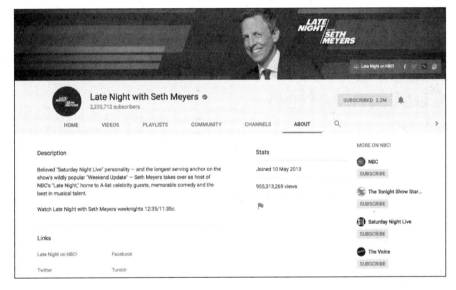

FIGURE 13-3:
A good example of an About tab on a YouTube channel from Seth Meyers. Here's where you can add your channel description.

To add or change your channel's description, go to your channel's main page and follow these steps:

1. **Click on Customize Channel.**

2. **Click on the About tab and then click on the Channel Description button.**

   An input box opens, enabling you to write a brief description of your channel.

3. **Type your description and click on Done.**

   You can edit this description at any time.

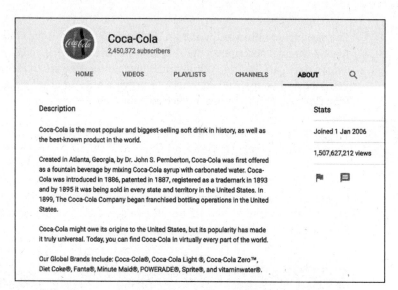

FIGURE 13-4:
Coca-Cola
provides a
great example
of a channel
description.

Digging Deeper into Channel Customization

You can do many things to customize your channel beyond just adding art, text descriptions, and social links. Your YouTube channel offers ways to initiate discussion, link to other YouTube channels, and make choices about how you'll display videos.

TIP

If you get lost at any point, click on your profile image in the upper-right corner of YouTube and click on My Channel from the drop-down menu to return to your channel.

About tab

In the About tab, you can see how many subscribers you have, the date you joined YouTube, and the description of your channel. In the About tab, you can

REMEMBER

» Add your email address so that people can reach you.

The email address you list doesn't have to be the one you use to access your YouTube channel.

>> Use a drop-down menu to select your location. (Choose your home country, where you are based.)

>> Add links to your website and social sites so that people find you on Facebook, Twitter, Instagram, LinkedIn, and other social sites.

Channels tab

You can add featured channels to highlight some of the channels you like the most or to informally connect your channel to other channels you may have.

Some YouTuber's have a primary channel for their videos, where they review new technology, and then a second channel that they use for videos like vlogging about their life and adventures. You also may have friends who have YouTube channels that you'd like to link to.

Similarly, some brands have a primary channel for their videos and then use other channels for one-off special advertising campaigns or initiatives, charitable efforts, or partnerships.

Warby Parker, an eyewear brand, has a primary channel for its videos about how its products are made, short films, TV spots, and its corporate social responsibility efforts (see Figure 13-5). The company also has a separate channel, WarbyParker-Help, for its customer service videos. On this channel are videos that tackle key customer questions around topics like prescriptions or its home try-on program.

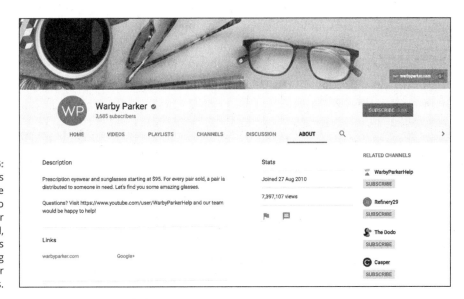

FIGURE 13-5: Warby Parker's primary YouTube channel links to its WarbyParker Help channel, which features videos tackling key customer service questions.

You can add featured channels by following these steps:

1. **In the Featured Channels section of your Channels tab, click on the Add Channels button.**

   A page like the one shown in Figure 13-6 appears.

FIGURE 13-6:
I renamed the section Channels I like and linked it to my two favorite channels: For Dummies and Wiley.

2. **Enter a channel username or URL and click on the Add button.**

   The channel appears in the list of Added channels.

   You can add either a channel username or a URL.

3. **Repeat Step 2 to add channels.**

4. **When you've added all the channels you'd like, click on the Done button.**

   The featured channels appear on the right side of your channel and in the Channels tab.

Discussion or Community tab

While you're setting up your channel, you may notice a Discussion tab, which sometimes appears as the Community tab.

The Discussion tab is an area where the channel owner, subscribers, and visitors can post text comments, such as status updates and replies. Most channels have a Discussion tab.

The Community tab typically appears when your channel reaches a certain number of subscribers and is rolling out increasingly over time. If you do have the Community tab, you'll be able to not only post text updates, but also create polls, post GIFs, and interact with subscribers and visitors. The Community tab is a more advanced version of the Discussion tab, allowing for images and links, not just text, to be posted (see Figure 13-7).

FIGURE 13-7: The Voice makes use of its Community tab by posting questions to engage its audience along with a fairly spectacular selection of animated GIFs from its show.

Here are some ideas to get you started posting in your Discussion or Community tab.

>> **State the purpose of your Discussion or Community tab.** Let people know what you'll be posting here and what you're looking for in return from them. For example, perhaps your Discussion tab will be used exclusively for feedback on your products and services, so you're looking for people to provide candid constructive feedback.

>> **Post your latest videos.** Use the tab to direct people engaging in discussion to your latest posting. You can also post videos from your archive when

relevant — for example, resurfacing something from the previous year, such as a fall recipe video you made.

>> **Promote any products or services you are offering.** Strike a balance when doing so because people aren't looking for the heavy sell here. If someone is asking a question about your product or service, provide a link directing them to it. Don't periodically blast promotional messages apropos of nothing.

>> **Ask people questions.** Use polls to ask questions like what your next videos should be or what they think about various topics. Maybe you're developing a new product that you want input on.

>> **Speak the language of the Internet with visuals.** Communicating using memes is common, and even the most conservative of brands can find that using memes is a fun way to create a rapport with their audience.

>> **Encourage people to act.** Perhaps you want people to rally around a cause, take some kind of action, or focus their attention on a topic.

TIP

When you first start your YouTube channel, the Discussion or Community tabs won't have a lot of action. Don't worry too much about spending a lot of time posting in this section until you get a volume of subscribers that warrant your time. Test posts occasionally to see whether people are seeing and responding to them.

TIP

For inspiration, follow the community posts of channels you subscribe to so that you can see how they're engaging with their audience.

Home tab shelves

YouTube offers a lot of flexibility to organize your channel, enabling you to merchandise your video content in a variety of ways and focus people's attention on what's important. Think of your other social channels, such as Facebook. Many of these channels are waterfalls of content, simply showing the latest posting in a never-ending stream of posts scrolling back into time. You may have the option to pin a post to the top of the page, but that's pretty much the limit.

With YouTube, you can craft your Home tab to appear how you'd like, focusing people's attention where it matters by using shelves. A shelf is a row of content, such as a playlist you want your audience to see.

The Channel shelf lets you group videos together in a specific way so that your audience can make easier decisions about what they want to watch. You can have up to ten shelves on one channel.

To group videos together:

1. **In the Home tab of your YouTube channel, click on Customize Channel.**

   You can now edit your channel's features, as shown in Figure 13-8.

FIGURE 13-8:
When you customize your channel, you see your channel with the addition of buttons that let you edit features and options.

2. **Click on the Add a section button.**

   A little section appears within the page. It features two drop-down menus: Content and Layout. The Content drop-down menu lists the options to craft your channel's layout:

   - *Videos:* You can create sections for videos, including your most popular uploads, a list of uploads in order of most recent, liked videos, and live streaming options.

   - *Playlists:* You can include playlists you've created, a single or multiple playlist, and more.

   - *Channels:* You can feature the channels you subscribe to as well as use a custom grouping option.

   - *Other:* You can create sections that contain recent activities and recent posts.

3. **From the Content drop-down menu, choose the type of shelf you'd like to create.**

4. **From the Layout drop-down menu, choose whether you'd like the shelf to be laid out horizontally in a row or vertically as a list.**

TIP

Your top row should match your marketing priorities, such as your campaigns in market or your best performing content.

Marketers should consider refreshing the layout of their channel periodically throughout the course of the year.

Editing home tab shelves

If you need to edit any of the shelves you set up, follow these steps:

1. **In the Home tab of the channel you want to edit, click on Customize Channel.**

   You see your channel with the option to edit features.

2. **Hover your cursor over the shelf you want to edit and click on the Edit icon.**

   The Edit icon is a pencil button that appear when you hover over the shelf.

3. **Change the content and layout of the shelf as you want.**

   See the preceding section for details on how to make these changes.

4. **Click on the Done button.**

TIP

   If you don't like what you see, instead of clicking on Done, you can click the Bin icon to delete the section or cancel to discard your edits.

Re-ordering channel sections

If you want to change the order of the shelves in your channel, you can easily move them around:

1. **In the Home tab of the channel, you want to edit, click on Customize Channel.**

2. **Hover your cursor over the shelf you want to edit and click the up or down arrow to move the shelf above or below other shelves.**

3. **Repeat as needed to move shelves up or down.**

Channel trailer

One of my favorite features of the YouTube channel is the ability to create what's known as a *channel trailer*, a short video that is shown to people who visit your channel but are not yet subscribers. This trailer video is an opportunity to pitch them your channel and show them a "best of" video that entices them to watch more of your videos and to subscribe.

TIP

The best trailer videos are short, lasting a minute or less, and keep things punchy and fun. Focus on what's really important to your audience and why your channel delivers to their needs.

To add a channel trailer:

1. **Create your video and upload it to your channel.**

   Visit Chapter 14 for details on uploading videos.

2. **In the Home tab of the channel you want to edit, click on Customize Channel.**

   You have the option to edit your channel for returning subscribers or new visitors.

3. **Click on For new visitors.**

   The Channel trailer button appears.

4. **Click on the Channel trailer button.**

5. **In the window that appears, choose one of your videos from your channel.**

6. **Enter the URL of the YouTube video.**

7. **Click on Save.**

   Your channel trailer is set!

TIP

Avoid making this a boring "Welcome to my channel" video introduction. Instead, get straight to the best content in a short and sweet video that sells viewers on you and your channel and encourages them to subscribe right then and there.

Making Money from Your YouTube Channel

You may be surprised to find out that your YouTube channel can be a money-maker. Most marketers aren't as concerned with turning their marketing channels into revenue streams, but that's not to say there aren't opportunities to do so that are worth considering.

Tons of YouTubers dedicate a lot of time and effort in creating channels with popular videos and are able to make a decent living from the revenue. Top YouTubers can pull in millions of dollars a year in revenue from their channels and a variety of ancillary sources.

TIP

The main thing to consider for marketers who want to participate in a program like the YouTube Partner Program (YPP) or other revenue generating techniques is whether there are any conflicting issues with treating your channel as a revenue source.

REMEMBER

If you're a marketer, you're primarily using YouTube as a marketing channel, and you don't need generating revenue from the channel to be a distraction if it's not a primary goal of your business. You may not like to have lots of ads running in and around your videos either. While you do have options to control these settings, the goal is to service your business needs. Generating revenue from YouTube is a business in itself.

The YouTube Partner Program

Introduced in 2007, the YouTube Partner Program (YPP) transformed the YouTube landscape. YPP enabled people creating and uploading videos to their YouTube channels to participate in ad revenue sharing. Suddenly, people who made content for fun could actually make money from their videos.

You can sign up for YPP if you meet certain eligibility criteria. If accepted, you start to earn money from advertisements that are served against your videos and from the YouTube Premium subscribers who watch your content.

THE YOUTUBER RICH LIST

Forbes regularly publishes its annual list of the wealthiest people in the world, and for the past few years, it's published the top-earning YouTubers. While these YouTubers make money from a variety of sources, including book deals and sponsorships, a big chunk of their massive revenue comes from their YouTube channels. In 2017, the list featured

- *Lilly Singh at $10.5 million*: Makes comedy, music, and acting videos as well as videos documenting her adventures as a philanthropist

- *Felix Kjellberg (PewDiePie) at $12 million:* Has the most subscribed to YouTube channel with 70 million subscribers, vlogs, and plays video games.

- *Dude Perfect with $14 million:* Pulls off seemingly impossible challenges and trick shots.

- *Daniel Middleton (DanTDM) in the top spot with $16.5 million:* Makes gaming videos.

To be eligible for the program, you need a channel that has reached more than 4,000 watch hours in the previous 12 months and has more than 1,000 subscribers.

TIP

The criteria to join the YouTube Partner Program can change from time to time as YouTube works to ensure the program delivers a quality experience. Check the most current eligibility criteria by visiting: https://support.google.com/youtube and searching for YouTube Partner Program.

Signing up for YPP requires the completion of four stages:

1. **Agree to the YouTube Partner Program terms.**
2. **Sign up for AdSense.**
3. **Set your monetization preferences.**
4. **Get reviewed.**

Agree to the terms

To sign up for YPP, start by following these steps:

1. **Sign in to YouTube and visit the YouTube.com home page.**
2. **Click on your account icon in the upper-right corner.**
3. **From the menu that appears, click on the Creator Studio button.**

   The Creator Studio interface appears.

4. **Under the Channel menu, click on the Monetization option to visit the Monetization subsection.**
5. **Click on Enable and follow the on screen steps to accept the YouTube Partner Program Terms.**

Sign up for AdSense

After you agree to the YPP terms (see preceding section), the next stage is to sign up for AdSense.

If you already have an AdSense account or want to set up an AdSense account associated with an umbrella account that owns multiple YouTube channels, visit https://support.google.com/youtube and search for *Setting up an AdSense account.* A helpful tool guides you to the specific set of steps to follow in these scenarios.

The following steps apply if you don't yet have an approved AdSense account yet or when you're creating a new association between a YouTube channel you manage:

1. **Visit www.youtube.com/account_monetization.**

   You're redirected to AdSense.

2. **Make sure you're signed in to the Google Account that you want to create an AdSense account for.**

   Check that the email address in the top corner matches the Google Account that manages your YouTube account.

3. **Accept the AdSense association and provide your contact information to submit your AdSense application.**

   You're redirected back to YouTube, and a message appears saying that your AdSense application has been received.

Set your monetization preferences

After you sign up for AdSense (see the preceding section), your next stage is to set your monetization preferences. You're able to set the types of ads you want to run on your videos and automatically turn on monetization for all your existing and future videos.

To set your monetization preferences:

1. **In Creator Studio, click on Status and features in the Channel Section.**

2. **In the left menu, choose Channel ⇨ Upload defaults to be taken to that subsection.**

3. **Check or uncheck the Monetize with ads check box next to Monetization.**

   You're asked to acknowledge some terms.

4. **Read the terms and click on the Got it button to proceed.**

5. **Check the boxes under Ads formats to choose the types of ads you want to show**

6. **Click on Save.**

TIP

For marketers, I recommend selecting not-monetized for each video that is uploaded automatically instead of choosing specific videos. Because you may be uploading your own ads to YouTube, you won't want other ads to run against them.

Get reviewed

After you agree to the terms, sign up for AdSense, and set your monetization preferences (see preceding section), you'll have met the program's thresholds to be reviewed. In the fourth and final stage, the YPP team reviews your application to ensure that it meets all of its criteria and policies, which includes the YouTube Partner Program Policy, YouTube's Terms of Service, and its Community Guidelines. YPP will let you know once your application has been reviewed.

If you're successful, you'll start to see revenue appear in your AdSense account.

Other ways to make money

Beyond using YouTube to promote sales of your products or services, or to grow brand awareness and product consideration, which both drive revenue, you can make money through YouTube in some other ways. While these approaches usually apply to YouTubers, marketers may be able to find creative ways to leverage them.

Patreon

Patreon is the name of an incredible third-party service. This membership platform uses the idea of patronage, where you can give money to YouTubers, just like rich aristocrats and royal families who paid artists to create works.

Patreon is primarily designed for creatives, such as YouTube creators, who set a monthly subscription style payment — for example, $5 a month. In exchange for contributing monthly, the fans get access to special content or features set by the creator such as early access to videos or shout outs. Patreon won't apply to all marketers. For example, if you're a large corporation selling the market's most popular brand of shampoo, it's going to be pretty hard to convince fans to give you money, no matter how much they like your content. However, some marketers will be able to find ways to apply Patreon to their business goals. Visit www.patreon.com to learn more and sign up.

Working with brands

Brands will pay YouTubers who exert a certain amount of influence over their audience to encourage people to buy their product or become aware of their brand. Visit Chapter 12 to find out more about collaborating on videos with YouTubers.

However, you may be a marketer who can create partnerships with other brands who want to reach your audience. That brand may pay you to access your audience if it's large enough, or perhaps you'll arrange a deal where you cross promote each other without exchanging money.

Merchandising

Many big brands will offer merchandise, branded clothing, accessories, and products of all sorts with the brand's logo emblazoned front and center. This technique is leveraged by popular YouTubers, such as PewDiePie. PewDiePie offers a range of merchandise, shown in Figure 13-9, so his 70 million plus subscribers can express their fandom and he can further monetize his audience. Marketers can take advantage of promoting their merchandise through their YouTube channel.

FIGURE 13-9: PewDiePie's merchandise store of clothing and accessories.

Crowdfunding

Crowdfunding is a method to source funds for a project or venture by asking your audience to contribute small amounts of money. TheUnsolicitedProject, (www.youtube.com/user/UnsolicitedProject), a YouTube channel with more than 400,000 subscribers, was able to successfully crowdfund to make its first feature film, surpassing its goals of funding by 300 percent.

Crowdfunding can be a great approach to fund projects if you're a marketer, especially if you work in creative fields, nonprofits, causes, and anything where crowdfunding feels uniquely applicable.

Two of the top crowdfunding platforms are Kickstarter (www.kickstarter.com) and Indiegogo (www.indiegogo.com.).

Chapter **14**

Publishing Your Videos

t's an exciting moment when you're finally ready to upload your video. All your hard work filming and editing is about to pay off. In this chapter, I walk you through the steps to upload and publish your video.

The process may seem simple at first, but some tips and tricks can help maximize your video's chances of success. YouTube also provides tools to add more advanced features to your videos like end screens and cards, which can provide interactivity and encourage viewers to watch more of your videos.

Writing Compelling Titles

A well-written title is the difference between a click to watch or being ignored. Title writing is crucial to the performance of your video because people scan YouTube for the video they want to watch, rapidly reading titles and making their choice. Your title should

» Stand out and grab attention compared with other similar videos

» Be an accurate description of your video

» Encourage and entice someone to click

TIP

If your title is misleading and your video doesn't deliver on its promise, people won't be happy and will let you know in the comments! Keep the title accurate and don't oversell it just to get more clicks.

YouTube limits your titles to 100 characters including spaces in total, but only about 50 characters of your title displays on the YouTube desktop home page. Make sure that you get the best information in the first half of your title.

The following sections describes some common title structures.

The hook, explanation, and information

In the hook, explanation, and information structure, you provide an initial hook to snag someone's interest, follow with an explanation of what the clip is, and finish with information about the show or channel. For example:

>> No Soup For You | Seinfeld | TBS (from TBS)

>> Fitness Body Transformation | Simple Guide from Fat to Fit (from Buff Dudes)

>> How I Grocery Shop! | Food & Meal Planning Tips! | Q&A (from Jordan Page's channel, FunCheapOrFree)

The question

Posing a question sets up your video nicely as the answer. It's intriguing and suggests an entertaining or informative explanation will follow. For example:

>> What Does Cake Batter Do In a Vacuum Chamber?

>> Can you travel Bali with $100? Keeping Paradise Affordable (from LostLeBlanc)

>> Would You Swim In This? (from The King of Random)

The statement

The statement structure is similar to formatting your title as a question (see preceding section). You're stating that your video will provide a compelling explanation of the statement:

- » Here's Why Old Mercedes Live Forever (from Hoovies Garage)

- » Testing My Dog's Trust On A Giant Suspension Bridge (from Drew Lynch)

- » Cher Is Not a Cher Fan (from TheEllenShow)

The clickbait

A trend you may have noticed on YouTube is the use of clickbait along with the use of disclaimers that a video is not clickbait. *Clickbait* is a piece of content designed to attract attention and get a click, often stretching the truth in order to get more clicks and potentially misrepresenting the content.

As people become increasingly aware of clickbait, a trend has arisen where video titles include "Not Clickbait", which can often be a sign that the video is in fact clickbait! Consider the following (I've left out the offending YouTube channels):

- » Buying Every Advertisement I See (NOT CLICKBAIT)

- » I got arrested! Not Clickbait.

- » I'm quitting this channel FOREVER!! *NOT CLICKBAIT*

WARNING

I can't really recommend this type of title, because I think it's a bit of a cheap and lazy way to get some clicks, but it can work. Use at your discretion!

Crafting a Quality Video Description

Your video description lives beneath your video and appears when people search YouTube. The description provides them with some extra details about your video and encourages them to choose your video over someone else's. (See Figure 14-1 for an example where I searched "How to knit a scarf.") The first two lines or so from each video's description appear beneath the title.

A great description

- » Uses the first few lines to describe the contents of the video and entice people to click. Include your most important keywords here, but use natural language; don't just list keywords.

- » Describes in more detail what's included in the video, such as what they'll learn.

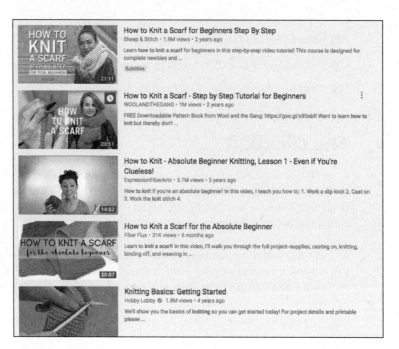

FIGURE 14-1:
The first few lines of your description help you encourage people to choose your video over someone else's. Make sure your description is compelling and accurate.

» Provides links to any resources you mention in the video and to your site and social media profiles. You can even include hashtags.

» Provides time stamps to let people know the various chapters of your video, helping them skip ahead to the relevant part.

» Encourages people to subscribe, comment, like, and share.

» Suggests other videos or playlists viewers may want to watch.

TIP

Some of your description will likely be a standard template you apply across all your videos. A standard template will save you time for each video you upload, but don't let one description apply to all videos — you'll still need to customize the description for each video. (Visit Chapter 15 to find out how to set a default description to apply to all your videos.)

Adding Tags

A lot of confusion and debate center around the role of tags. Historically, tags were used in search engines to help websites rank in the results pages. People quickly abused tags as a technique, and the search engines downgraded the importance of tags as an indicator of what the content is actually about and the subsequent priority of the site's listing.

TIP

YouTube still makes use of tags, but it's not clear how much they affect how your video will be found when people search. Having said that, the general rule is that if YouTube provides you with a feature, maximizing the use of that feature is a good idea as it probably does have an impact.

You can input tags, separated by commas. Tags should be

>> Short one- or two-word phrases, known as *keywords,* that describe your video. Consider adding between 10 and 20 keywords in total.

>> Specific whenever possible. Avoid generic tags that are too broad.

>> Include your brand, business, and channel name if you want. However, I recommend adding them to the end of the list.

>> Only accurate representations of what your video is about. Don't stuff in irrelevant tags because that can violate YouTube's policies.

For example, for the video "How to knit a scarf for beginners step by step," you can add the tags *knitting, scarf, scarves, knitting for beginners, how to knit step by step, knitting guide, knitting basics, knit stich, cast off,* and *knitting needles.*

TIP

YouTube likely uses your title, description, and tags in some way in its evaluation of your video that informs where it places you in the search results page. Maximizing these added pieces of information not only encourages people to click your video, but helps people find you in searches. For more about search engine optimization, or SEO, check out Chapter 15.

Customizing Your Thumbnail

The best approach is to create a thumbnail separately and upload it instead of using one of YouTube's automatic selections. This way, you can guarantee that you're maximizing your thumbnail's chances of being clicked

A great thumbnail

>> Clearly conveys the subject of the video and encourage the viewer to click

>> Makes use of bright color to stand out

>> Uses a person's face, when possible, because faces tend to get attention, or demonstrates an action taking place

>> Uses text to give extra information about the video and draws the viewer in

>> Is clearly and consistently branded and look like it's your brand's video

Make your custom thumbnail image as large as possible. Use a minimum resolution of 1280 x 720, in the format .JPG or .PNG. Keep the file under 2MB and use a 16:9 aspect ratio.

Test, test, test! Your thumbnails are something you can experiment with, so test to see which one best encourages people to click. You may discover that people are more likely to click on different colors.

TIP

Search Google for YouTube Thumbnail Maker, and you'll find lots of simple drag-and-drop tools and premade templates to help you make your YouTube thumbnails. These solutions are great if you're not a whiz with advanced graphics software. You can also use services like Fiverr.com to find people who can create your thumbnails for you.

Uploading Videos

Uploading your videos involves more than just clicking Upload and hoping for the best. You have lots of options and settings to ensure that your video is accurately uploaded and represented on YouTube, maximizing its chances of being found and watched.

To upload your video, follow these steps.

1. **From any page on YouTube, click on the video camera icon in the upper right-hand corner and choose Upload Video.**

   You're prompted to choose the files to upload.

2. **Choose the files to upload by either clicking the larger arrow icon to select files to upload or dragging and dropping your video files into the browser window.**

3. **From the drop-down list, choose whether the video will be public, unlisted, private, or scheduled.**

   It's a smart best practice to upload your video a day or so before you actually need it to go live and set it to unlisted or private initially. You can then take your time to make sure all the other information is complete and have any other team members review it before you make it available to the world. Just don't forget to change the setting to public later.

Your video starts to upload automatically, and a message will notify you when it's completed.

While it's uploading, further options appear so that you can add information to your video, as shown in Figure 14-2.

FIGURE 14-2:
While your video uploads, take the time to add information, such as a title, description, and tags, to your video.

REMEMBER

4. **Add a title, description, and tag.**

   The description field is limited to a maximum of 5,000 characters.

   For tips on creating these items, see the earlier sections on "Writing Compelling Titles," "Crafting a Quality Video Description," and "Adding Tags,"

5. **Add a thumbnail.**

   YouTube automatically chooses three potential thumbnails from the first few minutes of your video. You can click on one to set it as the thumbnail, or you can click on Customized thumbnail to upload your own thumbnail image that you created.

TIP

   If you don't see the option to upload a custom thumbnail, it's because your YouTube account isn't verified. Visit www.youtube.com/verify to verify your account using your phone.

   For more tips creating a thumbnail, see the section "Customizing Your Thumbnail," earlier in this chapter.

6. **Set the video's status using the drop-down list.**

   Your video can be

   - **Public:** Anyone can find and watch the video. Choose this setting when you're ready for your video to be seen by the world.

   - **Unlisted:** Anyone who has the link that you provide to them can view the video. A useful choice when you want to send the video to select people.

   - **Private:** Only those you invite can view the video. This option is the safest if you don't want people to see your video just yet.

   - **Scheduled:** You make the video live at a set time and date in the future. This allows you to schedule multiple videos ahead of time.

7. **Click on Add to playlist and select the playlists you want to add.**

   A list of playlists you've previously created appears. Simply check the box for any and all playlists that relate to this video to add them.

   REMEMBER

   Always add your videos to playlists, as playlists can surface in YouTube's search results. It's a bit like giving your video another chance to be found, and playlists encourage people to watch more of your content. Not assigning videos to playlists is a wasted opportunity.

8. **Add a translation by clicking the Translations tab.**

   Clicking this tab allows you to translate your title and description into other languages, which can help you reach more people around the world.

   TIP

   If you don't speak other languages, that's OK! You can use Google Translate or the YouTube community to add translation. Discover more about how to add translation and the benefits of translations and transcriptions in Chapter 15.

9. **Adjust any advanced settings for each video you upload.**

   The Advanced Settings tab, shown in Figure 14-3, has lots more options that you can tweak.

   TIP

   You can set many of these settings as a default to apply to your videos, which saves you time every upload. You won't need to make every choice time and again if you set your defaults. Check out Chapter 15 for details.

10. **When you finish adding information and adjusting your settings, click on Done.**

    Your video upload process is complete. A box appears and gives you the link where you can access the video. You can copy this link by placing your cursor in the box and selecting it to copy and later paste.

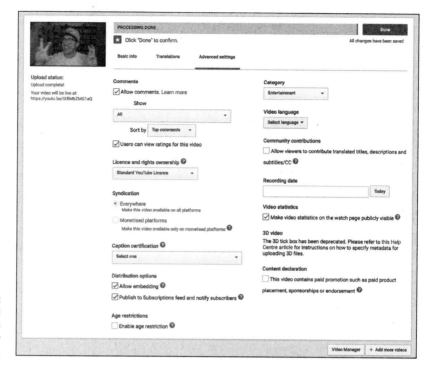

FIGURE 14-3:
Use the Advanced settings tab to tweak your video's settings.

TIP

Don't skip the step of adding information to your videos because titles, descriptions, and tags are crucial to helping people find your video in YouTube. Great titles and thumbnails are what will encourage people to click on your video.

Improving Your Videos with Advanced Customization

Your uploaded video appears along with all your other videos in Creator Studio Classic within the Video Manager section. Use the extra customization options here to improve and power up your video. Simply find the video you want to edit, click on the Edit button, and go to the tab you'd like to edit.

More than likely, you'll want to

>> Apply enhancements to your video

>> Adjust audio settings

>> Add end screens and annotations

>> Add cards

>> Modify your subtitles and closed captions

Applying enhancements

In the Enhancements section, you can blur people's faces and certain areas and trim your video.

Blurring

Blurring is helpful if your video contains people who did not sign a permission waiver allowing them to appear in the video. (See Chapter 11 for more on permissions when featuring people.)

To blur faces:

1. **Go to the Blur Faces section of the Enhancements tab and click on Edit.**

   An overlay popups while YouTube searches your video for faces. As it finds them, YouTube displays thumbnails of each face it finds in the video.

2. **Select any faces to have them blurred.**

3. **Watch the video again to verify that the faces have been accurately blurred and then click Save.**

You can also use blurring to blur specific areas, such as brand logos on people's clothing.

To blur a custom area, click on Edit under Custom blurring within the Enhancements tab, and then draw shapes over the areas you want to blur out (see Figure 14-4).

You can play the video, drawing shapes as needed. You see a timeline (also known as a *scrubber*), so you can have your blurred shape appear for more or less time. When you've drawn shapes and ensured that they persist long enough to blur the desired area shown on screen, you can just click the Done button when ready.

TIP

If at any point you want to undo your work, you can click on Revert to original. You can also click on Save as new video to make a copy with your edits.

FIGURE 14-4:
You can draw
shapes to blur
specific areas of a
video — for
example, if you
don't have
permission to
show something.

Trimming

Chapter 11 covers the more powerful editing options that most marketers will want to leverage. However, the Trimming feature, found under the Enhancements tab, is helpful for some basic edits to make cuts to your video.

To use the Trimming feature:

1. **Click on the Trim button.**

    You see a screen like the one shown in Figure 14-5.

2. **Add splits to your videos or delete sections.**

    You can add splits by playing the video and pausing it wherever you want one. Just click on the Split button to add a split. You can also use the timeline/scrubber to move around the video.

    If you split your video, an X appears above the split section. Click that X to delete that part of the clip.

    If you're unhappy with your changes, click on the Clear button to undo all edits.

3. **Click the Done button when you're finished editing.**

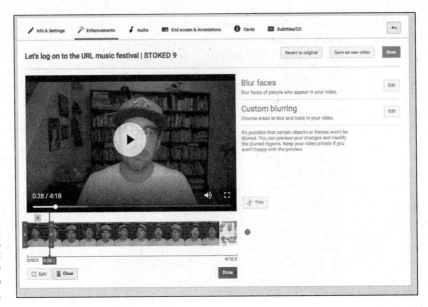

FIGURE 14-5:
The Trimming
feature is a basic
editing feature
you can use to
cut your video.

Adding audio

YouTube offers a deep library of thousands of royalty-free songs that you can use in your videos. In the Audio section, you can search the library and choose to add or replace the audio.

Adding end screen and annotations

*End screen*s (see Figure 14-6) are a fantastic way to promote your content and build your viewership. They work by adding suggested next steps to the final 30 seconds or so of your video.

To add end screens:

1. **Choose the video you want to edit and click on the End screen & Annotations tab.**

2. **From the Add element drop-down menu, choose the action you want to take.**

   You can add a video or playlist, add a message to encourage people to subscribe to your channel, promote another channel, or link through to an approved website.

   The element you add appears over the video, as shown in Figure 14-7.

FIGURE 14-6:
Oprah's YouTube
videos make use
of end screens,
encouraging you
to subscribe and
watch more
videos.

FIGURE 14-7:
The elements
you add appear
over the video
and can be
resized and
moved.

3. **Make your changes to the element.**

   You can drag to resize the element or move it around the grid to change its placement. You can select the element and hit the Delete key to get rid of it, and you can use the timeline to adjust when they appear and how long for.

4. **When you're done making changes, click on Save.**

TIP

The End screen tool lets you draw your own shapes, but using a template is much easier, saving you time and giving you a better result. When you click on the Use template button, the various template options appear. Click on the one you want to use and then click on the Select button.

When you add a video or playlist, YouTube lets you choose your most recent upload or a specific video or playlist. YouTube also chooses the video that's best for the viewer if you enable this option. This fantastic feature allows YouTube to select the video that it thinks your viewers will most want to watch next. I highly recommend trying this option!

TIP

If you're going to use end screens (and I recommend you do), include some additional footage to play at the end of your video so that your end screens don't appear over your video while your content is still playing.

After you create an end screen that you like, you can easily re-use it across other videos. Within the End screen and Annotations tab, you can click on Import from video to choose the end screen you'd like to apply.

WARNING

Annotations are text overlays that you may recall seeing on videos you've watched in the past. Although annotations live in the End screen & Annotations section, this feature was disabled in May 2017. With more people using mobile devices, YouTube found that annotations didn't work well on smaller screens and replaced annotations with cards (see the next section.) If you have videos that already have annotations, you'll see details listed in the Annotations subsection within the End screen and Annotations tab.

Adding cards

Cards replaced annotations and add interactivity to your videos. Cards point viewers to websites and show them custom images, titles, and calls to action. Viewers can hover over the video player and see the card icon (i). Clicking that icon allows them to browse all the cards on the video.

Card types include

>> **Channel cards** that link to your or another channel

>> **Donation cards** that can help you fundraise (only available in the United States at the time of writing)

>> **Link cards** let you link to approved websites and is available only to those in the YouTube Partner Program

- » **Poll cards** allow your viewers to vote
- » **Video or playlist cards** link to videos, playlists, a specific time in a video, or a specific video within a playlist

TIP

When you set up cards, a *teaser* — a little hint at a specific time in your video that cards are available — is included. Teasers are a helpful reminder that cards are there. As the video plays, space cards throughout rather than grouping them together.

Modifying subtitles/CC

Subtitles (also known as closed captions) help people watch without audio turned on and give YouTube more information about what's contained within your video. You can

- » Upload a text file containing a transcription or a timed subtitles file. That's a special file format that includes the text and the time code for when that text was spoken.
- » Transcribe the video yourself and have YouTube automatically sync the subtitles with the video.
- » Create new subtitles and closed captions. YouTube auto-generates text that you can edit as you watch the video.

See Chapter 11 for more about translations, transcriptions, and subtitles.

IN THIS CHAPTER

» **Harnessing the power of YouTube's Creator tools**

» **Benefiting from regularly auditing your channel**

» **Organizing your content with playlists**

» **Ensuring your account is in good standing**

» **Exploring copyright and community guidelines**

Chapter **15**

Channel Management

YouTube offers an incredibly powerful backend tool, currently named Creator Studio Classic, that enables you to manage your videos, playlists, and channel. It also offers advanced features, such as live-streaming, and helps you engage with the YouTube community.

In this chapter, you discover how you can use the Creator tools to tweak your settings, apply new defaults, and finely hone your channel's setup. You also find out about resource libraries for things like music and sound effects, discover how to regularly audit your channel to keep it fresh and accurate, ensure that you're maximizing your videos to appear in the search results, and become familiar with YouTube's stance on copyright and community guidelines. This chapter is all about keeping your channel healthy and in good standing with active management.

Introducing Creator Studio Classic

At the time of writing, Creator Studio Classic is the tool that most channel owners use in order to manage their channel. To access the tool, visit your YouTube channel and click on Creator Studio. (See Figure 15-1 for an example of Creator Studio.)

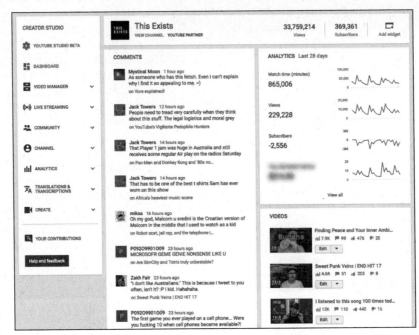

FIGURE 15-1:
The Creator
Studio Classic
interface.

YouTube Studio is the new tool in beta rolling out across YouTube channels and
will be replacing Creator Studio Classic. It contains many of the same features as
Creator Studio Classic, with new features and a new and improved layout.

The Creator Studio Classic tool houses a raft of features and settings:

>> YouTube Studio Beta

>> Dashboard

>> Video Manager

>> Live Streaming

>> Community

>> Channel

>> Analytics

>> Translations and Transcriptions

>> Create

>> Your Contributions

Dashboard

Your dashboard gives you a snapshot overview of your channel, including your total video views, your subscriber count, recent comments, videos, and an overview of your analytics with stats on watch time, views, and even revenue, if you have monetization enabled.

You can click on Add widget in the upper right-hand corner of your dashboard to customize the content that appears on your dashboard when you log in.

Video Manager

Clicking on Video Manager offers you three options.

>> **Videos,** where you can see a list of the videos you've posted, with the most recent list first. Marketers may find this particular snapshot handy because it shows you how many views, comments, likes, and dislikes your videos have, which makes it easy to compare their relevant performance. You can sort this list by clicking on the View in the upper right-hand corner and choosing Most viewed, Monetized, and other sort options from the drop-down list. You can also take bulk actions on this page or edit individual videos. (Check out Chapter 14 for more on the publishing and editing of videos.)

>> **Playlists,** a listing of your playlists that you can sort by newest or oldest, edit playlists, or create new ones.

>> **Copyright notices,** which gives you a listing of your videos that may have copyright issues. See the upcoming section "Being in Good Standing" for more on copyright.

Live Streaming

In the live streaming section, you can choose to start a livestream or schedule an event. You can also test your camera settings. (Check out Chapter 11 for more on setting up live streaming.)

TIP

Marketers should consider whether a livestream will help deliver against marketing and business goals. One of the trickiest things about livestreams is garnering decent audience numbers. Some interesting livestream applications for marketers can be live events, interviews with influencers and celebrities, or product launches.

Community

The Community section houses

>> Comments

>> Subscribers

>> Super Chat

>> Community Settings

>> Credits

Comments

The comments section allows you to see all comments posted across any of your video, with the most recent comment appearing first.

Being open to input is key. Use your videos to encourage people to

>> Comment on what they like or don't like about your product or service

>> Say whether they like your videos and offer suggestions for how to improve them

>> Comment on the ways in which they use your product in their lives

>> Ask any questions that you can answer

>> Suggest new ideas they'd like you to explore

>> Encourage conversations that provide helpful input to your business and marketing.

TIP

Don't feed the trolls! A *troll* is someone who comments to provoke or annoy you or other people commenting, and a popular adage on the Internet is "Don't feed the trolls." The idea is that you simply don't respond because responding gives the troll attention, and attention is the fuel for them to continue trolling even more. Don't take the bait, and the troll will go away.

TIP

If you're the community manager within a marketing team, this tool is the best place to start your day. You can easily scan for comments that may need a reply and get a general sense of the sentiment of the audience and their thoughts about your video content. You can delete and flag comments right from this page, without needing to visit each individual video. You also see tabs for comments that are Held for review and comments that are Likely spam, which you can approve, remove, or report.

Subscribers

The Subscribers section shows you a list of the most recent subscribers to your channel. This tool is helpful because you can easily click to subscribe to their channel right from this page. You can also sort the list to see who are your most popular subscribers.

TIP

Sort your subscriber list by most popular to see who is a fan of your channel. You may be able to reach out to them to collaborate or work together in some capacity. For example, if a popular YouTuber likes your channel, perhaps he would like to review your product or service. Chapter 12 has more information on collaborating with popular YouTubers.

Super Chat

A *super chat* is a feature that lets a fan highlight their message in a chat, so it's more applicable to fans. However, marketers may find creative ways to make use of it.

When you're live streaming, fans can chat directly with you in a chat window (see Figure 15-2). Super Chat allows those fans to pay to have their message highlighted with a color to make it stand out against all other chat messages and pinned in the chat window for a set period of time.

FIGURE 15-2:
Super chat is a feature that lets fans pay to have their chat message highlighted during livestreams.

TIP

If you're a marketer creating a livestream that features a celebrity or influencer, the people tuning in may want to use the Super Chat feature to highlight their message. This feature generates revenue for your channel.

Community Settings

The Community Settings section hosts a variety of helpful features to tweak how you want to engage and manage your community. You can

>> Add *moderators,* people who can remove comments and review your livestream chat

>> Add approved users who can manage features of your account on your behalf

>> Hide users, blocking people whose comments and live chats you don't want to appear

>> Enter a list of blocked words to stop comments that are closely related to those words

>> Block links by default — for example, if someone comments with a hashtag or URL, their comment will be held for review

>> Tweak your default settings as to whether you allow all comments, hold potentially inappropriate comments, or disable comments completely

TIP

I've worked with many conservative clients who want to disable comments across their videos because they worry about what people might say and that the overhead of managing comments will be too much to manage. My advice is to initially keep all comments enabled and to set expectations around how your brand will engage in comments by stating such in the video's description. See the "Comments" section, earlier in this chapter, for more information on how to manage comments.

Credits

Credits is a feature that enables you to tag collaborators in your videos, linking to their channel from your video. For example, if your video features a celebrity or YouTuber, you can tag them in the credits to link to their channel on YouTube. Note that this feature is available only to channels with at least 5,000 subscribers.

TIP

For marketers making ads, you can give credit to everyone who worked on your commercial, —for example, your director, composer, video editor, and more.

Channel

Within the Channel section, you can review and customize a variety of settings:

>> Status and features

>> Monetization

>> Upload defaults

>> Branding

>> Advanced options

Status and features

The Status and features tab provides an overview of your copyright and community guidelines status and any features that you're eligible for. As you grow your YouTube channel, additional features will become available to you.

Monetization

If you enable monetization for your YouTube channel, you can find helpful guidelines and information in the Monetization section. For channels that are part of the YouTube Partner Program, you can access the Creator Benefits program (www.youtube.com/creators/benefits) and directly chat to a support team who help YouTube creators.

You can review or change your monetization settings for future or individual videos, tweak your AdSense account settings, or even disable monetization or leave the YouTube Partner program (although I don't know why anyone would do that!) For more on the YouTube Partner program, see Chapter 13.

Upload defaults

The Upload defaults section is a huge timesaver. You can set the defaults you want implemented across each video you upload. You can, of course, override these settings when you're uploading a video (see Chapter 14 for more on publishing videos) but having your favorite settings set as defaults will save you lots of time each time you upload. You can set defaults for

>> Privacy, choosing from private, unlisted or public

>> Category, such as music, sports, and travel

>> The license that applies

>> Title, which is helpful if you have a standard title format you use

>> Description, where you can include standard text and links that appear in the description box for each video

>> Tags that apply to your videos

>> Comments and user ratings

>> Monetization, including if you want to include midroll ads (see Chapter 4)

>> The language the video is in and whether you'd like people in the community to help you with translating and transcribing your video

REMEMBER

For marketers, consistency is key, and setting your defaults is a great way to ensure a level of consistency against every video you post. For example, while each video will have a custom description, you can include a standard boilerplate description across all your videos. See Figure 15-3 for an example from Oprah Winfrey's OWN YouTube channel, which includes a standard description across all of her videos posted.

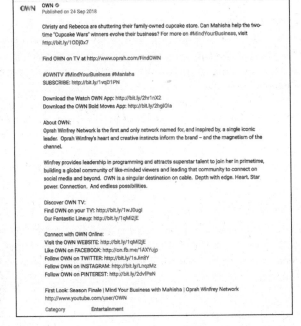

FIGURE 15-3:
A standard boilerplate description for each video provides consistency across all videos posted to the channel.

Branding

Marketers will love the Branding feature. You can automatically apply your brand's logo or other visual treatment as a watermark across all your videos. Including your logo or marque is a great way to give people a recognizable identifier to let them know they're watching your video.

Advanced options

In the Advanced options section, you can tweak settings to

» Change your account name and profile image

» Change your country setting

» Add channel keywords that describe what your channel is all about

» Disable interest-based ads so that personalized ads aren't shown on videos on your channel

» Link to your Google Ads account so that you can promote your videos through paid media (see Chapter 7 for more on Google Ads)

» Link to your associated website

» Set whether you want your channel to be recommended by other channels or display your subscriber count

» Link to your Google Analytics tracking ID (see Chapter 17)

Analytics

Spending time regularly looking at your analytics is a key component of successfully using YouTube for your marketing efforts. For a deeper dive into all things Analytics, see Part 6.

Translations and Transcriptions

When you visit the Translations and Transcriptions section, you see a list of your videos that community members have either translated for you or transcribed. Your videos can

» Have your video's title and description translated into other languages.

» Have the audio of the video transcribed, capturing whatever is said in the language it was said in, which enables people to see subtitles *(closed captions)* for your videos so they can watch without audio.

» Have transcriptions translated, allowing speakers of other languages to enjoy your videos.

TIP

Translating your videos can help you appear more often in the search results and reach more people around the world. If people who speak other languages or are living in other countries can enjoy your videos, consider asking community members to help you translate.

Google Translate is a fantastic tool that provides high-quality translations. Visit https://translate.google.com, enter some text, and then pick your language. You can even have Google Translate play back the translation through audio. I once had a conversation with a Romanian man and an Italian woman all at the same time using this tool!

TIP

Adding subtitles to your video may seem like a lower priority consideration because you'd assume that most people are listening to the videos they're watching. However, many people are watching videos on their mobile phones, so Google has started to auto-play videos with no sound, instead using captions to entice people to click and watch more with the full audio. Further, millions of people are hearing impaired and use subtitles regularly.

TIP

You can provide translations and transcriptions to other people's videos. If you click on Your Contributions on the left-hand side menu in Creator Studio Classic, you'll see a listing of the contributions you've made.

Create

In the Create section of Creator Studio Classic, you find an audio library with tons of free music and sound effects. YouTube knows that when people are creating videos, they want to use music and sound effects, but most folk don't have access to royalty-free sound that they can easily use. This library offers a deep and comprehensive selection of audio files you can freely use without worrying about running afoul of copyright laws and policies.

The library contains two tabs:

>> **Free music,** which lets you browse songs by genre, mood (such as happy, dramatic, or sad), instrument, and duration.

>> **Sound effects,** with categories from alarms to animals, horror to human voices, tools to transportation, and even weapons to weather.

When you find a music track or sound effect you like, you can download the file and use it in your video editing. (Discover more about video editing in Chapter 11.)

An additional section under the Create tab, named Music Policies, helps you search for popular music tracks that you may want to use in your videos and determine whether they're available for use.

Your contributions

Any subtitles and closed captions that you've contributed to other people's videos are listed in the Your contributions section.

Auditing and Updating an Existing Channel

Auditing your YouTube Channel at least once a year, or even as frequently as once every quarter, is a good idea. When you *audit* your channel, you're simply stepping through a series of questions to ensure that everything is setup to maximize all the features a channel offers.

When it comes to your channel, focus on these three areas:

» Artwork

» Text areas

» Organization of posted videos

Channel art

The *banner image* is the large image spanning the top of a channel. Look at your current banner and decide whether it still accurately represents you, your brand, your company, your marketing efforts, and your channel's overall purpose.

Consider updating your banner if

» **Your company's brand image or style guidelines have changed.** Ensure the banner is an accurate reflection of your brand.

» **You have a new marketing campaign, product launch, or seasonal initiative.** If you have an active marketing campaign or initiative, you may want to update your banner to reflect that. For example, if you run a garden nursery, perhaps you'll update your banner to feature imagery that matches the season, such as spring flowers or fall clean-up.

>> **You want a refresh.** Sometimes updating your banner keeps the channel looking fresh. People visiting your channel regularly will see that it's being actively maintained.

Updating your banner is also a chance to ensure your social media channels are up to date. If you've created any new social media channels or built a new website, ensure the links on your banner are accurate.

Chapter 13 details the steps to update your channel art.

Text areas of your channel

Text lives in a couple of areas of your channel:

>> **Discussion or Community tab:** Depending on which tab you have, you can post text comments, links, and, with the Community tab, images, such as GIFs. The Community tab is slowly replacing the Discussion tab across all channels. Check to see whether people have commented on this tab and like, dislike, heart, reply, or delete.

>> **About section:** The About section describes your channel and its content. It also describes your brand or company, so, take a look at what's written to ensure that it accurately reflects who you are and how you are using your channel. Consider updating the text if anything has changed.

Video organization

Probably the most important part of auditing and managing your channel is how you organize your videos, Time spent organizing is never wasted. Playlists are the way you organize videos, helping people navigate all your content and encouraging them to watch more of your videos.

Every time you upload a video, you should add it to an existing playlist or create a new playlist for it. Check regularly to make sure that you haven't forgotten to add all your videos to at least one playlist. Likewise, don't forget to remove unnecessary videos from playlists and make sure that you give the playlist a description.

TIP

Playlists can appear in YouTube's search results, so creating playlists is a great way to help people find your videos and is a key technique for SEO. SEO stands for search engine optimization, which is the process of attempting to influence where your search result appears. For more on SEO, see the nearby sidebar.

THE SECRETS OF VIDEO SEO

If you want your website to appear higher up in Google's search engine's results pages, you can use SEO techniques to influence its position. SEO is classically made up of three components: the content itself, the way its technically presented, and signals, such as links, that endorse the content. The tricky thing with SEO is that Google and YouTube won't tell you how to do it because then people would game the system. Instead, what experts know about SEO comes from their own experiments aimed to test out Google's various algorithms.

SEO in relation to YouTube concerns influencing where your videos appear in YouTube's search results. Almost every client I ever work with asks me questions about video SEO because they are all keen to see their videos appear higher in the search results. My answer is always the same: Representatives of Google don't comment on SEO techniques. I then say, somewhat unofficially, that YouTube provides all the clues in the tools it offers. Fully using those tools can help you maximize your YouTube search engine optimization. If clients press for more details, I explain that I think they should keep three things in mind:

- YouTube is really only ever concerned with one thing, and that's giving users a great experience with quality content that they want to watch. Watch time is a key factor and well worth considering as a lever of SEO. If your watch time is high, that's probably a good thing.

- YouTube offers a whole slew of features and tools to help you manage your YouTube channel and publish your videos. Using each of these features to the maximum extent will give you the best SEO result.

- Having your video listed in the search results doesn't really matter (although I fully recognize that it helps!) The key is that if you're a marketer, you have the chance to use YouTube's ad solutions to intercept the moments that matter when your target audience may want to hear from you. Sure, SEO is great, especially if you're a creator who wants to grow your audience, but the most important thing is driving your business goals.

If you're making great content, utilizing all YouTube's features, and considering how you use their ad solutions, you'll be maximizing your overall YouTube opportunity to meet your business needs — and that's what's most important.

Being in Good Standing

YouTube uses the concept of *good standing* for your account. *Good standing* is a sort of evaluation YouTube applies to your channel based on its rules and guidelines, ensuring you're being compliant. Accounts in good standing that meet various criteria get access to special features. Accounts not in good standing will have various warnings about their infractions, and certain features may be limited as a result.

YouTube reviews all your content to ensure that it meets its standards and applies *strikes* if you break a rule. Think of a strike as a warning. If you have strikes against your account, YouTube limits your access to certain features. For example, if you get a strike on an active livestream, YouTube may disable your livestream access.

WARNING

If you get three strikes your channel will be deleted.

The two types of strikes are copyright strikes and community strikes. To see whether your account is in good standing, navigate to your channel, click on Creator Studio, and then click on Channel. Select Status and features if it's not automatically selected to see whether you have any copyright or community guidelines strikes. If your account is in good standing, you can also see a list of features that you have access to as a result of your account status.

Copyright strikes

YouTube applies a strike when you upload a video that contains content that you do not own the copyright for. For example, if you upload a TV show or movie, that's a pretty obvious copyright strike waiting to happen. A common example of a copyright strike comes from people using music that they don't have the rights to on their videos.

If you receive a copyright strike, it's because the copyright owner has sent YouTube a complete and valid legal request asking them to remove your video. A copyright strikes is one way YouTube complies with copyright law so that the platform doesn't become the Wild West of bootlegged movies and music.

You can see specific details of your copyright strikes by navigating to your channel, clicking on Creator Studio, clicking on Video Manager, and then choosing Copyright Notices.

The good news is that YouTube is forgiving. When you get a copyright strike, it's a warning. You can resolve a copyright strike in three ways:

>> **Wait for it to expire:** Copyright strikes expire after 90 days, as long as you complete something referred to as Copyright School. Visit www.youtube.com/copyright_school to find out more about this requirement.

>> **Get a retraction:** Contact the person who claimed your video and ask them to retract their claim of copyright infringement.

THE POWER OF CONTENT ID

Content ID is a really cool tool that YouTube created to help copyright owners identify and manage their content on YouTube. Say that you're the legal copyright owner of a song. You can upload your content to YouTube's Content ID system, and YouTube then scans every video that anyone else uploads to see whether they're using your content.

By working with the studios and record labels to create a library of content that it can check people's video against, YouTube is able to easily flag things like TV shows, movies, and music. For example, every time someone uploads a video that includes a Michael Jackson track, YouTube's system scans the video and compares it with its huge library of official music content from the record labels. It identifies someone's videos uses a Michael Jackson song and can take a few actions depending on what the copyright owner has requested.

Copyright owners get to choose the actions that happen when someone uses their copyright, which is one of the reasons Content ID is so great. They can choose to block a video from being seen completely, *monetize* the video, whereby they share in the ad revenue of the ads running against the video, or simply track the video's viewership statistics. Say that someone uses your song in a video that becomes incredibly popular. You, as the owner of the copyright for the song, can choose to share in monetization rather than having the video removed. You get to make money without doing anything!

Content ID is available only to copyright owners who meet certain criteria. If you want to find out about qualifying for Content ID, visit https://support.google.com/youtube/answer/1311402.

>> **Submit a counternotification:** If your video was mistakenly removed because it was misidentified as infringing or qualifies as a potential fair use case, you can submit a counternotification. For more on this process, visit https://support.google.com/youtube and search for counter notification basics.

WARNING

Simply deleting a video does not clear your strikes. The best approach is to not use any copyrighted material in your videos.

Community strikes

Community strikes are the type of strike you may receive if users are flagging your content as inappropriate. The key difference between a copyright strike and a community strike is that your video isn't necessarily breaking any copyright rules. However, it is potentially infringing YouTube's community guidelines — for example, by being racist, sexually explicit, abusive, or offensive.

YouTube is a site that relies on user-generated content, so these guidelines are in place to ensure that the platform doesn't fill up with potentially offensive content. When a user flags a video, a YouTube team member reviews the video. Your video can stay on the site until reviewed. Users can report videos, comments, and channels as violating community guidelines.

If you get a community strike, you'll receive an email and see an alert in your account's channel settings with information about why your content has been removed. Strikes expire three months after they're issued. While you have an active strike on your account, you may not be able to access some features.

If you receive multiple strikes, here's what happens:

WARNING

» For your **first strike,** you may see some restrictions on your ability to do things like livestream.

Don't try to set up another account to livestream, as YouTube will know and may terminate your accounts as a result.

» For your **second strike** within a three-month period, you won't be able to post any new content to YouTube for two weeks. You get full access back after those two weeks.

» If you get **three strikes** within a three-month period, that's it. Your account gets terminated.

You can appeal strikes by navigating to your YouTube channel, clicking Creator Studio, and choosing Channel ➪ Status and features. In the Community Guidelines Status section, choose to appeal this decision.

After you submitted your appeal, you get an email from YouTube letting you know the result. If you didn't violate the community guidelines, YouTube will reinstate your video and remove the strike.

TIP

Read more about YouTube's Community guidelines at `www.youtube.com/yt/about/policies/#community-guidelines`.

6

Measuring Success

Chapter **16**

Ad Campaign Metrics That Matter

The biggest challenge people face when it comes to reporting is understanding which metrics really matter. Not all are equal, and metrics that matter can be something of a philosophical choice based on how you, as a marketer, think and operate.

It's my belief that amateur marketers neglect their reporting, whereas sophisticated marketers make time every day to understand how their target audience are responding to their campaigns, iterating, evolving, and optimizing. A marketer should know how the reporting tool works and how to interpret the data and act.

In this chapter, I walk through the reporting capabilities of the Google Ads interface. I also describe the various metrics that you can use to evaluate and improve the performance of your campaigns.

REMEMBER

The options you see in the reporting section can depend on the campaigns you've set up. Don't be alarmed if something isn't listed or if you choose a report and see no data.

Getting to Know Google Ads Reports

Within the Google Ads tool, you'll find a whole section dedicated to reports. Just look in the upper right-hand corner of the top menu bar for the labelled icon. You can look at your ad campaign performance through the lens of many different metrics. You need to regularly check how things are going so that you can be sure that your marketing budget is being spent wisely.

Using predefined reports

Google Ads offers a raft of predefined reports that will satisfy the needs of most marketers. To access these readymade reports:

1. **Choose one of your active campaigns by clicking Campaigns in the menu on the left side and choosing a campaign from the main window.**

   Details about that specific campaign appear.

2. **Click on Reports in the upper right-hand corner of the top toolbar.**

3. **From the drop-down menu that appears, choose Reports.**

   You see a list of any previously saved reports, along with an option to create a custom report.

4. **Click on View all to see the predefined reports.**

5. **Choose the report you'd like to view from the expandable list that appears.**

TIP

If you're not sure which report to start with, I suggest you look at the Campaign report, the Ad report, and the Audience report, which are all listed under Basic reports. These three reports tell you how much you're spending, what you're getting in terms of clicks, which ads are performing best, and which audiences are responding the most. That information is usually enough to make some educated choices as to what you may like to do more or less of as you optimize your efforts.

Basic reports

The Basic reports section of Google Ads, shown in Figure 16-1, contains lots of predefined reports that satisfy most marketer's needs. Your options for Basic reports appear first, with expandable boxes for other types of reports available. You can choose from the following reports:

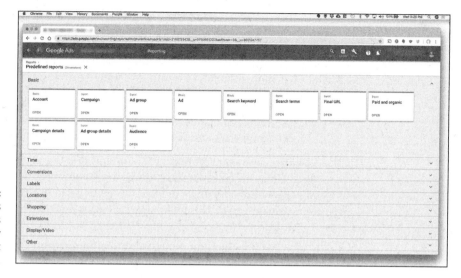

FIGURE 16-1:
The Basic reports
section contains
virtually every
kind of report
that you desire.

>> **Campaign** provides an overview of all your campaigns and your key campaign performance metrics, such as how many people have seen and clicked your ads and how much you've spent so far.

>> **Ad group** is similar to the Campaign report except that it sorts your results by your ad groups, not your campaigns. This report helps you see which ad groups are performing best regardless of which campaign they exist within.

>> **Ad** shows you which of your video ads are performing best. Look at this report, which I really like, to see if one ad is significantly performing better than others.

>> **Search keyword** and **Search terms** show you the performance of your keywords if you're running a search campaign. This report doesn't apply to video-only campaigns.

>> **Final URL** is an interesting report, showing you the performance of your campaigns and ad groups listed by the final destination webpage people clicked through to. If you're running campaigns to drive people to a variety of your webpages, this handy view lets you see which pages are getting the most or least clicks, along with how much those visits to your web pages cost in media spend.

>> **Paid and organic** concerns search campaigns and doesn't apply to video campaigns. It lets you see how often pages from your website are being shown in Google's organic search results listings and which search terms triggered those results to show.

>> **Campaign details** gives a more detailed overview of the way you've set up your campaigns. This report includes details on whether the campaign is

enabled, its type (video, display, search), your bidding strategy, and other campaign level settings. Campaign details is a nice overview if you're running many campaigns so that you can see the full picture of what you have active.

>> **Ad group details** is similar to Campaign details. This report gives you a snapshot of your various ad groups, such as whether they're enabled, the bidding strategy, and other ad group level settings. Use this report if you want a picture of the general makeup of all your ad groups.

>> **Audience** shows your campaign and ad group performance, but this time the data is split by the audiences you're targeting. For example, this report can easily show you if a particular affinity audience is performing better than others. Audience is another great report to look at regularly.

I don't think basic is the right way to describe these reports because it suggests they give you only basic information. In fact, they give you tons of great data that is typically of most interest to marketers. A better name would be "the most popular reports."

Figure 16-2 shows an example of a predefined Campaign report. Most reports take this format of showing a table of data. In this report, you can see the campaigns and their status (enabled, paused, or removed), how many clicks and impressions they have delivered, and other data. (*Impressions* is simply the number of times your ad was shown.)

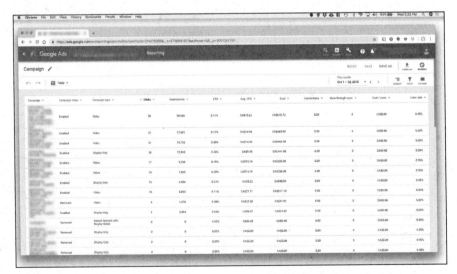

FIGURE 16-2:
Reports take the format of a table of data. You can sort by any dimension.

TIP

You can click the down arrow against any row header to sort the report by that dimension. For example, if you want to see your cheapest cost-per-click, click on Avg. CPC and sort from Low to High.

Time

In the Time section, you can choose to see reports based on day, week, month, quarter, year, and even hour of the day. The typical metrics of impressions, click-through rate, cost and so on are broken out by time dimension. This data is especially handy for marketers who are promoting retail locations with certain operating hours or any time-based need.

Conversions

If you're interested in ensuring that your campaigns deliver specific conversions, such as sales or downloads, you'll want to spend time in the Conversions report section. Most people use search and display campaigns to drive conversions, but you can use video ads to drive conversions, too.

You can choose from the following reports:

» **Conversion category** lets you see your conversions aggregated into various categories, such as all product sales, website actions, or in-app downloads.

» **Conversion action name** shows the conversions you've had sorted by the action that took place, such as website purchases, app downloads, or phone calls. For example, someone can convert when they take an action on your website, such as signing up for an email address or reaching the thank-you for purchasing page.

» **Conversion source** lets you see where the conversion took place. The conversion can come from an app or a potential customer clicking your phone number in the ad or your number listed on your mobile site. This report breaks out the different conversion sources as well as the number and cost of conversions.

» **Store visit** matches your advertising online to people who actually visit your physical location, such as your retail store, hotel, or auto dealership. Advertisers must meet specific criteria to be eligible for this report and need to contact a Google Ads representative to set it up. Visit https://support.google.com and search for "About store visit conversions" for more details.

TIP

You see conversion data if you have set up your campaign with conversion goals. See Chapter 7 for more information.

Labels

Labels is a bit of a weird report because at first it seems like a duplication of the reports listed in the Basic reports section. The labels section is a way of collecting various campaigns, ad groups, and ads into a new collection that you give your own unique name.

Ignore the ones that are already listed by default and instead set up your own labels. For example, I may want to create a label for my newest experimental campaigns, ad groups, and ads. I can choose to label any combination of campaigns, ad groups, and ads with "My Experiments" and easily see a report that pulls all of them together in one place, even though structurally they may exist in a variety of places within my Google Ads account.

TIP

I consider Labels a bit of an advanced feature within Google Ads reports, and most people won't need to make use of it. If you do want to try using labels, visit `https://support.google.com` and search for "Create, use, and manage labels" for details on how to set up labels.

Locations

The Locations report section is especially useful for marketers who are promoting their products or services that are bound to specific geographic areas — for example, if you're a chiropractor, a chain of restaurants, or a region-based car repair shop.

You can choose from the following reports:

>> **Geographic** is the report that breaks out the performance of your campaigns by user locations and locations of interest based on Google or Google Maps searches, sorted typically by clicks. You can see the country, region, area, city, and even zip or postal code where people are clicking the most on your ads.

>> **User locations** is similar to the Geographic report, but it shows only the actual physical locations of users, regardless of the locations they may have shown interest in. It's a subtle distinction, and I recommend using the Geographic report over the user Location report for most applications.

>> **Distance** shows you the distance between the location that triggered your ad and your closest business location. This cool report is used only if you're running search network and shopping campaigns.

TIP

If you're seeing people in some locations responding more to your video ads than other locations, consider whether you should tweak your campaign settings to focus more on that area or alter your creative to speak to people directly in that region.

Shopping

The predefined Shopping report appears if you've set up campaigns that use TrueView for shopping (see Chapter 7). In this section, you find reports for every possible dimension for shopping campaigns. Not all shopping campaigns use all these dimensions. You find reports for

>> **Category,** such as sports equipment

>> **Product type,** such as rackets

>> **Brand,** such as Wilson

>> **Item ID,** which is the number you use to identify the product you're selling

>> **MC ID,** which stands for Merchant Center ID and is the accompanying storefront you set up with Google to sell products

>> **Store ID,** so that if you have many stores you can assign them a Store ID

You may also see additional dimensions, depending on your campaign setup.

Extensions

In the Extensions report section are reports for sitelinks, call, app, offer, location, callout, and review extensions, along with many more.

Extensions appear only on ads running in the search network and don't apply to video ad campaigns.

Display/Video

The Display/Video section contains some of the most popular reports that apply specifically to display and video campaigns:

>> **Topic** shows you the performance of your campaigns sorted through the dimension of topic. In Chapter 7, I cover choosing topic targeting, which lets your show your ads on topically related sites within the Google Display Network.

>> **YouTube search terms** shows you the search terms that have triggered your ads to show. If you set up search terms for your campaign (see Chapter 7), you see which ones are performing best here.

>> **Automatic placements** shows you where your ad was served up based on Google's choice. When you first set up a campaign, you're able to either manually choose the placements of where you'd like your ads to appear (for

example, specific websites, YouTube channels, and mobile apps) or have Google automatically choose the placements for you.

» **Display and video keywords** show you the keywords and phrases that triggered your video (or display) ad to be shown.

Other

The Other section contains two miscellaneous reports:

» **Free clicks** is a report that sounds promising, but it isn't. Google Ads reports some clicks that are considered free. For example, for some video ad types if someone clicks your video ad to initiate playing, you won't be charged until the viewer watches the minimum amount of time. Other free click types include some website and image ad interactions.

My advice is to not worry about this report. It's collecting pretty minor interactions and doesn't yield useful information that can help you optimize your campaign as much as other reports.

» **Billed cost** shows adjustments that Google makes to specific media you've bought. Again, this report isn't the most useful, but it's helpful if you want to comb through the fine details of adjustments that were made to what you were charged.

TIP

Creating a custom report

While the predefined reports described in the previous sections should cover most people's needs, you can create your own custom report using only the data points that you are most concerned with (see Figure 16-3).

To create a custom report:

1. **In the Reports section, click on + Custom.**

2. **From the drop-down menu that appears, choose your chart type.**

   Your choices include table, line, bar, pie, or scatter.

3. **Drag and drop any number of metrics, such as campaigns or ad groups, from the menu on the left side of the screen to the main window.**

   The metrics are added to your report.

   It's a long list! Experiment with adding different dimensions until you're happy.

FIGURE 16-3:
You can create a
custom report
with any
dimension
you'd like.

4. **Name the report and click on Save.**

   You can access this report at any time or schedule it to be sent automatically. (For more on scheduling, see the section "Scheduling reports.")

Creating a custom dashboard

A *dashboard*, shown in Figure 16-4, is exactly what it sounds like: a handy single place where you can see the metrics that matter to you in one place. A dashboard can help you scan your data quickly and look for issues and opportunities. You can share dashboards with other people, which is a great way to focus a team's attention on the most important numbers.

1. **To create a new dashboard, click on Reports at the top of your account.**

2. **Click on Dashboards from the drop-down menu.**

3. **Click on the blue + icon to create a new dashboard.**

   Any previously created dashboards are listed on this page.

   You'll see a page with a series of grids and another blue + icon.

FIGURE 16-4:
Create your own
dashboard with
the most
important metrics
to you. It'll save
you time for
at-a-glance
check-ins.

4. Add notes, tables, charts, and scorecards to your dashboard by clicking the blue + icon.

   You're walked through the process of creating a custom report (see the previous section).

5. **Adjust the placement of elements so that they're to your liking.**

   As you build your dashboard, the elements you add behave like movable boxes that you can expand and contract. You can change where these elements appear and the amount of space they take up.

6. **When you're done, name the dashboard and save it.**

   You see your finished dashboard. You can edit it anytime to add, remove, and tweak your choices.

Scheduling reports

If you like a particular report and want to review it regularly, you can save time by scheduling it to be sent to you and any colleagues automatically.

1. **In the upper right-hand corner of the report you're viewing, click the Schedule icon.**

   The Schedule dialog box, shown in Figure 16-5, appears.

2. **Enter your email address or check a box to have the report sent to all account users with access to view reports.**

3. **Choose whether you'd like the report emailed one time only, every day, every week, or on the first day of each month.**

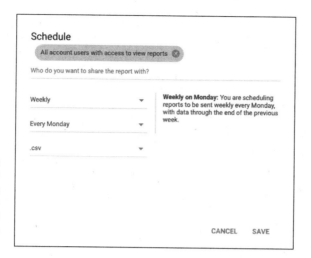

FIGURE 16-5:
Schedule your
favorite reports
to automatically
be emailed to you
and other team
members.

4. **Choose the file format you'd like to use for the report, such as .CSV or.XLS.**

5. **When ready, click on Save, and your report will be scheduled.**

Measuring the Metrics That Matter

All these reports contain lots of great data, but data can be useless if you don't know how to interpret the meaning and decide whether something is important. The challenge I've seen so many clients wrestle with is determining what numbers they should pay attention to. Sure, your video had a lot of views or likes, but did that matter to your marketing goals?

In Chapter 7, you can find a breakdown of the different goal-based campaigns you can easily create within Google Ads for your paid YouTube advertising efforts, along with details as to why you may choose a certain campaign type. In this section, I walk through each of these campaign types, suggesting the metrics that I think relate and matter most:

» Brand awareness and reach

» Brand and product consideration

» Website traffic and leads

While you can look at any and all metrics for a campaign, a handful of metrics usually matter more than others. These metrics tend to be the most important indicators that your campaign is delivering. Note that the metrics that matter most are all debatable because the ones that matter are what you decide and aren't necessarily the same for someone else. The real trick is knowing what matters to you and focusing on those numbers.

REMEMBER

You aren't limited to these campaign goal types. You can create your own custom campaign in Google Ads, which lets you decide what you want your campaign to deliver and how you'll determine success. Check Chapter 7 for details on setting up a custom campaign.

Brand awareness and reach metrics

Awareness is all about getting people to know who you are. If people don't know you exist, they can't buy your product or use your service.

Marketers interested in brand awareness and reach are primarily focused on showing their brand and message to as many people as possible. The idea is that one of the strongest drivers in getting a consumer to take an action, such as purchasing something, is the ability to simply know and recall the brand and product. If you can tell as many people as possible about your brand often enough so they remember, you'll deliver a successful campaign.

Think of the brands who sponsor athletes, partner with celebrities, or spend big budgets on TV spots during the Super Bowl, billboards in Times Square, or the YouTube Masthead. They're trying to reach large audiences.

Two main metrics matter for a successful brand awareness and reach campaign:

>> **Reach:** The number of how many people who see your ad

>> **Frequency:** How often people see your message

YouTube is a fantastic way to reach a large number of people, and based on your marketing needs, you'll need to decide how many people you want to reach. The number of impressions is the simplest measure of success in delivering awareness.

Another way of measuring how many people you reach is the unique reach metric. The unique reach metric includes the different users who saw your ad and the average number of times they saw your ad. For example, if I see your ad once, that's one person reached with one impression. If I see your ad again, that's one person reached with two impressions, which is a frequency of two.

TIP

You can view your reach and frequency data by adding those columns to a custom report and creating a table. If reach and frequency data is available to you, those options appear in your left-hand side menu. Look for them under Reach metrics. (For more on creating a custom report, see the section earlier in this chapter.)

A common question I am asked is "How many people should I reach and with what frequency?" Unfortunately, there is no one-size-fits-all answer to that question. Some marketers are lucky to find that they need to show their ad to a person only once or twice to make their target audience aware. On the other hand, other marketers may show their ads lots of times to people but not make much of a tangible impact. Only through testing can advanced marketers determine how many people they need to reach and the frequency of ads they need to deliver before they see the results they want. (For more on this topic, see the nearby sidebar on brand lift.)

TIP

Think of brand awareness as the foundation of your marketing strategy. Brand awareness, though, can often require a larger media budget and doesn't guarantee immediate results, such as sales. Larger, more established marketers can make use of brand awareness campaigns, whereas smaller advertisers just getting started or who need to focus on short-term results can focus on performance campaigns like conversion. See Chapter 7 for information on setting up your brand awareness and reach campaign.

Brand and product consideration metrics

After people are familiar with your brand, product, or service, the next step in the consumer journey is to encourage them to consider you as a viable option. Of the people who are aware of you, *consideration* is the subset of people who are now actively thinking "This might be for me."

Think about buying a car. Most people can name a lot of car brands, but when you start the process of searching for a new car, you usually have a handful of makes and models on your list that you're already considering. Some of the cars you are aware of have moved into an active consideration set.

How you measure consideration depends on what you're marketing, so consider the following as metric signals of increased consideration:

>> People clicking on your ad and investigating your website

>> Time spent on your product or service pages

>> Downloads of files like ebooks or guides that may educate someone before they consider making a purchase

>> Calls or inquiries for more information

>> Store visits, if someone is browsing but not purchasing

>> Email newsletter sign ups

» Follows on your social media profiles

» More views of your videos on YouTube

Other metrics may also signal that someone is showing more than just awareness of you and actively considering your brand, product, or service.

TIP

You can find reports for metrics like clicks on ads in your Campaign, Ad Groups and Ads reports, and for other metrics, such as which pages people visited on your website and how long they spent there, in Google Analytics. (For more information, see the nearby sidebar "Going further with Google Analytics.")

GOING FURTHER WITH GOOGLE ANALYTICS

While the reports in the Google Ads tool are comprehensive, how many people see your ad and interact with it is just part of the picture. People may click your video ad to visit your website or visit it on their own accord at a later date. To get the full picture, Google Analytics is the free tool from Google that provides deep reporting on your website and apps, and setting it up should be your top priority.

In Google Analytics, you can see how many people visit your site, how many people are new versus returning visitors, how long they spend on your site, what they look at, and whether they convert — for example, by purchasing something from you. Google Analytics captures everyone who visits your site or app and lets you know where they came from, such as from a paid ad, a piece of video content, your social profiles, by email marketing or by typing your web address directly.

Visit http://analytics.google.com and use your Google account to sign up. You'll be asked to add a tracking code to your website, and within a few hours, you'll start to see real-time and historical data.

You can find my favorite report in Google Analytics in the left-hand side menu by choosing Acquisition ⇨ All Traffic ⇨ Source/Medium. The "Source/Medium" report shows you where your visitors came from before arriving at your site. This report shows you every single source of traffic that sent someone to your site. You can uncover some real marketing gems. When I was working at MTV, I found an entertainment site buried in this report that was sending our site a few hundred people a month, sometimes a few thousand. I emailed the editor of the site and agreed to send him advance notice of content we'd be posting to the site. He started to link to us more and regularly sent more than 200,000 people a month, without it costing me anything! Proof that Google Analytics is an important tool to help you grow!

BRAND LIFT

How you actually measure increases in awareness and consideration requires an advanced approach. *Brand lift* is a measure of how your video ads are affecting the perceptions and behaviors of your target audience. It's a sort of macro view of how all your YouTube engagement metrics are impacting your audience's awareness of your brand, their ability to recall your ad, and interest in and consideration of your brand or product. Brand lift is essentially a methodology to see if your YouTube efforts are delivering the change in the target audience you'd like to see, going beyond the typical metrics of how many people saw your video ad. Brand lift is measured in two ways. The first is to isolate a random group of people as a control group and not show them your ad. Another group, the exposed group, sees your ad. After a short while, a one-question survey is provided to both groups to see whether the exposed group has been impacted by your marketing efforts.

The second way to measure brand lift is by looking at how people's search behavior has changed — for example, whether more people are now searching Google.com for your brand and product.

Google offers a service called Brand Lift Study to those of you who have Google Ads accounts with the support of a Google representative. You can call the Google Ads support center to ask whether you qualify or read more about the criteria at `https://support.google.com` by searching *brand lift studies for video campaigns.*

TIP

In Chapter 7, you can find out how to set up a campaign with the goal of brand and product consideration, a campaign type that presents you with preset options to help people who are researching the kinds of things you offer to find and engage with you, leading to consideration.

Website traffic and leads

You may be a marketer who wants to grow the number of people visiting your website, or you may be focused on getting *leads,* visitors who are prospective buyers of your product or service and who will convert to a purchase or similar action.

Marketers interested in these campaign types should focus on two main measures of success:

>> **Clicks,** which is the total number of people who clicked through to your website. You can find this metric in lots of Google Ads reports, especially in your Campaign report.

>> **Conversions,** which is the total number of people who took the action you defined as a conversion. (See the nearby sidebar "Conversions" for more on conversions.)

TIP

When you're looking at how many clicks your campaign delivered, look at your average cost-per-click. This metric appears in the Campaign reports and is the average amount each click cost you.

Marketers should decide what they consider to be a reasonable price to pay for each click. Usually, that amount is calculated based on the value of those clicks as they convert to something like a purchase. For example, if I find my cost per click is $1 per click and I get 100 clicks, I will have spent $100 of my media budget. If I know five of those people will convert to buy a $200 product, I'll have made revenue of $900, based on sales of $1,000 worth of product minus the $100 of marketing cost for the clicks. That's a great return! If no one purchases, I have to decide whether those 100 clicks were worth it by some other measure or whether I wasted my marketing budget.

TIP

If you want more people to convert, consider optimizing your *landing page,* which is the page people arrive at after they click on your ad. The landing page should be easy to read, give them all the information they need to decide along with links to learn more details if needed, offer compelling reasons to purchase immediately with an easy way to add your product to their cart and check out. A lot of information is out there on how to optimize landing pages, so you can do a search to find some tips if your landing page isn't doing a good job of converting.

TIP

Although video ad campaigns can be an effective driver of both website traffic and leads, I recommend setting up both a search and a display campaign, which can be effective driving traffic. Search and display campaigns are easier and quicker to set up and often deliver a cheaper cost-per-click.

CONVERSIONS

The concept of a conversion is an important metric for success, especially when you're interested in traffic and leads. A *conversion* is that moment when someone takes an action that moves him from being a potential customer to an actual customer.

Conversions aren't limited just to actions like purchasing a product and can include things like signing up for emails, subscribing to your YouTube channels, calling your store or booking an appointment, writing a review, or taking any number of actions where the person actually does something that has meaningful value to you. You can define what you consider a conversion when you set up your campaign (see Chapter 7).

TIP

In Chapter 2, I describe a classic consumer journey where your target audience becomes aware of you, starts to consider and engage with you, eventually purchases from you, and becomes a loyal advocate of your brand. In this chapter, I cover the metrics for success for Google Ads campaigns that deliver awareness, consideration, and leads that convert to a purchase or action, but that's only part of that complete consumer journey.

A content strategy is a great driver of engagement, loyalty, and advocacy. You can refer to Chapter 9 for more information on how to develop a content strategy. Chapter 17 has details on content metrics that matter and includes how you can measure engagement, loyalty, and advocacy marketing results.

Think of it this way: You'll use your video ad campaigns to attract new customers (increasing awareness and consideration), you'll use the video content on your YouTube channel to further engage them, your ad campaign to convert them (to something like a purchase), and your content to keep them coming back as loyal fans. You can craft this intertwining flow however you want, deciding the role you want ads versus content to play. Overall, a complete YouTube marketing strategy combines both advertising campaigns and a content strategy working symbiotically.

Optimizing Your Ad Campaign

If you look at your reporting on a regular basis, you can identify opportunities for *optimization,* or ways to improve the results of your campaign as it delivers.

If you're not seeing the numbers you want, consider the variables you can tweak and the levers you can pull. For example, you may need to increase your budget or tweak your campaign bid settings, target a different audience, or change your ad creative. Re-evaluate every choice you make when setting up your campaign after you have some data telling you what is and is not working.

Tweaking your creative

When you launch your first campaign, you may be using only one video ad. As data comes in, look to see how it's performing and consider

>> Testing different versions of your video ad by making some small edits

>> Trying different titles and thumbnails

>> Making sure that you have a really compelling call to action to encourage someone to click

>> If you're using TrueView (see Chapter 4), seeing how many people are skipping the ad

>> Developing theories about what worked or didn't work and using these theories to inform the next video ad you make

REMEMBER

Your video ad is probably the biggest lever you can pull on to improve your campaign performance. Take a look at the YouTube Ads Leaderboard (`www.thinkwith google.com/advertising-channels/video/leaderboards`) for inspiration on what makes great video ads and check Chapter 6 for more best practices to make great creative.

Experimenting with ad formats

You can experiment with quite a few different ad formats to see which one works best for you. If you've made a video ad for only one format, such as TrueView, consider making edits of your video so that you can use it in other ad formats. (See Chapter 4 for an overview of ad formats.)

For example:

>> Make a shorter version of your video ad so that it's only 15 seconds long.

>> Make an even shorter version of your video so that it's a 6-second bumper, an ad which works great on mobile devices.

>> Make a longer video if people are watching your video ad to completion, which suggests that people like it!

>> Run companion display ads when your video ad is playing to reaffirm your message and encourage clicks.

Targeting new audiences

Improving your video ad creative and maximizing your use of ad formats available are probably the two best levers to improve your campaign's performance (see the preceding two sections). However, the third lever is to ensure that you're talking to the right people. (Chapter 7 covers the different options you have available to target audiences.)

Tweak each of your audience targeting settings to see whether you can improve your results:

>> Use demographic targeting to target people based on gender, age, and other criteria, such as household income.

>> Specifically target people based on their interests and habits with affinity targeting.

>> Reach people based on whatever they're currently looking to purchase using in-market audiences, life events, and custom intent.

>> Remarket to people who have previously interacted with you in some way, which can be a powerful targeting method.

TIP

Some marketers keep their targeting broad initially and then make refinements to their campaign after they see who is responding to their ads. This strategy is often referred to as a *run-of-site strategy*, where you let your ads run anywhere on a site (like YouTube) and then optimize as you go.

Modifying campaign settings

You can play with a lot of variables and settings in Google Ads, which can have a big impact on results. How you set up your campaign can make a big difference. Consider

>> **Targeting all the relevant locations and languages and devices.** Opening up your campaign to reach a broad audience is a great way to find who responds. You can narrow down who you target later.

>> **Letting Google automatically manage options where possible.** Google always optimizes your campaign's delivery based on your goals.

>> **Not overly limiting your campaign initially with too many options.** Keeping things broad can help you find the best settings as time goes on.

TIP

Chapter 5 discusses the benefits of buying media yourself versus using an agency partner to help you. If at any point you find yourself feeling overwhelmed or unsure, consider reaching out to an experienced partner for help. Most quality service providers have set up many campaigns and can easily find ways to optimize your campaign for you.

TIP

The Recommendations section within Google Ads periodically provides automated optimization suggestions uniquely based on your campaign's performance. Check this page regularly.

Altering bidding and budgets

The performance of your campaign can come down to the basic issue of budget. My last recommendation for optimization, after exhausting all others, is to increase your budget. If you make a great ad, choose smart targeting options, and set up your campaign but it's not delivering, your bidding strategy and budgets may need to change. For example, if your ad is performing but isn't reaching enough people, increasing your budget can help get your ad in front of more people. Chapter 7 details all the bidding and budget settings you can tweak.

Here are a few changes you can make to your bidding and budgets:

>> **See whether small incremental bid increases help more people see your ad.** You don't need to increase your budget by a lot immediately.

>> **Look to see whether your daily budget is big enough.** Perhaps your video ad is shown in the morning and exhausts your budget. Adding more daily budget can help your video ad show up more often.

>> **If you're reducing your audience to a more focused group, you may need to increase your bids to ensure that you win in the auction to reach those people.** Often, the more targeted your audience, the more competitive your bid will need to be.

>> **If you're finding your bids aren't winning in the auction, you may need to increase your budgets and bids.** You may be targeting a competitive area. If so, either increase your budgets and bids or consider targeting different audiences that are lower competition.

TIP

The single best tip I can provide to help optimize your campaign is to look at your reports daily. The Google Ad's solution can be a bit overwhelming due to its comprehensiveness, which sometimes puts people off, but you'll be surprised at how quickly you'll learn your way around the tool and start to see opportunities.

TIP

Google offers a TrueView Optimization Playbook at www.thinkwithgoogle.com/products/youtube-trueview, which is an excellent guide to more advanced optimization techniques. This PDF, listed at the bottom of the page, is well worth the read.

Chapter **17**

Content Metrics That Matter

After you create and upload your videos to your channel, you can look at your reports to see what people are responding to. This data can help you develop ideas for your next videos so that you maximize your chance to grow your audience. Just like the data and reporting discussed in Chapter 16, some metrics matter more than others. Knowing the difference is key so that you can focus on growth.

In this chapter, I walk through the reporting features of your YouTube channel, help you determine which metrics are the ones you should pay the most attention to, and show you ways to improve and optimize your content efforts.

Getting to Know YouTube Analytics

The YouTube Creator Classic tool has a fully featured Analytics section, with lots of reports to help you understand how your video content is performing. Figure 17-1 shows the Overview page you see when you first click on Analytics in the left-hand side menu of the Creator Classic tool.

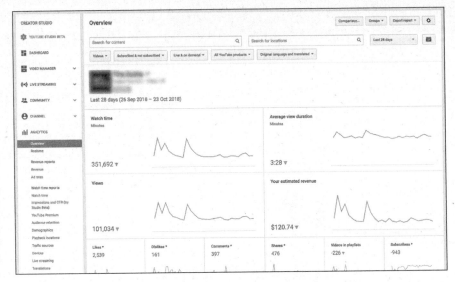

FIGURE 17-1:
The Overview
page in the
Analytics section
of the YouTube
Creator Classic
tool.

Some of the most important reports on this dashboard are for

>> Watch time

>> Average view duration

>> Views

>> Estimated revenue (if you're in the YouTube Partner Program)

>> Your Top Ten videos

Use the Overview page for an at-a-glance look of how your channel is performing and then use the left-hand side menu to dive deeper into the more detailed reports for each of these within the three main sections of reporting:

>> Revenue reports

>> Watch time reports

>> Interaction reports

At the time of writing, YouTube Creator Classic is the fully featured tool you use to manage your YouTube channel. However, it's slowly being replaced by YouTube Studio, a new tool in beta. All the reports listed in this chapter will appear in a similar form within the YouTube Studio tool.

You can view real-time data in the Realtime section, which shows you view counts from the last 60 minutes. The reports update every 10 seconds, which is great if you find one of your videos is *going viral*, meaning that it's taking off and being shared around the world.

TIP

You'll be able to export any of the reports in this chapter by clicking on the Export Report button in the upper right-hand corner. Use this feature if you want to share your reports with others.

TIP

In Chapter 2, I cover how marketers can use YouTube to deliver to their business goals, describing a classic consumer journey starting with awareness of your brand and ending with loyalty and advocacy. You can use paid advertising campaigns using Google Ads (see Chapter 7) for awareness, consideration, and conversion, and you can use a content strategy (see Chapter 9) to drive engagement, loyalty, and advocacy, but please don't think that these two things are mutually exclusive. They work together and overlap to such an extent that the lines where an ad becomes content and vice versa can blur. You can use ads and content in any combination to deliver to any marketing goal. I make this distinction only to keep things straightforward for marketers getting started with YouTube.

Revenue Reports

If your channel is part of the YouTube Partner Program, you see a section labelled Revenue reports (see Figure 17-2). This section details how much money your channel is making you and consists of two reports:

>> **Revenue:** You can see in Figure 17-2 that this channel has made a total of $120.74 in the last 28 days. Of this amount, $100.43 came from sharing in the ad revenue of the ads that YouTube sold and ran against this channel's videos, and $20.31 came from people who subscribe to YouTube Premium (YouTube's ad-free subscription service.)

>> **Ad rates:** The Ad Rates section lets you know the approximate CPM (cost per thousand) that YouTube is able to charge for the ads running against your videos.

TIP

If you scroll down either of these pages, you can see a listing of your videos sorted by revenue. This listing is a great way to see which videos are making you the most money so that you can make more of them!

FIGURE 17-2:
Check the money
you're earning
from your
YouTube channel
in the Revenue
reports section.

Watch Time Reports

The Watch Time Reports section is where you should spend most of your time because it contains the best reports to help you determine what's working and what's not. Along with the Interaction reports, which are described later in this chapter, it'll give you a sense of how much people are engaging with your content.

Watch time

WARNING

A common mistake is thinking that videos views are the most important metric for success, but that's not the case. The most important metric is *watch time,* which is the aggregated amount of time your viewers watch your video. Watch time doesn't have a more specific definition because it's part of the algorithm's magic formula, but the general idea is that YouTube likes videos that encourage people to watch longer. Longer doesn't necessarily mean that you have to make videos that are longer because watch time accrues for all your videos watched in any particular viewing session.

Just like with Google's search engine, which ranks web pages that are the best answers to someone's search query, YouTube is rewarding videos that are the best answer to what people want to watch. The lesson is simple: Make videos that people will want to watch.

The Watch time report shows you the total amount of watch time (in minutes) that your videos have delivered in a set time period. You want that number to increase to improve the performance of your channel.

You can scroll down to see a list of your videos. Click a video to see a page with a more detailed watch time report. This detailed report gives you a sense of what content viewers actually watch, as opposed to videos that they click on and then abandon.

WARNING

The Watch time report also shows you how many video views you've had. Some people are tempted to inflate their view counts by buying views from nefarious sources. Don't. You risk being banned from YouTube and having your channel dinged or deleted.

Impressions and click-through rate

The Impressions report tells you how many times your videos' thumbnails were shown to people and then how often those viewers clicked through to watch those videos (the CTR or *click-through rate*). You are able to see how much watch time those impressions and clicks led to (see Figure 17-3).

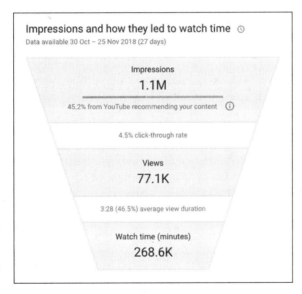

FIGURE 17-3:
A funnel graphic from the Impressions and click-through rate report.

You see the sources of where your thumbnails where shown, giving you a sense for how people are finding your videos. You also see when videos

>> Appeared in browse features, such as the home page or subscription feed

>> Were suggested videos next to or after another video has played

>> Were found through a YouTube search

> » Were promoted on other people's YouTube channels — for example, when another channel shares your video on its Community or Discussion tab
>
> » Were played within your or other people's playlists

TIP

Well-crafted titles and compelling thumbnails are one of the most important ways to encourage people to click to watch your videos. Chapter 14 provides detailed recommendations on how to maximize their impact. Try tweaking your titles and thumbnails with a new upload, experimenting until you find an approach that works really well. If your click-through rate increases, your title and thumbnails are working harder for you.

YouTube Premium

The YouTube Premium report gives you a further breakdown of how much watch time and how many views your videos have had from people who subscribe to YouTube's ad-free subscription service. I don't think this report is important.

Audience retention

A much more important report than the YouTube Premium report (see preceding section) is the Audience retention report. I love this report because it shows you how much of your video people watched.

For example, in Figure 17-4, you can see that this video lasted 9 minutes and 18 seconds, and the average view duration was 4 minutes and 40 seconds, or 50 percent. If you look at the graph, a steady line declines, which is pretty normal. You can click on Relative audience retention to see how well this video retains viewers compared with your other videos.

TIP

If you see a big drop at some point during one of your videos, play the video back to see what happens at that moment that causes people to abandon watching.

Demographics

The Demographics report gives you a breakdown of the people who watch your channel (you can choose specific videos, too) based on their age and gender. You can also click to see their geographic region.

TIP

If you see that your videos are popular in other countries, consider translating those videos into their languages to reach more people (see Chapter 15).

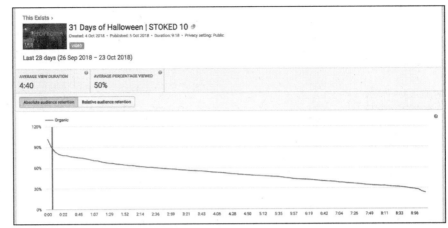

FIGURE 17-4:
The Audience
retention report
shows you when
people stop
watching your
videos and how
many watched to
the end.

Playback locations

The Playback locations report tells you where your video was watched, such as on YouTube, embedded within a website, or on your channel page.

TIP

Most people will view your video on the YouTube watch-page (that's what YouTube calls a *video page)*, but I like to check the report to see whether the video was embedded somewhere. That data can help you find the websites that like your content enough to link to it. Consider how you can use those sites in the future to send more traffic to your videos.

Traffic sources

The Traffic sources report builds on the Impressions and Playback location reports, showing you all the places where people found and watched your video sorted by the watch time generated. Figure 17-5 shows you a list of the different traffic sources that drove this channel's watch time.

Devices

The Devices report shows you what type of device your audience is using when watching your videos. More people use mobile phone devices instead of desktop computers or tablets, so even though you're probably filming and editing your videos on your computer, make sure that you watch your videos on your phone so that you can see what they look like on a mobile device.

Traffic source ⓘ	Watch time (minutes) ⓘ ↓	Views ⓘ	YouTube Premium watch time (minutes) ⓘ	YouTube Premium views	Average view duration
☐ Browse features ⓘ	105,585 (30%)	25,626 (25%)	9,641 (32%)	2,277 (31%)	4:07
☐ Suggested videos ⓘ	88,338 (25%)	21,598 (21%)	7,190 (24%)	1,476 (20%)	4:05
☐ YouTube search ⓘ	73,406 (21%)	29,427 (29%)	3,276 (11%)	1,032 (14%)	2:29
☐ Channel pages	31,660 (9.0%)	8,257 (8.2%)	2,163 (7.3%)	564 (7.6%)	3:50
☐ Playlists	14,557 (4.1%)	3,738 (3.7%)	2,392 (8.0%)	810 (11%)	3:53
☐ Other YouTube features	10,418 (3.0%)	2,248 (2.2%)	2,929 (9.9%)	630 (8.5%)	4:38
☐ External ⓘ	9,856 (2.8%)	4,660 (4.6%)	412 (1.4%)	152 (2.0%)	2:06
☐ Playlist page	6,773 (1.9%)	1,965 (1.9%)	728 (2.4%)	210 (2.8%)	3:26
☐ Direct or unknown ⓘ	5,018 (1.4%)	1,813 (1.8%)	378 (1.3%)	105 (1.4%)	2:46
☐ Notifications ⓘ	3,721 (1.1%)	1,174 (1.2%)	425 (1.4%)	141 (1.9%)	3:10
☐ Video cards and annotations	1,499 (0.4%)	372 (0.4%)	100 (0.3%)	25 (0.3%)	4:01
☐ End screens ⓘ	863 (0.2%)	156 (0.2%)	95 (0.3%)	15 (0.2%)	5:31
				1–12 of 12	

FIGURE 17-5:
Use the Traffic sources report for a detailed understand of how people are finding and watching your videos.

TIP

When you watch your video on a mobile device, you'll see if anything doesn't quite work. For example, if you're using text overlaid on your video, make sure that it's readable on a mobile phone. While most people will have sound on, consider how you can make your video watchable without the sound by using captions or on-screen visuals. The real test for maximum mobile viewability is if people can enjoy your video on public transit without sound required!

TIP

You can experiment with different lengths of video to see whether your audience prefers shorter or longer videos. The Devices report shows you the average view duration. For example, you may have an average view duration of 3 minutes on mobile phones, but 5 minutes for people watching on TVs.

Live streaming

You see data on the Live streaming report if you've run a livestream with metrics appearing between 48 and 72 hours after your livestream has ended. You see the data you'd find in your Watch time reports, such as how many people watched and how long for, but also how many concurrent users you had and interactions in the chat window. Visit Chapter 11 to find out about live streaming.

Translations

You can use the Translations report to see how many people are viewing the translated versions of your videos.

TIP

If your videos can be enjoyed by audiences in different countries, I highly recommend using the Translations and Transcriptions feature to increase your audience numbers. Check out Chapter 15 for more on this feature.

Interaction Reports

The reports found within the Interaction reports section give you a sense for the overall health of your channel and your community of fans. If Watch time reports, described earlier in this chapter, tell you about who is viewing your videos, the Interaction reports tells you who is engaging.

Marketers should strive to encourage as much interaction and engagement as possible with their content, and looking at these reports can give you insight as to what people are responding to.

Subscribers

I love the Subscribers report, which tells you how many new subscribers you've added and how many you've lost. Of course, the idea is to steadily increase your number of subscribers over time and reduce the number of people who unsubscribe from your channel. Take a look like Figure 17-6 to see a lifetime report for a channel's subscribers. You can see the number of subscribers, along with how many have been gained and lost. Don't be alarmed to lose subscribers, you'll always have some attrition, just make sure you're growing over time.

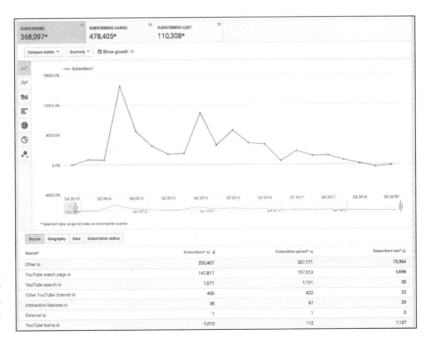

FIGURE 17-6: Look at your Subscribers report to see how many people you've added and lost.

TIP

If you're seeing more people unsubscribe from your channel, think about any recent changes. For example, YouTubers who may have a strong fan base often see an increase in people unsubscribing when they start to experiment with their format and try new things. Sure, seeing people leaving your channel can be painful, but don't let that stop you from experimenting with different formats. You may find that you ultimately reach a larger audience with this new format.

TIP

Know the value of a subscriber. Subscribers to your channel are more likely to see your videos recommended to them on places like their YouTube home page, and that's a gift to marketers that keeps on giving. It's effectively saving you the marketing cost of acquiring them again, and it's a nice proxy metric for encouraging loyalty. Think of your subscribers as your loyal fans. There's a real marketing dollar value in subscribers, so work to obtain them and keep them. Chapter 15 has some tips on subscribers.

Likes and dislikes

Likes and dislikes is a great report to look at because it quickly tells you which of your videos are the most liked and disliked. This invaluable information informs what you should be making more and less of.

It's simple: Make more of the videos people like, and less of the ones they don't.

Videos in playlists

The Videos in playlists report tells you how many of your videos exist in other people's playlists. Being in someone's playlist gives your video more chances for people to see it. Playlists appear in search results, so having your video appear in people's playlists potentially increases your chances of being found.

TIP

I have yet to come across an example where someone asks their viewers to put their videos in their playlists. Everyone asks for people to subscribe, like, comment, and share, but try experimenting with asking people to put your videos in their playlists.

Comments

The Comments report lets you see the videos that received the most comments. Real talk: Comments on YouTube can be helpful, but they can often be pretty snarky and unnecessarily mean. It's just a fact.

WARNING

Some people who make videos like to court controversy as a surefire way to get more comments, and comments are inherently helpful because they're indicators to the algorithm that something of interest is happening with the video, which may mean it appears more often in the search results. However, proceed with caution. Don't make controversial content just to get comments if it's not the right thing for you, your channel, and your marketing goals.

For more on comments and how to manage them, check out Chapter 15.

Sharing

A common misconception is that if you make a video and ask people to share it, they'll share it with two people, and those two people will share it with another two people, making for an exponential sharing pattern that creates a viral sensation and nets you millions of views. The reality is that getting people to share videos is very hard, and so people's expectations of a snagging a viral video are often left unmet. Sure, always encourage people to share your video, but ask yourself: "Would I share this?"

The Sharing report display how many shares you've had and for which videos. If some of your videos appear to be more shareable, ask yourself why and consider learning from them. Look at your least shared videos and make less of them!

I like to think of the sharing metric as a proxy metric for advocacy, taking your most loyal and passionate fans and enabling them to advocate on your behalf. Always make sure you encourage people to share your videos at every opportunity. Chapter 10 has more guidance on how to make your video shareable.

Annotations

Annotations are a feature that is no longer available. However, if you have videos that still have annotations on them, you can see details on how many people clicked on those annotations. If you don't have videos with annotations, this report will be empty.

Cards

Cards are the replacement for annotations, and the Cards report gives you details on how people are interacting with them, for example, how many times they clicked on one of your cards.

Check out Chapter 14 for how to add cards to your videos.

End screens

The End screens report tells you how many people click on your end screens. Aim to encourage as many end screen interactions as possible because they're one of the best ways to get people to subscribe and watch more of your video content.

For more on setting up end screens, check out Chapter 14.

Using Reports to Optimize Your Videos

Growing a YouTube channel takes time, and no hard and fast rules guarantee success.

REMEMBER

Your goal is to leverage YouTube as a marketing tool, so don't let yourself get distracted by trying to make more videos and get more views if they aren't helping meet your business goals.

Regularly looking at your reporting can help you see what is and isn't working. While it's best to look at all your reports in detail, if you only have a limited amount of time, I suggest viewing certain reports based on your goals.

Increasing watch time and views

If you're not getting a lot of watch time or views, check Chapter 14 to ensure that you're maximizing your discoverability chances when you upload your video and Chapter 7 to consider using paid media to boost your videos. Don't forget to check the report on audience retention to see whether people are abandoning your videos early, which may be a sign they don't like something about your content that you can modify moving forward.

TIP

People may abandon your videos for a variety of reasons, such as not liking the content or because your video is too long. Decide what you think may be the issue and tweak your next video to see whether it performs better. For example, I once worked with two YouTubers who made videos together. People would abandon the video when one of the YouTubers was on screen because they just didn't like him! Experimentation is the only way to find out what works.

Growing your audience

Chapter 19 lists some of the most popular YouTubers, who can be great sources of inspiration when it comes to how to grow an audience. These YouTubers work hard to tap into what people are interested in watching and rapidly iterate to perfect their approach. Marketers can potentially learn from their efforts, and if you can't beat 'em, join 'em — Chapter 12 discusses how you can work with YouTubers and influencers to reach new audiences.

Buying paid media is always going to be a top suggestion for those who want to grow their audiences on YouTube, especially marketers. With so much competition and so many great videos available, using paid media (see Chapter 7) can help you guarantee reaching the right people.

Getting more subscribers

If you'd like to get more subscribers, check that you're following the advice in Chapter 10 around content fundamentals, especially the key principle of being authentic. People will subscribe to you if they like your content and think it's genuine.

You can also try experimenting with the different formats outlined in Chapter 8 to see whether people prefer different videos from you. I've interviewed many YouTubers who have spent years building their channels only to find that things really popped when they switched up their format. Your format choice is a key driver as to whether people will subscribe because they want to watch more from you in the future.

Look at the channels you subscribe to or ask your friends and colleagues who they subscribe to. Ask yourself why you or your friends subscribe to these particular channels. Looking at other channels who have successfully grown their subscriber base can give you clues as to how you can encourage your audience to subscribe to you.

Maintaining your YouTube Channel

Chapter 15 details the ongoing channel and community management techniques you should follow. Active maintenance of your channel — for example, to make sure that your videos are always listed on playlists —can help ensure growth. If in time you find that your channel doesn't seem to be delivering to your marketing needs, consider referring to Chapter 9 to think (or rethink) your content strategy.

Your YouTube channel's overall health is fed by the videos you publish, so keeping a regular schedule where you consistently upload is key. Check out Chapter 10 for tips on how to make sustainable choices that help you stick to a consistent upload schedule.

7

The Part of Tens

Avoid the most common mistakes marketers make.

Understand what success looks like.

Focus on the audience and the creative.

Keep the faith and don't give up.

Learn from the world's top YouTubers.

Chapter **18**

The Ten Biggest Mistakes People Make

YouTube has so much to offer, and its potential to deliver to your marketing needs is limitless. Unfortunately, marketers tackling the channel often develop hasty approaches that aren't thought through in an effort to just get started, or, worse, they overwhelm themselves with analysis-paralysis by trying to figure everything out before starting.

I've seen the same mistakes made time and again with clients of all sizes, and you can be forgiven for falling into the same traps. In this chapter, I list ten of the most common mistakes so that you can avoid making them.

Trying to Do Too Much

YouTube is a search engine, a community, an advertising platform, a content destination, a subscription service, and much more. It's unlike any other digital platform, and it's always evolving and changing. The result is that marketers can't easily recognize YouTube as one thing or another, leading to confusion as to how to use it as a marketing channel.

Even the most expert of marketers can make the common mistake of trying to do everything possible on YouTube. The goal for every marketer is not to have a YouTube strategy simply because it's a box their boss wants them to tick, but rather to have a YouTube strategy that delivers to the needs of the business. You can use YouTube selectively as required. Nothing states that you must do everything listed in this book.

Further, when you evaluate your business needs, the resources you have available, and all the various marketing techniques you can employ, you may decide that you don't need to leverage YouTube at this present time.

REMEMBER

Successful marketing is about delivering against business needs, not having marketing activity occurring in every possible channel or medium for a false sense of completeness.

If you're confident that YouTube is a tool you'd like to leverage in your marketing, the best way to avoid the mistake of trying to do too much is to pick your lane. You can be

>> An advertiser running ads on YouTube

>> A sponsor running your ads in specific placements or working with influential YouTubers

>> A content creator where you make your own videos

>> A publisher where a major focus of your business is the content you create

Check out Chapter 1 for more details on how to pick your lane.

TIP

In the unlikely event that you decide not to use YouTube for your marketing, at the very least, set up your channel so that you have it registered. As you won't actively be using YouTube, you can use a single simple video or the channel artwork to point people to other spaces where they can find you instead. People may be searching YouTube expecting to find you, so at least have a minimal presence in place.

Failing to Set Success Criteria

Regardless of the marketing channel in question, failing to set success criteria before you start is a common mistake. Marketers may have an idea of the campaign they'd like to deliver, along with a loose idea of what success looks like, but the more specific you are, the more likely your campaign will be a success.

Marketers must determine the specific key performance indicators they will use to measure a platform like YouTube and ensure that those KPIs are the right ones to deliver against the business goals. (For more on KPIs, see Chapter 2.) Time and again, I've seen CEOs asking their marketing team to deliver lots of video views or channel subscribers, but the question to ask is "Why is that important?" If views or subscribers translate into sales, then they're probably good metrics for success, but if they don't deliver to a business goal, you'll be wasting your time.

TIP

Think through what you'd like YouTube to deliver for your business and set the appropriate KPIs. For example, if you want YouTube to help grow your brand awareness, you'll be interested in maximizing the number of people you can reach as cost efficiently as possible. If you're looking to drive sales, you'll want to ensure that the ads you run on YouTube compel people to click through and purchase.

Knowing what you need YouTube to do and setting those measures of success will ensure that you don't waste time creating videos that don't do anything for your business. At the end of any campaign, the question you'll be asked by the big boss is "So what did it do for the business?" Marketers who spend a lot of time and money developing videos that don't meet the right success criteria are destined to lose their jobs.

Forgetting about the Audience

Even though I emphasize YouTube's potential as a marketing channel, don't fall into the trap of thinking it's a traditional marketing space where you can use a megaphone to simply shout out messages. Your potential audience can skip your ad if it's not interesting or navigate away to watch or do something else. Marketers must work harder than they've done in the past to deliver really great ad creative and video content that the audience wants to see.

Marketers easily make the mistake of getting caught up thinking about marketing strategies, business jargon, reports, data, processes, agencies and more, forgetting that, ultimately, you're trying to talk to a real person and show them that you have something on offer they may like. It's all about the audience, and neglecting to keep their needs and wants in mind can lead to ad creative and video content that just doesn't resonate with them. Chapter 3 walks you through developing audience insights that can ground your efforts.

TIP

Identify a unique and compelling insight about your target audience and then focus on building your creative upon it. You'll find you've created something that resonates with them.

Neglecting to Make Creative for YouTube

A challenge marketers face is the increasing need to make more creative for more marketing channels than ever before.

The marketing channels used to be just TV, print, and radio. Now new digital platforms appear every few years, while existing digital channels evolve. For example, the video requirements for YouTube are different from Facebook and Instagram, and they change when YouTube creates new ad formats. It's hard to be a marketer! You have a lot to consider and keep up to date with. Having said that, the benefit is that your marketing efforts can be more effective and efficient than in the past.

Marketers I've worked with fall into the trap of thinking they can upload their TV ad to YouTube and that it'll work just fine, or that the video they make for their website is good enough to run on YouTube and in social channels. Better results with the performance of creative come when the channel or platform is kept in mind. Sure, making creative specifically designed for each platform or channel requires more work, but it's worth it. Make sure you that when you're making video creative for YouTube, you keep in mind what makes creative work on the platform.

Chapter 6 details how to make ad creative that works on YouTube, and Chapter 10 covers creative fundamentals for video content.

Thinking Paid Media Is Optional

Perhaps the most common mistake I have encountered with previous clients is that you can post videos on YouTube, and they'll magically find an audience for free. Sure, it's possible that anyone can find your video, but with millions of videos available on YouTube, it's more likely that it'll be lost in the sea, never to be seen.

Using paid media may seem daunting, especially for smaller marketing teams and individuals with smaller budgets, but you can spend just a few hundred dollars and see results. YouTube offers a ton of control so you can ensure that your paid media budget is working for you. If it's not, you just turn it off.

Chapter 7 covers the Google Ads solution and how you can set up a paid media campaign.

Copycatting

Copycatting is a real pet peeve of mine. I've had numerous clients who have seen another advertiser's successful campaign and said "I want that." Sure, simply copying the idea of another advertiser can work, but often it doesn't. Great creative and content are original works, not just copy-and-paste jobs.

I see this same mistake when I meet people who say they want to be YouTubers. I ask them what they'd like to make videos about, and the answer is invariably "Oh, probably just makeup tutorials." Newsflash! No one wants to see your makeup tutorial. Lots of people are already doing a great job of making zombie-taco makeup tutorials, so don't just copy someone else. Instead think of something you uniquely can create. Great marketing stands out when it's original and compelling, so avoid copycatting another person's work.

Chapter 4 walks you through the blank canvas that YouTube's ad formats offer, and Chapter 8 lists tons of different types of content videos you can make. Just make sure you bring your own unique approach to everything you do.

Ignoring the Basics of Quality Video Production

In the past, quality of things like picture and audio weren't quite as important as they are today. When online video was nascent, quality wasn't the best, but now people watching videos on YouTube expect a certain level of quality.

A friend who is a YouTuber recently made a video where his audio had a couple of glitches. It didn't seem like a big deal, so he uploaded the video but then got flamed in the comments by his fans. It turned out people really do want a baseline level of quality, so ensure that any video you create

>> Is in focus, clear, and high definition

>> Has audio that is clear and free from glitches

>> Has smooth and professional editing

WARNING

Gone are the days of turning on your webcam and making videos, as professional level equipment is now available to everyone. It's an easy mistake to think that YouTube doesn't require professional level quality, but when the 14-year-old kid at home is making movie-level videos, they're setting the bar higher for everyone.

Chapter 11 walks you through how to create video, including the gear (equipment) you'll need along with options for editing.

Making Once, Distributing Once

If you make a video but only post it to one place, you're missing an opportunity. Sure, even though I believe you should tailor your video creative to YouTube (and tailor it differently to other channels), you can find ways to make simple tweaks and adaptations to your video so that you can post it in as many other places as possible.

I've worked with marketers who do a great job of creating videos for YouTube, even running high-performing paid media to support their campaign, but forget that they can tap into lots of other potential distribution channels to reach a bigger audience.

For example, after you upload your video to YouTube, you can

>> Post it to your blog and embed it on your website

>> Link to it from your social channels

>> Email it to customers in your next newsletter

>> Play it at events or in retail locations

TIP

Ask yourself the question "Does the video, in its current iteration, work in another channel?" If your video works just as well somewhere else, post it! If a tweak will help, then take that extra step. For example, if you want to play a video you've made in a retail location, you may not want the sound to be always playing, in which case you can tweak the video by adding subtitles.

Giving Up Too Early

I admit this one is a big ask because I'm asking you to not give up even when things might feel hard. The fact is, YouTube is one of the more complex marketing channels to tackle — after all, that's why I wrote this book. I've had many clients and friends who have wanted to give up, and my advice is to keep at it.

Smart marketers know when to make changes to their plans and pivot away from channels that don't perform. That said, YouTube needs at least a full year of conscientious effort before making the decision to reduce, revise, or abandon efforts. Marketers should start small, be consistent, and be persistent.

"Oh, he tried the YouTube thing, and it didn't work" a friend once said to me, referring to a mutual friend who wanted to be a YouTuber. It's not that YouTube couldn't have worked for him; it's that he gave up too soon and that he didn't really know what he was doing. It's a real shame when I hear this kind of thing, because I know YouTube can work incredibly well. People who think it's not working usually just need extra support and guidance so that they can start to see results.

Slacking Off Optimization

Real talk: Don't even bother using YouTube for your marketing if you're not going to commit to optimization. This advice is true of most other digital channels, too. Their major benefit is that anything you create and publish will yield data that you can use to iterate and improve. You must

>> **Test, test, test!** Try different ideas and see what works better. For example, test thumbnails and titles to see which people click on more. Chapter 6 talks about testing methodologies.

>> **Use all the YouTube features available.** They'll ensure that you've optimized your chances of being found. Part 5 covers all the features YouTube offers for your channel, video publishing, and community management.

>> **Look regularly at your analytics and develop ideas for what to do next.** Your data will be your gold mine, revealing insights about what works and what doesn't. Chapters 16 and 17 expand on the analytics tools you should be spending some serious time exploring.

Chapter **19**

The Ten Most Popular YouTubers

Massively popular and equally wealthy, the top YouTubers rake in millions each year from their legions of fans, thanks to sharing in YouTube advertising revenue, partnership deals, merchandise, and more.

It's surprising that videos showing someone playing a computer game or giving their dog a makeover can be so successful and lucrative, but these YouTubers have perfected the art of making the kind of video content that people like to watch. Don't underestimate them. Their content may seem to be on the lighter side, but each of these personalities has developed a magic formula that combines their charisma, creative skills, and content into a money-making fame machine. In this chapter, I walk through ten of the top YouTubers and reveal how they got started finding a path to reach billions of people with the niche they've carved out for themselves.

In this list, I focus on the top YouTubers by subscriber count who are individuals either based in the United States or popular in the U.S. market. I exclude musicians like Ed Sheeran and Katy Perry, channels like 5-Minute Crafts, and companies like WWE and instead stick to YouTube personalities.

TIP

You can check out lists of top YouTubers and influencers on other platforms using a great tool called Social Blade at https://socialblade.com.

PewDiePie

PewDiePie, whose real name is Felix Arvid Ulf Kjellberg, lives in my old hometown of Brighton, on the South coast of the UK. He's a Swede who first became popular on YouTube with his computer-game playing videos.

With a whopping 70+ million subscribers — more than the entire population of the UK — PewDiePie makes gaming commentary, comedy, vlog, and meme videos in a unique, almost stream-of-conscious style. He's odd, bizarre, funny, and charismatic, and people love his videos, as evidenced by his 18.9 billion video views. Take a moment for that to sink in. That's the equivalent of every single person in the world watching 2.5 of his videos.

Despite sometimes encountering controversy, PewDiePie has reigned supreme as the most subscribed YouTuber since 2013, with no signs that he'll be supplanted. Estimates place his annual income around $12 million per year.

Dude Perfect

Coming in second on the list of most popular YouTubers, the group Dude Perfect has 35 million subscribers (so, just over half of PewDiePie's) and consists of five friends (Tyler, Coby, Cory, Cody, and Garrett) who make incredible sports and comedy videos. Dude Perfect focuses on pulling off seemingly impossible challenges like their extremely popular trick shot videos.

Their most viewed video, Ping Pong Trick Shots 3, has 170 million views and was sponsored by Oreo. The guys even hold some Guinness World Records.

Smosh

Anthony Padilla first created Smosh as a website in 2002 before YouTube existed. His friend Ian Hecox joined him, and in 2005, they started posting videos on YouTube. In 2017, Padilla left Smosh to pursue other projects., However, the channel continues under Hecox, catering to an audience of 23 million subscribers.

Smosh videos are mostly comedy skits and sketches, along with music, gaming, and animated videos. "Beef 'n Go" is their most popular video, posted in 2008, with a massive 103 million video views.

Markiplier

Markiplier is the channel of Hawaiian born Mark Edward Fischbach, who makes gaming, comedy, and vlog videos, often yelling. When writing this chapter, Markiplier was live-streaming himself playing a game called Amnesia: The Dark Descent and was using YouTube's Super Chats feature to raise money for cystic fibrosis.

The "SCARE ME for CHARITY" livestream had more than 25,000 people watching Markiplier play, with many fans donating hundreds of dollars in support, often in exchange for shout-outs to their friends and family.

Nigahiga

Ryan Higa's channel Nigahiga has more than 21 million subscribers and started with lip-sync videos before moving into comedy. Many of his earlier lip-sync videos were removed as YouTube started to crack down on copyright infringements, so Higa started to post original compositions.

"Nice Guys," published in 2011, is the channel's most popular video with more than 77 million views. It's an original music composition about how nice guys finish last.

Ninja

Tyler Blevins runs the channel Ninja, which features him playing games such as Fortnite, the battle royale-style multiplayer game. (which also happens to be my favorite game!)

Ninja streams on the gaming platform Twitch (where Blevins has 11 million followers) and has 18 million subscribers on YouTube. Fans flock to the videos to learn how to play and enjoy the commentary. His gameplay videos can top 36 million views.

JennaMarbles

An early YouTuber, Jenna Marbles (Jenna Nicole Mourey) hit big with her 2010 video "How To Trick People Into Thinking You're Good Looking," which now has more than 67 million views.

Jenna's channel has more than 18 million subscribers, and her vlog and comedy videos have netted over 2.8 billion views. A second channel, JennaMarblesVlog, has 1.7 million subscribers. Jenna features Mr. Marbles, her chihuahua, and Kermit, an Italian greyhound, prominently in her videos.

Logan Paul Vlogs

Logan Paul started his career as a Vine star before moving to YouTube. TheOfficialLoganPaul is the channel where Paul posts short films and comedy sketches, with an audience of 5 million subscribers. However, his channel Logan Paul Vlogs has a massive 18 million subscribers.

Although Paul has weathered several controversies that have led to him taking a hiatus and having certain projects cancelled, he's worked through them to come out the other side.

Interestingly, In February 2018, Paul participated in a highly publicized amateur boxing match against another YouTube personality, KSI.

Shane

Shane Dawson started his YouTube career uploading sketch comedy videos featuring original characters, amassing hundreds of millions of views. However, since 2015, Dawson has focused more on conspiracy theory and documentary style videos and has grown to more than 18 million subscribers.

Dawson's popular documentary series about YouTuber Jeffree Star features five videos that total close to 100 million views. The follow-up documentary series features YouTuber Jake Paul (see the next section).

Jake Paul

Jake is the brother of Logan Paul (see preceding section), making their YouTube success a real family affair. The Jake Paul Productions channel has 17 million subscribers. Like his brother, Jake first rose to fame through the now defunct platform Vine, but also on a Disney Channel TV show.

Paul's videos have more than 5 billion views, and mostly comprise music videos and vlogs. Jake participated in a boxing match with Logan against KSI and KSI's brother. It was a brother versus-brother event!

Index

About the Author

Will Eagle is a seasoned brand, marketing, and digital professional, having worked at Virgin, MTV, Leo Burnett, and Google. At Google, Will was a brand strategist focused on helping Google's biggest advertising clients understand how they can use YouTube to meet their marketing needs. Will was Google's Chief Facilitator at the PartnerPlex in Mountain View and an advisor to the portfolio companies of Capital G, Google's late stage venture capital fund.

Born in the UK, Will worked in London before moving to Toronto in 2004 and then to Los Angeles with Google in 2015.

Will lives in a cabin in rural Ontario, Canada, and loves creative approaches to problem-solving at scale, slow cookers, spending time in nature, and playing Fortnite.

Dedication

For Jim Lawler.

Author's Acknowledgments

My deepest thanks to: Damon Dean for 5 a.m. dog-walking phone calls; Yotam Dor, Bob Cornwall, and Mark Swierszcz for early feedback that helped make sense of everything; Tom Burke and Christopher Johnstone for the writer's retreat at their beautiful home in upstate NY and the creative support; Sam Sutherland and Ashley Carter for many philosophical YouTube conversations and drinks; Chris Mayell for his invaluable data and unlimited access; Jay V. Del Rosario for his editorial eye; Gabe Verkade for perspectives; Franny and Matt and Neha Sharma for everything; Marissa Orr Gottfried for our weekly conversations to keep me sane; and my Google and YouTube colleagues for the love, support, and snacks.

Publisher's Acknowledgments

Executive Editor: Steve Hayes
Project Editor: Kelly Ewing
Copy Editor: Kelly Ewing
Technical Editor: David Barr
Editorial Assistant: Matthew Lowe
Sr. Editorial Assistant: Cherie Case

Production Editor: Magesh Elangovan
Cover Image: © Rawpixel.com/Shutterstock